CW00547631

Contents

Trade Like Warren Buffett

John Wiley & Sons

Founded in 1807, John Wiley & Sons is the oldest independent publishing company in the United States. With offices in North America, Europe, Australia, and Asia, Wiley is globally committed to developing and marketing print and electronic products and services for our customers' professional and personal knowledge and understanding.

The Wiley Trading series features books by traders who have survived the market's ever-changing temperament and have prospered—some by reinventing systems, others by getting back to basics. Whether a novice trader, professional, or somewhere in-between, these books will provide the advice and strategies needed to prosper today and well into the future.

For a list of available titles, please visit our Web site at www.WileyFinance.com.

Trade Like Warren Buffett

JAMES ALTUCHER

WILEY

John Wiley & Sons, Inc.

Library of Congress Cataloging-in-Publication Data

Altucher, James.
    Trade like Warren Buffett / James Altucher.
        p. cm. — (Wiley trading series)
    ISBN 978-0-471-65584-8 (cloth)
    1. Investments. 2. Buffett, Warren. I. Title. II. Series.

    HG4521.A4559 2005
    332.6—dc22

                                                        2004020828

To Sam Vitiello and Seymour Altucher,
two great fathers.

Acknowledgments

F
irst off, I would like to thank Warren Buffett for having such a rich and varied career as to create the material that was then used for this book. I hope I learned something.

Dave Morrow and Jim Cramer at *TheStreet.com*, and Steve Schurr and Lionel Barber at the *Financial Times*, have nurtured the environments that have allowed me to write and interact with other investors and writers. *RealMoney.com* and the *Financial Times* have been great homes for my articles and I'm grateful. George Moriarty, Gretchen Lembach, Aaron Task, and Adam Batchelder have had the grueling task of editing and reediting my articles at *TheStreet.com* and they have helped me have a lot of fun in the process.

Michelle Donley, Karen Ludke, and Omid Malekan all have helped me in various stages of editing this book and all three have had no shame when telling me which chapters and passages could be a lot better. Thanks for creating a whole lot more work for me and I hope I can return the favor some day!

As usual, Dan Kelly has been both sounding board and psychiatrist throughout the writing and production of this book. Particular thanks for following up on that bounced email to Debbie, enabling us, for once, to be fooled by randomness.

Special thanks to Tim Melvin for pointing out to me Buffett's personal holdings.

Michael Angelides, Neal Berger, Jay Kaplowitz, Worth Gibson, Stephen Dubner, Joel Gantcher, Cody Willard, and Jim Moore and too many others to mention have all played key roles in encouraging and developing my other activities while I have been writing this book. Pamela van Giessen of Wiley has continued to be a great support and confidante throughout this entire process and I am greatly appreciative. And finally, Anne, Josie, and Mollie deserve special thanks for having put up with yet another summer of writing a book. I hope to make it up to them ten-fold.

CHAPTER 1

Does Warren Buffett Trade?

My favorite holding period is forever.

—Warren Buffett

F irst, I have to apologize in advance. This book barely mentions Coca-Cola or the *Washington Post*. I also don't really talk about the many fine companies that Berkshire Hathaway has bought over the past three decades (See's Candies, the Pampered Chef, Dairy Queen, National Furniture Mart, and others). There are many excellent books that cover these topics. And while Warren Buffett has made billions of dollars from these investments, I don't think I can add to the already great dialogue that has taken place on these topics.

Nor is this book really about value investing. There are many definitions of value investing and many treatises on value versus growth. But even Buffett has stated that on the whole, the distinctions between value and growth are nonsense. This book is about the various ways that Buffett has applied the concept of "margin of safety" outside of his buy-and-hold strategies. He has had a longer and more diverse investment career than just about anybody. There are several people in the world (fewer than ten, actually) who have had more years' experience than Buffett at picking stocks, but I can think of no one who has traded and invested with a more diverse group of strategies over the past fifty years. It is these strategies that I write about. Many of them are normally thought of as "trading" strategies instead of the buy-and-hold investing for which Buffett is famous.

When I went to the Berkshire Hathaway annual meeting in 2003 I had no idea what I would encounter. I met one man who bought 200 shares of Berkshire Hathaway in 1976 for $15,000, give or take. He sold half of those shares a year later for a solid double (who can blame him?) and today the remaining shares are worth over $9,000,000. He now hangs out skiing in Tahoe for most of the year.

I asked him why he had bought those shares and he said that he had heard of Warren Buffett while growing up in the same town as him, had heard he was smart, and liked the insurance industry. One can argue that this man I had spoken to was an incredible investor. He had turned $15,000 into $9,000,000 over the course of 25 years—a 50,000 percent return!

Not everyone at the meeting was as lucky. Most of the people at the meeting were fairly recent owners of their shares and were either mildly up on their investment or flat. At the time of this writing Berkshire Hathaway is close to making an all-time high, so hopefully most of these people have held onto their shares. Throughout the meeting I asked people why they were there. After all, it was the most popular annual meeting in the company's history, with approximately 15,000 people in attendance. Some people were there because they just wanted to see Warren Buffett. What zeitgeist had he been tuned into all his life that he could start with $100 and compound it into $40 billion? While at the same time maintaining his home-spun humility and simple lifestyle (he still lives in the same house he bought 40 years ago for $30,000).

Buffett supposedly found these incredible deals through the principles of value investing. Again, there are many good books out there about value investing that try to explain Buffett's value approach.[1] At the end of this

---

[1]The most famous of the books is Robert G. Hagstrom's *The Warren Buffett Way: Investment Strategies of the World's Greatest Investor*. Others include *How to Pick Stocks Like Warren Buffett: Profiting from the Bargain Hunting Strategies of the World's Greatest Value Investor* by Timothy Vick and *How to Think Like Ben Graham and Invest Like Warren Buffett* by Lawrence Cunningham. All of these are good books that focus on investing in companies with solid management, good corporate governance, high return on equity, a good brand, and so on.

book I try to provide a comprehensive suggested reading list of the major books written about Buffett.

However, Buffett achieved much of his early success from arbitrage techniques, short-term trading, liquidations, and so on rather than using the techniques that he became famous for with stocks like Coca-Cola or Capital Cities. In the latter stages of his career he was able to successfully diversify his portfolio using fixed income arbitrage, currencies, commodities, and other techniques. And further, in his personal portfolio he tended to stick to the style of deep value investing that marked his early hedge fund years.

This book is titled *Trade Like Warren Buffett*, and the phrase alone brings up several contradictions in the traditional mythos about Buffett.

First, Warren Buffett supposedly does not trade. He finds an undervalued gem, then buys and holds onto it forever. After all, it takes a million years to turn a piece of coal into a diamond, and a good company should always bare that in mind. For example, Buffett bought Gillette in the 1980s and, to his credit, many multiples later, he still holds onto it. After all, people will always shave, so the demographic for Gillette is approximately 3,000,000,000 citizens of this planet. How can you go wrong holding this stock forever?

Exhibit 1.1 represents the holding period of some of the Berkshire Hathaway trades that Buffett held for less than five years.

Second, the world of trading usually evokes images of day traders, fingers on the trigger, ready to scalp stocks for a few ticks several dozen times a day. Seldom do people think of Warren Buffett, known for holding onto stocks for years, when the subject of day trading comes up.

However, the texture of value investing now is very different than when Warren Buffett was making his early profits, let alone when Benjamin Graham and David Dodd wrote their classic text *Security Analysis*. Back then, there was only a limited set of eyes that had the access to information, not to mention the desire, to locate companies that fit a certain deep value criterion. But today if I want to sift through six thousand stocks to find some that fit specific earnings, ROE (Return on Equity), P/E (price over earnings ratio), and other criteria, then I can easily do so with any number of stock screeners online. And, believe me, countless value investors are doing just that. The information arbitrage that existed in the 1960s and earlier is nearly nonexistent today.

Buffett would spend hours going through *Moody's* reports on each stock, sifting for the gold among the dirt. And, after spending hundreds of hours

EXHIBIT 1.1   Some Berkshire Hathaway Trades Held for Less Than 5 Years

Company	Industry	Year of Purchase	Time Held (Years)
Kaiser Aluminum	Metals and Mining	1977	4
SAFECO	Insurance	1978	4
RJ Reynolds	Tobacco	1980	4
Time	Publishing	1982	4
Guinness	Beverages	1991	3
Knight-Ridder	Publishing	1977	2
ABC	Broadcasting	1978	2
FW Woolworth	Retail	1979	2
ALCOA	Metals and Mining	1980	2
Pinkerton's	Professional Services	1980	2
Cleveland-Cliffs Iron	Metals and Mining	1980	2
General Dynamics	Aerospace	1992	2
Capital Cities	Broadcasting	1977	1
Kaiser Industries	Metals and Mining	1977	1
Amerada Hess	Oil	1979	1
National Detroit	Banking	1980	1
Times Mirror	Publishing	1980	1
National Student Marketing	Financial Services	1980	1
Arcata	Paper	1981	1
GATX	Machinery	1981	1
Crum & Forster	Insurance	1982	1
Exxon	Oil	1984	1
Northwest Industries	Diversified	1984	1
Beatrice	Food	1985	1
Lear Siegler	Aerospace	1986	1
Gannett	Publishing	1994	1
PNC Bank	Banking	1994	1
McDonald's	Restaurants	1996	1
Travelers	Financial Services	1997	1

doing that (an activity that might now take one hour, tops), he would have to then figure out how to actually buy the shares he wanted. For instance, when Buffett was trying to buy shares of Dempster Mining he had to drive to the town where they were based and convince locals to sell their shares to him. There was no liquid market out there like there is now. So when he bought the shares, he *had* to hold them for longer then he might have wanted to.

So, value investing the way Buffett and Graham practiced it no longer exists today. There are thousands of mutual funds and hedge funds competing for those arbitrage opportunities, not to mention retail investors with access to the Internet.

During Buffett's hedge fund years (between 1957 and 1969) there were some years in which more than half his profits came from what he called "workouts"—special situations, merger arbitrage opportunities, spin-offs, distressed debt opportunities, and so on. Playing with semantics, we can argue that all of those opportunities represented "value"—that is, buying something that is cheaper than what it was worth—whether it was a spread between two securities, a distressed bond, or a stub stock that everyone ignored. However, these situations are not usually described as value investing.

Instead, over the past two decades we have seen Buffett dip his investing prowess into commodities (his foray into silver in 1997), fixed income arbitrage, many instances of distressed debt through the use of *private investment in public equity* (PIPE) vehicles, merger arbitrage, relative value arbitrage, and so on. In addition, Buffett has made his first forays into technology investing, owning over the past few years a number of shares in telecommunications services company Level Three and the debt of e-commerce company Amazon; the latter is a company that had never produced a dime of earnings when Buffett first invested in it, let alone an easy means by which someone could compute future cash flows.

There are three stages to Buffett's investment career, and we will focus on techniques used inside each of those phases.

THE EARLY YEARS

Buffett's hedge fund years were when he built his fortune from essentially nothing to about $25 million at the time he was interviewed by Adam Smith for his 1971 classic, *SuperMoney*. During this time Buffett had three techniques:

1. The cigar butt technique, into which category Berkshire Hathaway (in its original form) fell. This meant buying stocks that were selling for less than tangible assets. Buffett would sometimes accumulate enough shares that eventually a change of control would occur, giving him direct power over how the assets of the company would be disposed.

2. Value investing, but combined with some of his partner Charlie Munger's ideas on growth and the potential of brands. This resulted in Buffett's American Express play, among others.

3. Special arbitrage situations, workouts, distressed debt, merger arbitrage, spin-offs, and so on.

THE MIDDLE YEARS

The 1970s and 1980s were the decades when Buffett made the full transition from successful hedge fund manager to operator, asset allocator, and insurance company magnate. Why the insurance business? And why did he leave the hedge fund business? We know now in retrospect that he was a very good market timer, although prone to being early, just as Bernard Baruch said, "I always sold too soon." So it could be argued that Buffett's departure from the hedge fund business right before an essentially flat decade was a sign of good market timing. However, I don't believe this.

I believe that Buffett did anticipate a potentially horrendous decade for stock market returns, and in fact, 1973–74 was the worst downturn since the 1930s. But I don't think that Buffett would have stopped his hedge fund for fear of poor market returns. Rather, he was always more enthusiastic in his annual letters to his partnership investors when the market was doing its poorest. He prided himself more on outperformance than absolute performance. A return of 20 percent in a year when the market was up 30 percent would have been a disaster for him. Far better would be to return five percent, with the market returning –20 percent for the year. So the fact that the market was about to make a strong downturn would not have been the impetus to cause him to wind down his hedge fund and go into the insurance business.

Rather, I think he saw an opportunity unlike any he had encountered in the past and he wanted to pounce on it. The way Buffett's partnership was structured, he took a 0 percent management fee and 25 percent of all profits. As an example, if his fund had $5 million in it and he returned 20 percent, or $1 million, for his investors, then he would take 25 percent of that, or $250,000 of that, as his fee.

However, an insurance company is much more attractive to a master asset allocator like Buffett. An insurance company works like a hedge fund except Buffett gets to keep 100 percent of the profits. People "invest" their money when they pay their premiums and only get to take their money out again upon illness or disaster. In a well-run insurance business the "cost of float" is ideally zero; that is, you spend no more in payouts than you take in premium. In this way, all profits go to the owners of the business. If the cost of float is zero, then the economics of the insurance business are much better than the economics of a hedge fund.

Rather than retire to a lifetime of bridge playing, Buffett ended up buying for $40/share most of the Berkshire Hathaway shares that he had originally bought for his investors (profitably for them at prices ranging from $7 to $16 per share). Then, while Buffett used Berkshire as his base, the rest of the 1970s became a rollup of insurance companies, regional banks, and other cash-producing assets ranging from the Nebraska Furniture Mart to See's Candies.

It was during this period that he became less focused on his workout plays and more focused on his "control" plays like the insurance companies, furniture companies, and chocolate companies he was buying and his "generals"—the big value plays like Coco-Cola and Gillette that ultimately created billions of dollars in investment profits for Berkshire.

There is no one way to sum up Buffett's investment style during this period. Early on, he was certainly interested in buying companies for less than their book value. The Washington Post is a great example, where he began accumulating shares at a fraction of their liquidation value. Later on, however, particularly in the 1980s, his methods were much less quantitative and bordered on highly subjective. A case in point is Coca-Cola, which Buffett began accumulating in 1988; he ultimately became the largest shareholder. Coke was trading at 13 times earnings, hardly a discount to the market at that time, which was trading around 10 times forward earnings. That said, Buffett was convinced, and he was right, that Coke was trading at a huge discount based on the future earnings of the company.

"The Middle Years" are perhaps the least interesting period for me. However, this period (the 1970s and 1980s) is the subject of countless books on Buffett. Hagstrom's book *The Warren Buffett Way*[2] set the tone and documents Buffett's stock picks during this period.

---

[2]*The Warren Buffett Way*, Robert Hagstrom (Wiley, 1993).

I repeat the following refrain throughout the book: It is not possible to trade exactly like Warren Buffett. The goal is to use whatever means possible to approximate his trading by attempting to quantify the term "margin of safety".

THE LATER YEARS

The 1990s and then the 2000s created an interesting dilemma for Buffett, one that no other company has ever faced. He simply had too much cash to put to work. As much as he loved finding quality companies and stocks, the world was just too small for him at this point. In lectures that he occasionally gave to college students he would often sentimentally reflect that if he had less money he could still return 50 percent a year in arbitrage situations. But with $50 billion to put to work this was just impossible. Nor is it easy to go through the market and find the slim pickings. Let's say a $1 billion company is trading at a cheap price and Buffett is able to buy 10 percent of it. Assume that it then goes up 100 percent for him over the next year—a truly remarkable return. It would still only increase the book value of Berkshire Hathaway by 0.2 percent.

Instead, the 1990s saw several trends developing in Buffett's style. First there was a flight to safety. In the late nineties, when the world was haphazardly buying everything with dot-com written all over it (author disclosure: I was, too), Buffett was diversifying into bonds, into silver, fixed income arbitrage, and ultimately foreign currencies.

So given the fact that Buffett's investment career has spanned five decades and multiple styles and disciplines, is it possible to "trade like Warren Buffett"?

IT'S TOO LATE

It is not possible to trade exactly like Warren Buffett. The best we can do is approximate his approach, plead in each trading situation for the margin of safety that Buffett always demands, and try to develop our own approaches that are, if not exact replicas, at least Buffett-like. But why can't we trade like him? To summarize the three main reasons:

1. **The Internet has changed everything.** Every SEC filing, every news report, every inside transaction, and every earnings release is instantly posted to the Internet and available to the tens of thousands of investors who are looking for low price to book, high return on equity companies. Although many studies have come to the conclusion that too many retail investors are naive, the reality is that there are many good investors out there who know how to make use of the information at their fingertips. No longer does an investor have to dig through tattered old filings to find the next Dempster Mining and then drive around Nebraska to find random shares in it.

2. **Arbitrage spreads have narrowed.** The "workout" trades that Buffett mastered in his hedge fund days are no longer as easy to accomplish as they once were. When Buffett started out, only a handful of hedge funds existed that were attempting to use those techniques. Now there are over 7,000 hedge funds trying to squeeze the blood out of every arbitrage situation. While the opportunities still exist—opportunities that we will examine in depth in later chapters—they are of a much different breed then what Buffett first encountered.

3. **People don't give us money.** Warren Buffett has enormous deal flow. Every day opportunities are placed in front of him, and often the types of deals are not those that are available to the average investor. The flipside to this is that he also has a lot of bad deals put in front of him, and it takes acumen to sift through these questionable opportunities to find the gems. However, his gems might be 10-carat diamonds, whereas the average investor needs to settle for a few inclusions and work his or her way up from there.

IT'S NOT TOO LATE

But don't despair. The key thing to focus on is Buffett's constant desire for a margin of safety. With each style of investing that he delves into, he consistently requires a certain degree of safety; investors who attempt to apply his techniques should do the same. Also, the average investor has several advantages over Warren Buffett, both the Buffett from his early hedge fund years and the Buffett of the 1990s and 2000s.

1. **The Internet.** The same phenomenon that was listed as a disadvantage above is also an advantage. The reality is that it is easier to research any investment possibility under the sun. It is also easier to quantify and back-test various approaches to verify that an approach has at least been statistically sound in the past. Buffett has a great appreciation for the quantifiable side of investing; it would be interesting to see what he could have done had he had the capabilities of the Internet behind him when he started.

2. **Size is important.** Buffett is simply too big. He cannot enter into a position easily without causing the entire world to react accordingly. For instance, when he started buying up silver he wasn't simply making a small investment. He ended up becoming the largest investor in silver since the Hunt Brothers, controlling not just a small amount, but 25 percent of the entire world's above-ground supply. And still this was just a tiny, miniscule drop in the bucket for the Berkshire Hathaway portfolio. Getting into and then out of this market was no easy task for Buffett either. Silver, which had been in a slump for years, jumped 30 percent when it was discovered that Buffett was making an investment.

   No wonder Buffett likes to tell people to buy and hold. If investors feel like selling something that Buffett owns, there is almost zero chance Buffett can get out before the other interested sellers do. Clearly, if everyone had a philosophy of "buy and hold forever," it would be much better for Buffett's investments, since he can't really sell. The reality is that during his career he has done much selling and has held even some core value plays (McDonald's and Disney are great examples) for short periods of time.

The fact that the average investor is much more nimble is a huge advantage, although it is an advantage that cannot be treated lightly due to the damage it can cause. Many studies have been done that show that the average retail investor is damaged by too high a turnover in his or her portfolio. Ultimately, though, it is better to have the option than to not have it at all.

The remainder of this book is mostly broken down by investment style.

THE INVESTMENT STYLES

Merger Arbitrage

Buffett made significant use of merger arbitrage (buying the stock of a company being acquired and selling short the acquirer) in his hedge fund days from 1957 to 1969. As recently as the 1998 Berkshire Hathaway conference he stated that if he only had a small amount to play with he could still earn 50 percent a year using merger arbitrage techniques.

Relative Value Arbitrage

"Relative value" is a catch-all phrase that takes advantage of any discrepancy between the spread in values between two assets. A great example (which Buffett did not play as far as I know) was when 3COM (Nasdaq: COMS) spun out Palm (Nasdaq: PALM) and the shares 3COM owned in PALM were worth significantly more than the entire market cap of 3COM. Buying 3COM and shorting PALM was a straightforward exploitation of that discrepancy and had a fair amount of margin of safety associated with it. Of course, the spread could get worse before it gets better. For example, Eifuku, a hedge fund in Japan that was wiped out in less than two weeks in 2003 from applying these techniques), but hey, that's what makes it so much fun.

Bonds

Buffett has spoken several times over the past 40 years about the merits of the Federal Reserve model in market timing. More recently, when the economy was slowing and the market was getting significantly overvalued relative to interest rates, Buffett made the impressive move of switching his portfolio so he was heavily weighted in bonds. Masterfully, he did this without incurring any tax penalty at all (that is, he didn't have to allocate out of stocks and into bonds).

We will look at the merits of various applications of the Fed model and some studies that have been done in this area; included in this book are interviews with several managers who focus on investing in bonds.

Fixed Income Arbitrage

As much as Buffett has a distaste for derivatives and leverage, he does dip his toes into the world of fixed income arbitrage, the idea of buying and selling different interest rate derivatives with different time payoffs. What is fixed income arbitrage, how does Buffett invest in it, what are the advantages and disadvantages? While this is normally considered a very solid and safe way to invest, it should be pointed out here that Long-Term Capital Management, the highly pedigreed hedge fund that lost billion of dollars in 1998, also felt this was a very safe way to invest the money of their investors.

Stocks

I didn't want this to be a book "like all the others," and most other books about Warren Buffett focus on his stock-picking techniques. However, the reality is that this topic cannot be ignored in any work about Buffett. What I hope to offer to the dialogue is an examination of studies done on the techniques that Buffett supposedly uses for his stock picking.

And finally, we will examine and study the principle of mean reversion. The commonly quoted aphorism is to "buy when there is blood in the streets." Buffett and Graham both recount the story of Mr. Market, who is always buying when things are too expensive, and selling when things are too cheap. Mr. Market is often crushed by the idea of mean reversion. Without focusing specifically on value investing, can the average investor quantify an approach to mean reversion that still carries with it the concept of margin of safety?

Commodities

Buffett has never been a big fan of investing commodities. However, he has several times made the plunge, most recently with silver. Many people who trade commodities do so based on the technicals, chart reading, and pure systems trading. It is interesting to see how Buffett applies his principles of value investing to commodities.

Currencies

Currencies have never been a popular Buffett investment. In fact, Buffett only began buying currencies in the past year. "Buy what you know" is the slogan of Buffett fans, and Buffett knows the United States better than he knows any other country. We will explore what made him finally invest in foreign currencies later in this book.

Finally, the book concludes with a suggested readings section that catalogs the primary books that discussed or influenced Buffett.

CHAPTER 2

Graham-Dodd and a Dose of Fisher

Warren Buffett claims to be "15 percent [Philip] Fisher and 85 percent Benjamin Graham." You could make the argument that the inverse is true, although I take Buffett at his word and think he is correct, particularly when you look at the activities of his hedge fund from 1957 to 1969 and the activities of his personal portfolio. (Not to mention his overriding philosophy of always looking for a margin of safety.)

Let's begin with a few notes about Fisher. Philip Fisher, the author of *Common Stocks and Uncommon Profits*, advocated buying a focused portfolio, a few companies with above-average potential. How is it possible to determine above-average potential?

- Focus on growing sales.
- Focus on expanding research and development (R&D) since that will keep the company ahead of the curve and capable of growing sales in the future.
- Demographics need to be monitored. Is the market for this company going to continue to grow?
- Management should be strong and communications with shareholders should be direct and honest.

How does one get the low-down on management? This is what Fisher refers to as "scuttlebutt." Interview customers, management, employees, other investors, journalists, and so on. Get the information any way you can.

Fisher was also a big fan of focus investing. This is the idea that people should only buy a few stocks. The idea makes intuitive sense in that you can only focus on a few stocks at a time anyway. If you were in 200 stocks it would be much harder to follow all of the movements of each stock, and it becomes much more likely that, in the best-case scenario, all you do is track the overall market.

There has been interesting research recently on several of Fisher's criteria. For instance, looking at the R&D expenses of a company is not always helpful. The way a company expenses research and development might be just an accounting trick. However, there is a way to look at R&D in a way that is correlated with future stock market performance.

According to CHI Research, a consulting firm that focuses on studying the intellectual property of companies, a company's patent portfolio is a predictor of future stock performance. The quality of the patent portfolio can be assessed by, among other things, the statistics related to forward citations to the patents. A forward citation is a note on the front of a later patent that states which prior patents the patent pending is improving upon. The more patents the patent is improving, the more well-spent the R&D dollars were in creating that patent.

From 1989 to 1998, CHI constructed a test, selecting the 25 companies most undervalued based in part on patent quality indicators such as highly cited patents and short technology cycle times, that is, shorter than the average for their industries.

As we can see in Exhibit 2.1, the patent/R&D–heavy companies steadily outperformed the S&P and even outperformed the Nasdaq by a wide margin during 2000, when tech stocks were down by a wide margin.

In fact, CHI Research itself has a patent for its method of picking a stock portfolio based on the quality of the patent portfolio for each stock (see Exhibit 2.2).

The issue about diversification is a tug-of-war between Graham-Dodd purists and Fisher purists. Fisher advocates a "focused portfolio" approach, that is, a portfolio with just a few stocks in it so that it is easier to follow, research, and manage them. Graham-Dodd advocates more extensive diversification. Fisher's point—a valid one—is that the more stocks in your port-

EXHIBIT 2.1 Portfolio Performance

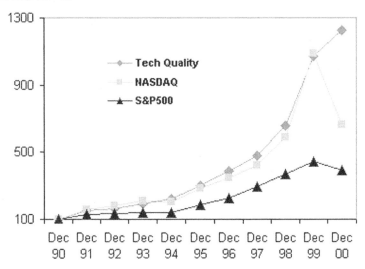

Source: Reprinted from the CHI Research website, http://www.chiresearch.com, 2004.

folio, the harder it is to follow them. As Buffett has stated, "Wide diversification is only required when investors do not understand what they are doing." And Robert Hagstrom, in his books *The Warren Buffett Portfolio* and *The Essential Buffett*, has done some excellent research on the value of a focused portfolio.

Academic research in this area received a boost from a paper by two University of Michigan professors, Clemens Sialm and Lu Zheng, and one of their Ph.D. graduate students, Marcin Kacperczyk.[1] Their conclusion after looking at all mutual fund data from 1984 to 1999 was that actively concentrated portfolios perform better than funds with diversified portfolios. They also tend to outperform the market, despite the evidence that actively managed funds in general (including the ones with high diversification) tend to underperform the market. The outperformance occurred both in the 1980s and 1990s, and was sector-independent (so it was not just technology).

---

[1]"On the Industry Concentration of Actively Managed Mutual Funds," by Clemens Sialm, Lu Zheng, and Marcin Kacperczyk, *Journal of Finance*, 2005.

EXHIBIT 2.2

---

(12) **United States Patent**   (10) **Patent No.:**   **US 6,175,824 B1**
Breitzman et al   (45) **Data of Patent:**   **Jan. 16, 2001**

---

(54) METHOD AND APPARATUS FOR
CHOOSING A STOCK PORTFOLIO, BASED
ON PATENT INDICATORS

(75) Inventors: Anthony F. Breitzman, Cedarbrook;
Francis Narin, Ventor, both of NJ (US)

(73) Assignee: CHI Research, Inc., Haddon Heights,
NJ (US)

(*) Notice: Under 35 U.S.C. 154(b), the term of this
patent shall be extended for 0 days.

(21) Appl. No.: 09/353,613

(22) Filed: Jul. 14, 1999

(51) In. Cl.† G06F 17/68

(52) U.S. Cl. 705/36; 705/10; 705/35;
705/37

(58) Field of Search 705/36, 10, 35,
705/37

(56)   Refences Cited

U.S. PATENT DOCUMENTS

5,761,442 * 6/1998 Barr et al. 705/36
5,819,238   10/1998 Rembolz.
5,934,674 * 8/1999 Bukowsky 273/278
5,978,778 * 11/1999 O'Shaughnessy 705/36
6,035,286 * 3/2000 Fried 705/36

OTHER PUBLICATIONS

"Techo File: Data Mining for the Soft Assets". Invester
Relations Dec. 1996.*
Stobbs Gregory: "Turning the Corporate Patent Portfolio
Using the Latest Software Tools". MapiT Briefing Report,
Manning & Napier, Jun. 1997.*
McGuire, Craig: "The Next Level of Proprietary Protect-
tion", Wall Street & Technology, Jan99, vol. 17 Issue 1, p52,
1p."
J.S. Perko et al.: "The Transfer of Public Science to Patented
Technology: A Case Study in agriculture Science". Journal
of Technology Transfer, vol. 22(3) 65–72, 1997.*

CHI Research, Inc. Introduces Tech–Line Analysis Tool
Technology, Information Today, V 15, n 9, p 66, Oct. 1998.*
Deng, Z., Lev, B., and Narin, F. "Science and Technology as
Predictors of Stock Performance" (Financial Analysts Jour-
nal, vol. 55, No. 3, May/Jun. 1999, pp. 20–32).
Rosenberg, N. and Birdzell, Jr., L.E. "Science, Technology
and the Western Miracle" (Scientific American, vol. 263,
No. 5, Nov. 1990, pp. 42–54).

(List continued on next page.)

Primary Examiner—Tod R. Swann
Assistant Examiner—Jagdish N Patel
(74) *Attorney, Agent, or Firm*—Akin, Gump, Strauss,
Hauer & Feld, L.L.P.

(57)   ABSTRACT

A portfolio selector technique is described for selecting
publicly traded companies to include in a stock market
portfolio. The technique is based on a technology score
derived from the patent indicators of a set of technology
companies with significant patent portfolios. Typical patent
indicators may include citation indicators that measure the
impact of patented technology on later technology. Technology Cycle Time that measures the speed of innovation of
companies, and science linkage that measures leading edge
tendencies of companies. Patent indicators measure the
effect of quality technology on the company's future performance. The selector technique creates a scoring equation
that weights each indicator such that the companies can be
scored and ranked based on a combination of patent indicators. The score is then used to select the top ranked
companies for inclusion in a stock portfolio. After a fixed
period of time, as new patents are issued, the scores are
recomputed such that the companies can be re-ranked and
the portfolio adjusted to include new companies with higher
scores and to eliminate companies in the current portfolio
which have dropped in score. A portfolio of the top 10–25
companies using this method and a relatively simple scoring
equation box has been shown to greatly exceed the S&P 500 and
other Indexes in price gain over a ten year period.

63 Claims, 11 Drawing Sheets

Source: Reprinted from the CHI Research website, http://www.chiresearch.com, 2004.

The reason for this is clear: With a portfolio of just a few stocks, it is possible that the active manager is able to obtain better information about each stock than if the manager had 200 stocks in his or her portfolio. This information advantage results in better performance on the whole, which is precisely Buffett's (and Fisher's) point.

GRAHAM-DODD

Although the book *Security Analysis* by Graham and Dodd fills up more than 700 pages, the basic message can be summarized by the phrase "margin of safety."

In the chapter "Survey and Approach," the authors state: "An investment operation is one which, upon thorough analysis, promises safety of principal and a satisfactory return. Operations not meeting these requirements are speculative."

And Graham admits a few paragraphs later that "The phrases *thorough analysis, promises safety,* and *satisfactory return* are all chargeable with indefiniteness," although their basic points are clear. If someone gives you an inside tip that stock XYZ is going up, then clearly you have not yet done thorough analysis. If you leverage up your portfolio 200 percent and buy just one stock, then you probably have not promised yourself much safety. And if you lose money, then chances are your return was not satisfactory.

But let's look at Graham's approach to safety more closely, since I think this is the underpinning of all of Buffett's trading and investing, whether it is in stocks, bonds, arbitrage situations, or even insurance.

Graham and Dodd state, "The *safety* sought in investment is not absolute or complete; the word means, rather, protection against loss under all normal or reasonably likely conditions or variations." And then a few sentences later the authors add, "A safe stock is one which holds every prospect of being worth the price paid except under quite unlikely contingencies."

However, as Graham later notes when discussing the fates of the fixed income bonds offered by railroads before the Depression, "even a high margin of safety in good times may prove ineffective against a succession of operating losses caused by prolonged adversity."

So what are we to do? Graham states later in the chapter on fixed value investments, "The only effective means of meeting this difficulty lies in following counsels of perfection in making the original investment. The degree of safety enjoyed by the issue, as shown by quantitative measures, must be so far in *excess* of the minimum standards that a large shrinkage can be suffered before its position need be called into question. Such a policy should reduce to a very small figure the proportion of holdings about which the investor will subsequently find himself in doubt."

He gives as an example the General Baking Company bonds paying 5.5 percent interest. The company itself earns 20 times the amount of its annual interest payments. Graham notes that this is safe and that if the earnings per year decline to only four times the interest payments, then it might be worth finding a safer investment.

Graham-Dodd likes stocks that trade below their liquidating value, where the liquidating value is roughly all of the current and long-term assets minus all of the current and long-term liabilities on the balance sheet. As they state in the chapter "The Significance of the Current-Asset Value" in *Security Analysis*:

> *The phenomenon of many stocks selling persistently below their liquidating value is fundamentally illogical. It means that a serious error is being committed either: (a) in the judgment of the stock market; (b) in the policies of the company's management; or (c) in the attitude of the stockholders toward their property.*

During the Depression, all of these items were applicable. The market as a whole was going down as speculators pulled their money out en masse. Management, not anticipating how bad things were getting, was dissipating their assets. And even long-term investors, in need of cash just to survive, were pulling money out of stocks regardless of any value in the stocks. However, ultimately, these types of stocks were what Graham called "investment bargains." Specifically:

> *Common stock which: (a) are selling below liquid asset values; (b) are apparently in no danger of dissipating these assets; and (c) have formerly shown a large earning power on the market price may be said to truly constitute a class of* investment bargains. *They are indubitably worth considerably more than they are selling for, and there is a reasonably good chance that this greater worth will sooner or later reflect itself in the market price. At their low price these bargain stocks actually enjoy a high degree of safety, meaning by safety a relatively small risk of loss of principal.*

One possible criticism is that these types of plays no longer exist. They existed in the Great Depression, but never since. However, we will see in the case of Buffett's personal portfolio that he was able to play these situations even in the late 1990s. We will look at more Buffett examples in a moment.

But first, my own foray into this phenomenon occurred on December 11, 2002, when I wrote the following article on thestreet.com's sister site Street Insight.

The Cash Index, James Altucher, Street Insight, December 11, 2002

Let's look at a couple of rules from the greats. Benjamin Graham's favorite rule was to find companies that were trading for less than cash and then hold onto them until they were trading for more than cash. Warren Buffett's two rules are: Rule #1: Don't lose money. Rule #2: Don't forget rule #1. Warren Buffett was a student of Graham's for many years. As Buffett put it, "the secret to success is figuring out who to be the batboy for." Buffett was Graham's batboy and Buffett's rules for investing are directly related to the "margin of safety," as Graham put it, that you get when you buy stocks that are debt-free and trading for less than the cash in the bank.

It sounds simple-if someone is holding a check with your name on it, it is probably worthwhile to figure out how to cash that check. At first glance, it seems mystifying. Why doesn't someone just buy all the shares of the company and then put the cash in his pocket? It is never that easy and the way to make money in arbitrage situations, even as simple as these, is to conduct thorough risk management and due diligence on the stocks involved.

When looking at these stocks, it is important to accept the first premise: they are trading for less than cash for a reason. And that reason is that the market thinks they will run out of cash and eventually declare bankruptcy, rendering the shares worthless (hence the negative enterprise value).

Some of the risks involved include:

- **Inaccurate reflection of "cash on hand" in their books.** Future cash commitments can be tied up in leases, severance packages, unprofitable deals that have cash penalties to back out of, etc.

- **Business model destined to fail.** Management might be obsessed with pursuing until the bitter end a business model that has no chance of turning profitable. Great examples from the past include MTHR (MotherNature.com), TGLO (theglobe.com), VSTY (VarsityBooks.com), which never could shake the chains of their strategy until the money ran out.

- **Management with no incentive to return value to shareholders.** In some cases, management has direct control over the millions of dollars sitting in the bank. Why would they give that up just to end up unemployed?

Some of the possible exit strategies that can be enjoyed by holders of companies trading for less than cash include:

- **Management-led buyouts.** Not always the best strategy for the shareholder (MBOs are the only legal form of insider buying), but we will look at a case below where on an annualized basis we think the risk/reward is there.
- **Business turnaround.** While rare, the cash does give management the opportunity to step on the brakes without worrying about a crash and see if they can turn the business around. A notable example was TSCM, which earlier this year traded below its cash levels and has since rebounded.
- **Dividend to shareholders.** The board does have legal responsibility to create shareholder value when possible and there have been cases where the board has determined the only way to do that is to dividend out the cash to shareholders.
- **Takeover candidates.** Assuming the cash in the financials is accurate and the business model has some potential for survival, many of the stocks listed below are either potential takeover candidates or are already in the process of being taken over, in which case a very direct merger arbitrage analysis can take place. Recent companies trading below cash that have been taken over include VCNT, taken over by Microsoft, presumably to help them compete with the MapQuest product offered by AOL Time Warner.
- **Reverse merger.** The company can decide to eliminate its existing business lines and merge with a profitable company. A recent example is SOFN, which went from $120 million in cash to about $60 million when they wound down their broadband businesses and then merged with a profitable insurance company, causing a 40 percent jump in their stock price.

When developing the cash index presented below, we established eight selection criteria and weighted them accordingly. Our goal was to take out, as much as possible, some of the risks mentioned above, as well as to look for companies that could be considered possible takeover candidates.

1. **Market cap < cash.** Obviously a criterion, but more importantly, that cash had to be made up of only cash in the bank plus short-term investments. We left out companies with little cash but significant inventory or long-term investments.

2. **Debt/Equity < 0.20.** If management is to have any chance of turning the situation around, they cannot be plagued with debt commitments or debt

covenants. Also, the lack of debt gives the stockholder some degree of confidence that bankruptcy isn't in the near future.

3. **Market Cap + Annual Burn Rate < Cash.** I like to know that if the company continues to burn money at its current rate, then the company can still be liquidated a year later so I can ideally get my money back, at the very least.

4. **Some stability in revenues and earnings.** Ideally the company will already have begun a turnaround (profits this year as opposed to losses last year) but my primary concern is that revenues are still not dropping at a rate of 50 percent a year with losses still doubling. In some cases revenues will drop, but losses will decrease because the companies are winding down their businesses. That is fine for us.

5. **A reasonable belief that the sell-off in the stock was partly irrational.** While not a quantitative measure, it is useful to look at the situation and understand at a glance why the company's shares sold off and why that sell-off might have been "guilt by association." For instance, hundreds of Internet companies went bankrupt, but not every company whose shares sold off will go bankrupt. Later, we will look at examples from the Internet, software, and aviation industries. A company that recently went past its cash levels, and so is not included on this list, is CAMZ, a software company which catered to the IPP industry (a double whammy in the eyes of shareholders who initially sold off their shares).

6. **Favorable arbitrage analysis.** In the instances below where the company has already accepted a takeover offer, we want to make sure that owning the shares right now still has a high likelihood of having a favorable annualized return.

7. **Insider buying.** While not a requirement, it is nice to know that senior officers and directors in the company feel as we do: that the company should be trading for higher than its cash levels.

8. **Institutional ownership.** We like to see mutual funds with above-average track records that focus on value opportunities swooping down onto these opportunities. Among the mutual fund families that we look for include: the Royce Funds, the Clipper Fund, Heartland, and Artisan.

The Cash Index as of December 11, 2002 included: PCYC, CLRS, AMIE, PRTS, FAVS, VCLK, NTRT, GEMS, STRD, CPCI, and IATV (see Exhibits 2.3–2.13 for a discussion of each stock). (Each exhibit reflects the price and attributes that caused me to write about it on December 11, 2002.)

EXHIBIT 2.3 PCYC

Pharmacyclics is a pharmaceutical company focused on the development of products that improve existing therapeutic approaches to cancer and atherosclerosis.

Price	Cash/Share	Book/Share	Cash	Market Cap
$3.53	$7.10	$7.26	$114 million	$57 million

- $27–29 million annual burn rate.
- Warren Kanders, chairman of Armor Holdings, and a shareholder activist who successfully won a proxy to be on CLRS's board has recently started a similar battle to be on PCYC's board.
- Insider buying from the CFO last May at higher prices than current.
- Royce funds own 450,000 shares.

Source: Reproduced with permission of Yahoo! Inc. © 2004 by Yahoo! Inc. YAHOO! and the YAHOO! logo are trademarks of Yahoo! Inc.

EXHIBIT 2.4 CLRS

Clarus Corporation develops, markets, and supports Internet-based business-to-business e-commerce solutions that automate the procurement, sourcing, and settlement of goods and services.

Price	Cash/Share	Book/Share	Cash	Market Cap
$5.65	$6.88	$6.37	$107 million	$88 million

- Warren Kanders successfully won his fight to be on the board of directors and sell off all of their revenue-producing (and money-losing) assets.
- $10–12 million annualized burn.
- Significant insider purchases by several directors, including Kanders.
- Recently hired Morgan Joseph & Co. Inc to look into possible reverse merger opportunities.
- Significant increase in institutional ownership over the past month (422,000 more shares bought than sold by institutions).

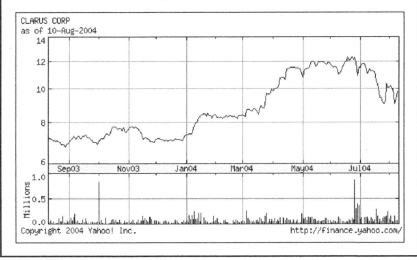

EXHIBIT 2.5   AMIE

Ambassadors International organizes, markets, and operates international and domestic travel programs

Price	Cash/Share	Book/Share	Cash	Market Cap
$8.74	$10.71	$11.49	$105 million	$85 million

- Most recent quarter was profitable, suggesting a turnaround in the business
- Stock sold off, in part, because of recent spin-off where shareholders chose to keep shares of the spun off company. Many people bought into the original company because of the student travel business, which has now been spun off as EPAX.

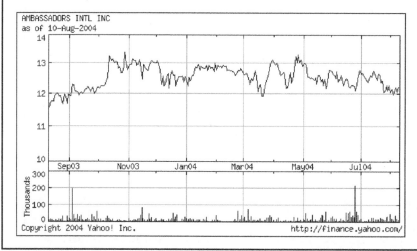

Source: Reproduced with permission of Yahoo! Inc. © 2004 by Yahoo! Inc. YAHOO! and the YAHOO! logo are trademarks of Yahoo! Inc.

EXHIBIT 2.6 FAVS

First Aviation Services, Inc. is one of the leading suppliers of aircraft parts and components to the aviation industry worldwide, and is a provider of supply chain management services, including third party logistics and inventory management services, to the aerospace industry.

Price	Cash/Share	Book/Share	Cash	Market Cap
$3.92	$4.52	$6.40	$32 million	$28 million

- $1.65 million EBITDA, $68,000 net income in the most recent quarter.
- Sales down 4% Year over Year (YoY) in the most recent quarter, suggesting some stability despite worldwide slump in the aviation industry.
- CEO and several directors recently purchased shares.

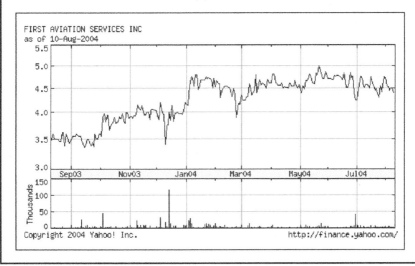

EXHIBIT 2.7   VCLK

ValueClick offers marketers and advertisers traditional and interactive media and advertising technology solutions.

Price	Cash/Share	Book/Share	Cash	Market Cap
$2.82	$3.00	$2.97	$266 million	$245 million

- $75 million share buyback program.
- Small pro-forma profit last quarter.
- Institutional ownership has risen 50% in the past 3 months.
- Royce & Associates, Al Frank Fund among the top mutual fund holders.
- If the company retires the shares that are part of the buyback and price remains the same, the market cap could go as low as $180 million, making this trade at a significant discount to cash for a profitable company.

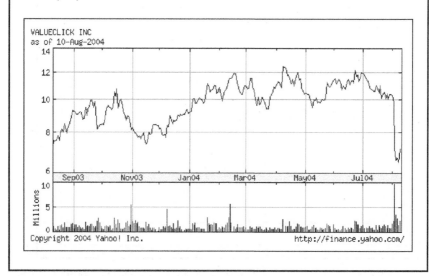

Source: Reproduced with permission of Yahoo! Inc. © 2004 by Yahoo! Inc. YAHOO! and the YAHOO! logo are trademarks of Yahoo! Inc.

EXHIBIT 2.8 NTRT

Netratings provides Internet measurement services.

Price	Cash/Share	Book/Share	Cash	Market Cap
$6.62	$7.80	$9.28	$250 million	$232 million

- $30 million annualized burn.
- Revenues rose 10% YoY.
- Clients increased Quarter over Quarter (QoQ) from 740 to 827.
- Renewals include Yahoo! and AOL.
- Acquisition spree makes predicting future cash levels hard (five done for mostly cash in the past 8 months), but NTRT is emerging as leader.
- Although clearly the dot-com bubble has deflated, it is interesting to note that e-commerce sales are up last month 34% YoY.

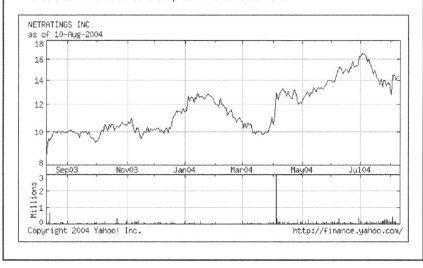

EXHIBIT 2.9   GEMS

Glenayre provides unified messaging services.

Price	Cash/Share	Book/Share	Cash	Market Cap
$1.33	$1.63	$1.67	$106 million	$87 million

- $77 million in annual sales, $5 million annual burn which is down 87% YoY.
- Heavy insider purchasing since June—the president, two directors, two senior officers of the company.
- The Royce Fund family is a large mutual fund shareholder.
- Integration of Glenayre's unified messaging services with Rim's wireless platform recently announced. Just as RIM devices have become the standard among corporate users of wireless data devices, we feel that GEMS software will become the standard for wireless unified messaging.

Source: Reproduced with permission of Yahoo! Inc. © 2004 by Yahoo! Inc. YAHOO! and the YAHOO! logo are trademarks of Yahoo! Inc.

EXHIBIT 2.10 CPCI

Ciprico provides storage for digital media.

Price	Cash/Share	Book/Share	Cash	Market Cap
$3.81	$5.09	$6.70	$24 million	$18 million

- $31 million sales, $6.5 million burn.
- 40% YoY sales growth in the most recent quarter.
- Losses decreased 31% compared with prior year quarter.
- Sales to military increased 80% YoY in prior quarter.
- Heartland Value Fund is a large mutual fund shareholder.
- CFO bought shares a year ago.

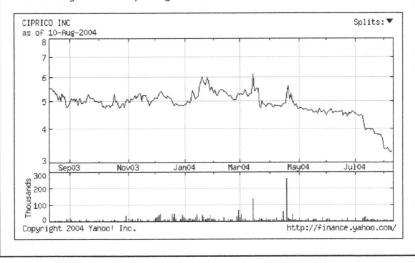

Source: Reproduced with permission of Yahoo! Inc. © 2004 by Yahoo! Inc. YAHOO! and the YAHOO! logo are trademarks of Yahoo! Inc.

EXHIBIT 2.11   STRD

Strategic Distribution, Inc. provides proprietary maintenance, repair and operating supply procurement, and handling and data management solutions to industrial sites, primarily through its In-Plant Store (R) program.

Price	Cash/Share	Book/Share	Cash	Market Cap
$1.33	$1.65	$1.73	$23 million	$18 million

- Profitable in the most recent quarter ($0.6 million vs. $–3.4 million last year).
- Eliminated unprofitable contract with Kraft that accounted for almost half of their revenues.
- Royce Micro Cap fund a significant mutual fund shareholder.
- $284 million in sales last year.

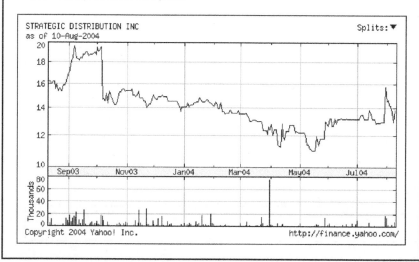

Source: Reproduced with permission of Yahoo! Inc. © 2004 by Yahoo! Inc. YAHOO! and the YAHOO! logo are trademarks of Yahoo! Inc.

EXHIBIT 2.12 PRTS

Partsbase, Inc.

Price	Cash/Share	Book/Share	Cash	Market Cap
$1.33	$1.65	$1.73	$23 million	$18 million

- Annualized burn rate of $3.7 million.
- Offer on the table for $1.41 from a company formed by Robert Hammond, PRTS's CEO. A definitive merger agreement was signed in August 2002. A higher offer, for $1.55–1.65, was presented by AVL, but the board has rejected it.
- If the merger closes by January 1, the annualized return for sharebuyers at current prices is 72%.

EXHIBIT 2.13 IATV

ACTV, Inc.

Price	Cash/Share	Book/Share	Cash	Market Cap
$0.73	$1.15	$0.75	$64 million	$40 million

- Has signed definitive merger agreement with OPTV, which is majority owned by Liberty Media.
- OPTV also trades under cash levels ($135 million cash, $98 million market cap).
- The deal, to be done in OPTV shares, currently has a value of $1.07 if the deal closes today with OPTV at $1.46, implying a spread of 34 cents to sharebuyers today.

Within six months of writing that article, the basket of stocks I recommended was up over 100 percent as the market not only jolted upwards in the aftermath of the Iraq War but also began to realize the value of the cash portfolios of these companies. I mention this article as prime evidence that these situations still occur when the notorious "Mr. Market" takes an aggressive view toward selling.

This brings us back to the topic of diversification. All of the above examples were interesting in that they were trading below their book value and had reasonably safe criteria in terms of the rate by which they were dissipating these assets. However, I still was not willing to put all of my chips in one stock.

Graham notes that when a company is trading below its market value, one of two things should happen (note the word "should"):

1. The market will once again value the company on the basis of its liquidating value or higher.

2. The company's management, if they can't turn the business around, will liquidate the business and return the proceeds to investors.

All of this is based on the notion of mean reversion. If a company were trading well above book value, then it would imply that the market was giving high value to the company's earnings. If the earnings were of such high quality then eventually competition would set it, driving down the quality of those earnings, and the market would respond accordingly. Similarly, if a company were trading below book, then the market would not place any value on the company's business, eventually causing potential competitors to look for other opportunities and industries, which in turn would drive up the quality of the company's business (since all competitors are elsewhere).

However, there is always the danger that management doesn't care about the shareholders but instead enjoys sitting on the assets of the company and using it for their personal benefit. Diversification is the tool that we can use to reduce the risk of corrupt, or at best, uncaring, management.

To quote Graham and Dodd again, this time from the chapter "Theory of Common Stock investment" in *Security Analysis*: "Finally, [the investor] will rely...upon diversification to average out the effects of unforeseeable future developments..."

And then they state: *"Purchase of a single common stock not an investment"* (italics their emphasis). They add:

> *Group Purchases May constitute an Investment Operation—Group purchases of selected common stocks at attractive prices will very probably fall under our original definition of investment in Chap IV ("An investment operation is one which, upon thorough analysis, promises safety of principle and a satisfactory return").*

It is interesting in the paragraph above that one diversifies and *then* there is a valid investment operation. In other words, they separate the idea of diversification from the idea of safety. Buffett is able to combine the ideas from *Security Analysis* with Fisher's ideas of a focused portfolio by reintegrating diversification into the concept of margin of safety. In other words, diversification is one possible means of acquiring that safety. But if you have other means of getting the desired degree of safety, then it reduces the need for diversification.

A great example from the Buffett historical portfolio is that of Sanborn Map. In the 1960 letter to his limited partners, Buffett mentioned that there was one situation that constituted 35 percent of the portfolio of the partnership. This would not have been considered by Graham to be an investment in the spirit of their approach since it was not diversified, despite having many of the other characteristics that Graham typically recommended. As was typical with Buffett, he did not reveal what the stock was in 1960 that took up so much of the partnership's assets. However, in the 1961 letter he did unveil this mysterious stock and put up his reasons for the investment.

Sanborn Map was the MapQuest of the early twentieth century. The company started in 1866 when Aetna Insurance employed D.A. Sanborn to map a town in Tennessee. In the first year of business, 50 towns were mapped out. By 1873, 600 towns were mapped out. By 1920 they had over 1,000 employees and had production facilities in Chicago, San Francisco, and New York. The maps were incredibly detailed—showing underground pipes, fire hydrants, and so on, so that they were of great use to fire insurance companies. Starting around the 1950s the map business began to falter. Rising competition and little need for the insurance companies to constantly update their maps forced Sanborn to downsize.

Starting around the 1930s, however, Sanborn began putting their profits into an investment portfolio that, over time, grew substantially. By 1958, when Buffett started accumulating the stock, the investment portfolio was worth more than the market price of the company. As Buffett put it in his 1961 letter:

> *Let me give you some idea of the extreme divergence of these two factors. In 1938 when the Dow-Jones Industrial Average was in the 100–120 range, Sanborn sold at $110 per share. In 1958 with the Average in the 550 area, Sanborn sold at $45 per share. Yet during that same period the value of the Sanborn investment portfolio increased from about $20 per share to $65 per share. This means, in effect, that the buyer of Sanborn stock in 1938 was placing a positive valuation of $90 per share on the map business ($110 less the $20 value of the investments unrelated to the map business) in a year of depressed business and stock market conditions. In the tremendously more vigorous climate of 1958 the same map business was evaluated at a minus $20 with the buyer of the stock unwilling to pay more than 70 cents on the dollar for the investment portfolio with the map business thrown in for nothing.*

In other words, Buffett felt he had a substantial margin of safety based on the fact that the investment portfolio was worth far more than the company was being sold for on the stock market. Additionally, the company was still profitable, although the profits were deteriorating. Moreover, the value of the maps was not going away anytime soon, even if the company had to downsize. The maps were so detailed and useful that there would always be some sort of market for them. In fact, the company still exists today and still serves the insurance community.

Additionally, the income from the investment portfolio was such that there were absolutely no worries regarding the financial viability of the company. What concerned Buffett, though, was that while dividends were being cut during the period of downsizing, Buffett "could never find any record of suggestions pertaining to cutting salaries or directors' and committee fees." Since directors did not own enough of the stock, they were therefore less concerned about the price of the stock than Buffett, who ended up either owning or allying himself with about 40 percent of the company's stock.

It is this control that gave him an extra level of safety. He knew that once he was in control he could arrange an appropriate liquidation of stock. Once he obtained enough shares to influence a shareholder vote, he worked out with the board a plan to separate the investment portfolio from the map business. All shareholders who wanted to were taken out at fair value, and Buffett made a significant profit on his investment. And to anybody who thinks Buffett doesn't understand technology at all, his 1961 letter contains an interesting foreshadowing of the future of the map business when he states: "There appeared to be a real opportunity to multiply map profits through utilization of Sanborn's wealth of raw material in conjunction with electronic means of converting this data to the most usable form for the customer."

If anything, diversification would have hurt Buffett's efforts to turn this investment into a profitable one. Left to its own devices, the board of Sanborn would have done nothing to unlock shareholder value. In order for Buffett to fully realize his margin of safety he could not have stood by passively. He needed to actively negotiate with the other shareholders to take control, and then once in control, to develop the plan and execute it for unlocking that value. If he had been in 50 other similar situations with other companies, there is no way he could have spent the time and effort needed to do it. If anything, his focus was his margin of safety.

A more famous example in the Buffett mythos is that of the Dempster Mill Manufacturing Company. The company, started in 1880, was a major manufacturer of windmills and farm implements.

Buffett accumulated his 70 percent voting block in the company from 1958 to 1962 at an average price of $28 per share. At the time the company had $9 million in sales, limited profitability, and tangible assets of about $75 per share. Buffett made the point in his first letter to investors where he mentioned Dempster that the price of the overall market was meaningless for Dempster. If General Motors went up, for instance, it didn't necessarily follow that Dempster would go up. Because he owned 70 percent of the shares and there were very few other shareholders, there was no real public market for the stock. So he began to value the stock based on what he felt the liquidation value of the business was, plus any value he thought was left in the underlying farm equipment business.

Since Buffett now controlled the company he was very focused on unlocking the value. He decided to install new management in the company in early 1962. This resulted in the hiring of Harry Bottle to take over the company. From the 1963 letter to investors in the Buffett Partnership, he writes: "A good friend, whose inclination is not toward enthusiastic descriptions, highly recommended Harry Bottle for our type of problem."

This is the first mention in the Buffett letters of Charlie Munger (the "good friend" mentioned earlier). Munger ended up being Buffett's partner for the next 40 years and participated in the decision-making of almost all of Buffett's significant investments henceforth. Harry immediately cut costs and began selling off the inventory as well as the company's unprofitable facilities. Also, with the newfound cash on the balance sheet obtained from these liquidations, Buffett began investing this cash in a portfolio almost identical to that of the Buffett Partnership. This was his first experimentation into the model that proved very successful later on when he took control of textile manufacturer Berkshire Hathaway.

By the end of 1963 Buffett, with Bottle's help, was able to basically sell off all the assets and realize a profit of $80 per share on his initial investment of approximately $28 per share.

Again, this is an example where Buffett had two alternative routes for increasing his margin of safety once he found a company trading significantly below book value:

1. He could buy up shares in the company and then diversify his risk by buying many more similar situations and hoping for the best.
2. He could take control of the company, find effective management, sell off the assets, and realize his profits.

With both Sanborn and Dempster, he chose the latter approach. We have seen this in other chapters where Buffett always has a "back door" to his trade in order to justify his margin of safety. For instance, in the Arcata/KKR merger arbitrage situation mentioned in Chapter 5 on merger arbitrage, Buffett figured that either he would make money if the Arcata deal went through, or he would make money because Arcata was undervalued anyway. With some of these liquidation situations, Buffett figured he would either make money because management will realize the benefits of selling off assets to achieve shareholder value, or *he would become management and unlock it for them.* In both cases there was also no immediate danger of assets being dissipated. In fact, both companies, Sanborn and Dempster, were still mildly profitable and increasing their tangible assets, albeit more slowly than they had in the past.

Other examples throughout this book can be found of Buffett taking the Graham-Dodd approach. And by Graham-Dodd I'm not just referring to the idea that you should always buy a stock when it trades at ⅔ book value and then sell when it trades higher than book value. I also want to emphasize the idea that you should not make an investment unless there is a guaranteed margin of safety. In every instance, whether it is an arbitrage, a fixed income instrument, a stock, or even the purchase of someone's life insurance policy, Buffett always reaches for that extra element of safety. He always asks the question, "What if my initial premise, the initial reason for making this trade, is wrong?" He then asks, "And what if the next reason is wrong?" And so on.

CHAPTER 3

Equities

Warren Buffett has repeatedly stated that when he buys shares of a company, he thinks of himself as an "owner" of that business rather than as someone who simply wants to flip those shares for a small profit (i.e., a trader). As stated in Chapter 1, there are many occasions where Buffett does take a rather short-term (less than forever) view of a stock, and he occasionally takes short-term profits or losses. However, that does not diminish the deeper sentiment expressed in his statement that you should not buy a stock unless you can put yourself in the shoes of an owner of that business and be able to say, "This business is going to generate a return worthy of my investment."

The best example is that of the old-fashioned lemonade stand. When you set up a lemonade stand you outlay some cash for the table, cups, the first batch of lemonade, and maybe the sign that you put up the street pointing people in your direction. Whether or not your initial outlay of cash was a good investment is directly related to whether this lemonade stand is a good business. Several factors play a role:

- For each dollar you put into the business, will you expect to eventually make that dollar back plus additional money (the return on your investment)?

- Could you have taken the same money and had a better investment elsewhere (either in setting up another business or simply putting the money in a savings account)? A corollary to this is that a "better investment" can also mean an investment with a similar return but less risk.

As simplistic as it sounds, this is how Warren Buffett evaluates all his stock buying and selling decisions. He doesn't do anything based on sophisticated technical analysis, volume indicators, chaos theory, or neural networks. However, the reason it is hard to get high stock market returns is that for a somewhat complicated business, the predictability of what the business is going to earn (and what other alternative investments are going to earn) is very complicated.

At this point most investors snap their fingers and say, "Aha! Let's break out the dividend discount model." A business should be valued on the basis of its total cash flows from here to eternity, discounted by whatever the risk-free rate is. Why the discount? Well, assume that your business can earn five percent a year forever and that I can get a five percent return, forever, from Treasury bills. Your business is essentially worthless, then, since as long as the U.S. government is here to stay, putting my money in T-bills will be a better choice for me than putting it in a risk-filled business.

Example: My Story

My own example of the dividend discount model coming into play occurred in early 2000. I had started a wireless software company and at the time "wireless" was a favorite buzzword among investors. Despite the fact that we had minimal revenues and were burning money at a fairly quick rate (we were, after all, a startup company), we were already being wined and dined by every investment bank and analyst. On one occasion a group came in from a tier one investment bank to pitch us. The head of the group started off by saying that Mr. X (a well-known analyst now barred from the securities industry) would cover our stock despite the fact that we were a wireless software company and he was an e-commerce/consumer analyst. Then came the fun part: valuation.

The junior member of the team broke out his dividend discount model. Apparently we were going to stop losing money within a year (thank God!) and then start growing earnings per share at a rate of 25 percent a year compared with a risk-free rate of nine percent. That miraculous growth (about as miraculous as miracle hair growth cures from carnivals of the 1920s) would continue for 10 years (why not?) and then slow down to a more terminal growth rate of 10 percent. It all sounded good, but the reality never quite matched the pretty picture this analyst created (although fortunately the company still exists, as compared with most of its peers).

So the question is, if the intrinsic value of a business can be determined by its future cash flows, then how can we improve the predictability of those cash flows? Note that if investors could truly predict cash flows, then Warren Buffett would never have been able to achieve his above-average market returns. The key is not only to find companies where the cash flows are somewhat predictable but also to find companies where, for whatever reason, the market perceives those cash flows as being at-risk. The more risk the market perceives in those cash flows (or the more unpredictable those cash flows are), the higher return an investor must demand to compensate for that risk.

For example, American Express in 1963 fell victim to the notorious Salad Oil Scandal. Anthony DeAngelis, a New Jersey meatpacker who started a company called Allied Crude Vegetable Oil Refining, was sending supposed shipments of vegetable oil to a warehouse in Bayonne, New Jersey, which then issued receipts for the oil. With those receipts, DeAngelis was able to obtain up to $175 million in financing (on the basis of $60 million worth of vegetable oil as collateral) and then use that money to speculate on vegetable oil futures. The whole thing fell apart (as these things usually do) when DeAngelis lost it all on his speculation and had to go bankrupt. The company that vouched for the warehouse receipts and allowed DeAngelis to obtain his financing was American Express.

When American Express did an audit to collect their collateral, they found that instead of $60 million worth of vegetable oil there was only $6 million. The vegetable oil had been watered down to make it appear as if there were more. To their credit, American Express very quickly made good on the hundreds of millions of dollars in potential liabilities, but this also created a very big black hole on their balance sheet, temporarily wiping out all shareholder equity.

Shares in American Express fell from $60 to $35 over a two-month period. Shareholders and speculators were both playing a momentum game (if it can fall $2 today, it will probably fall $2 tomorrow) and some had legitimate fears that American Express was going bankrupt. To some extent, these fears were not entirely irrational. If American Express management was lax enough to let this scandal happen, who knows what other problems might lie underneath?

First, however, Buffett was comforted by management's instant and honest response to the losses, taking the hit, and indemnifying many of the third-party victims to the scandal.

Second, Buffett recognized that this scandal had nothing to do with American Express's core businesses—the traveler's checks and credit card businesses.

Third, Buffett is always impressed by businesses where a large float can provide liquidity to the underlying operations of the business, as in, for instance, the insurance business. The traveler's checks business involves consumers paying cash up front to American Express; American Express pays out that money at some future unspecified date. In the meantime, American Express can do whatever it wants with customers' money. This idea of a float-based business is almost like getting a zero-interest loan. Eventually, American Express has to pay all the money back, but with no interest charges attached. The cost of financing doesn't get any better than this (at least until the 2003 SQUARZ bonds that Buffett himself put out—the first negative-interest bonds in history).

Finally, Buffett wanted to see what the consumer perception was of American Express's problems. He went out to Ross's Steakhouse in Omaha, stood behind the cashier all evening, and watched as customer after customer used their American Express cards to pay for their meals. He was able to conclude two things:

1. The American Express brand was not affected at all by the scandal; in fact, it was stronger than ever. This idea of brand strength was used by Buffett repeatedly (starting with this incident) over the next 40 years as a "gut" predictor of future earnings.
2. It was clear that the merchants were not worried about being paid by American Express. In other words, the Salad Oil Scandal was a one-time hit against earnings, but the underlying business was strong and getting stronger.

Buffett started accumulating shares at $35 apiece and sold them between two and four years later. Five years after the incident, American

Express shares were trading as high as $185 a share. Note that this was not a long-term buy-and-hold "forever" investment for Warren Buffett, even though it had many of the characteristics of his buy-and-hold investments later on: strong brand, predictable earnings, strong moat, and so on. But at this point, the cash Buffett had to put to use, which consisted of the money in his hedge fund, was a lot smaller and allowed him to be more nimble. Taking advantage of this nimbleness in a way that he can no longer do due to his enormous size allowed him to go in and out of trades as needed, taking profits and moving on to the next opportunity.

What created the phenomenal trading opportunities (and excesses) of the dot-com era from 1997 to 2000 was directly related to the notion of intrinsic value. Basically, people had no idea what these companies would make. However, it was clear that the Internet was a revolution on par with the printing press. Suddenly, the cost of commerce got much cheaper. People could shop from their homes, implying that the bricks-and-mortar approach of setting up stores everywhere, and the costs inherent with that kind of business, were not necessary for the winners in the Internet commerce gain. Additionally, the Internet also decreased the costs of communication as well as the costs of software development, since network protocols and interfaces were built into the underlying ideas of the Web. With all of the costs out of the picture and a potential customer base in the billions, the earnings created would be phenomenal and so would the returns—if it were possible to pick the winners.

The idea that the Internet was a bubble is often implied by Buffett adherents but not necessarily by Buffett himself. He simply states that he had a hard time valuing these companies simply because he was not a computer expert. He had no way of determining what the future cash flows of these companies would be or which companies would be the winners. Nor does Buffett take a "VC-style" approach to his investing. Buffett likes to make as few bets as possible; with luck every bet pays off. A typical venture capitalist portfolio might have 20 investments, with 10 failures, eight break-even investments, and two home runs. What happened in the so-called Internet bubble is that the public became venture capitalists instead of value investors. Many of the companies did turn out to be worthless. But the basic idea was correct. There were enormous opportunities in the Internet space, as evidenced by eBay's earnings just a few years after its inception (see Exhibit 3.1).

Never have a company's profits grown this quickly so soon after its birth. Does this mean that all of the Internet speculators were correct and

EXHIBIT 3.1 eBay's Earnings over the Past 5 Years

Year	Earnings (in millions)
1999	$10.8
2000	$48.3
2001	$90.4
2002	$249.9
2003	$441.8

Buffett was wrong? Absolutely not. It is just a different approach. And the eBays of the world happen once in a lifetime; Buffett's results, however, have stood the test of time over a 50-year period. I was always very surprised with all of the investors who consistently turned up their noses at the Internet and refused to even acknowledge that the potential was there. Even in the summer of 2003, Barron's had a cover article suggesting that perhaps Yahoo!, Amazon, and eBay were in another bubble; the magazine picked the exact companies that would end up doubling their earnings growth yet again over the next year.

That said, Buffett likes to keep it simple. He looks for earnings predictability with companies that might be distressed but whose quality of business still remains high. Why might investors (Mr. Market) be putting more risk on the future earnings flow than Buffett? Here are a few reasons:

- **Market risk.** In recent years the market has become fearful that a future terrorist attack might slow down the U.S. economy and put pressure on even predictable earnings streams. As detailed in Chapter 12, Buffett does not care so much for market or systemic risk, assuming that there is no real event that can so drastically change the value of all securities in the market that he worry too much.
- **Fear of corruption.** When the Enron scandal broke in late 2001, the shares of many energy companies, even the most conservative utilities, fell in sympathy despite the enormous predictability of those earnings. In Chapter 7, we will see how Buffett took advantage of this market fear to place a private investment in a public utility.
- **Litigation risk.** In the tobacco industry, the market and earnings have always been predictable but the fear of mass class-action litigation has often kept the price lower than would be suggested by any measure of intrinsic value.

- **Setback in the business.** When mad cow disease surfaced in England, shares of McDonald's reacted, reaching multi-year lows. Investors had to assess whether this would have a permanent effect on the business. If the answer was "no," then the assumption would be that the shares would go back to where they were before the stock started to fall—about a 50 percent return. If the answer was "yes," then one had to assess how far the stock had yet to fall. If the stock had another 10 percent to go, but you felt there was more than a 20 percent chance that the market had already discounted enough the effects of mad cow disease, then the buying was certainly worth it.

The risks of investing go on and, in each specific case, are usually fairly straightforward. When a market or stock starts to sell off there are usually countless news articles, Internet message board postings, and television commentators documenting the rise and fall of once-proud companies. The Internet has closed the information gap and has made it possible to quickly assess the veracity of any story quickly. Similarly, very standard tools can be used to examine the predictability of future cash flows.

Note that we are talking about future cash flows and not necessarily price/earnings (P/E) ratios. In Chapter 11 I discuss the pros and cons of trading based on P/E ratios, but this section necessitates a few comments first. The P/E ratio refers to the price the stock is currently trading at divided by its net income per share. For instance, if a stock trades at $20, has 30 million shares outstanding, and earned $30 million last year, then it trades at a P/E ratio of $20 × $30 million divided by 30 million shares outstanding, or 20. Many people also look at the earnings yield, which is simply the P/E ratio upside down, or E/P. In the above example, the earnings yield would be five percent. The earnings yield is what the company could potentially pay out to shareholders if it did not reinvest its earnings in the business. If the earnings yield of a given stock is much higher than Treasury bill interest rates (that is, if the P/E ratio is low), then many investors think that the stock constitutes a good investment. We'll look at this later in Chapter 12.

Note that the E in this equation might not be real earnings at all, but a modified definition of earnings, which might include various non-cash charges such as depreciations, amortization of goodwill, and (should a company do this) options-related expenses. Also, for each company, the method for booking revenues varies significantly and is often an issue. The same can be said for how expenses are booked. For example, can a marketing expense be amortized, as Worldcom tried to do to the tune of billions of dollars? AOL was notorious for doing this throughout the 1990s but it didn't slow down the rise in their stock price. Worldcom, however, almost instantly went bankrupt when their accounting discrepancies were exposed.

P/E ratios also do not tell you anything about the predictability of future earnings, the quality of current earnings, or the fundamentals of the business. Nor do we have any reason to believe that Warren Buffett looks at the P/E ratio. In fact, many of his acquisitions are occurring precisely when earnings are falling and the P/E ratio is skyrocketing higher. In chapter 11, I take the analysis one step further, and examine whether P/E ratios are truly predictive of the future.

What tools can be used, then, in helping predict future cash flows?

- **Growth of the U.S. economy.** In general, if the U.S. economy grows at a certain percent a year, then the cash flows of the market are most likely growing at the same rate, give or take one to five percent. The market has grown slightly faster than the economy only because the multiple over those cash flows has grown slightly over the years. If stocks go up much faster than the U.S. economy, as happened in the 1990s when the gross domestic product (GDP) was growing at approximately six percent a year and the Nasdaq was going up almost 30 percent a year, bad things can eventually happen.
- **Operating Margin, Return on Equity (ROE), or Return on Capital (ROC).** A study by John Schmitz and Sean Cleary on what fundamental criteria have been the most predictive for stocks on the Toronto Stock Exchange from 1989 to 1998 determined that return on equity and operating margin were consistently among the top factors for every time period. The higher the ROE and operating margin, the more likely a stock would go up in the next period.

Return on equity is defined as the net profits of a firm divided by the total amount of equity invested in a firm. In our lemonade stand example, if someone started with $15 ($10 for the table, $3 for the first set of cups, and $2 for the first batch of lemonade) and earned $10 in the first day, then the ROE would be 66 percent. If the stand's owner has a high operating margin (gross profit over sales), then he or she would presumably need to reinvest relatively little of the profits in order to sustain the current level of profitability. Companies with a high fixed asset base, where assets are depreciating and occasionally need to be replenished, will suffer severely if the operating margin is hurt for any reason or if the business slows in general.

Does this mean Buffett simply does a screen on all public equities and buys companies with high ROEs and high operating margins? Absolutely not. In some cases, Buffett bought companies that were experiencing declining earnings (The Washington Post is a good example), but Buffett believed in management and in the industry. In one case (Coca-Cola), Buffett bought a business that had suffered in the past. He wanted to capitalize on the turnaround despite the fact that the business was neither cheap, nor was there necessarily a catalyst that was going to drive up the stock price. In another case (GEICO), Buffett bought into a business that to all outward appearances was completely falling apart, but he had a belief in the underlying fundamentals of both the business and the industry. The lesson we can take from all this is that there is no one formula for success.

CHAPTER 4

Current Holdings

T his chapter provides a list of Buffett's current known holdings, along with some statistics and background about each one.

AUTOMATIC DATA PROCESSING

Symbol: ADP (NYSE)
Date Purchased: 2003

ADP is the world's largest provider of outsourced payroll processing services. Despite 10 years of steady revenue and earnings increases, the stock dipped in 2002–2003 during the general market decline. Buffett and/or Berkshire Hathaway started to accumulate the shares. He played it for the small dip and subsequent rise, and then got rid of the shares in the first half of 2004.

DOVER CORPORATION

Symbol: DOV (NYSE)
Date Purchased: 2001

EXHIBIT 4.1   ADP

Year	Revenues	Net Income	Margin	Book/Share	ROE
4-Jun	7399.5	935.6	12.6	NA	NA
3-Jun	7147	1018.2	14.2	$9.03	19
2-Jun	7004.3	1100.8	15.7	$8.17	21.5
1-Jun	7017.6	924.7	13.2	$7.53	19.7
Jun-00	6287.5	840.8	13.4	$7.29	18.3
Jun-99	5540.1	696.8	12.6	$6.43	17.4
Jun-98	4798.1	605.3	12.6	$5.64	17.8
Jun-97	4112.2	513.5	12.5	$4.54	19.3
Jun-96	3566.6	454.7	12.7	$4.02	19.6
Jun-95	2893.7	394.8	13.6	$3.64	18.8

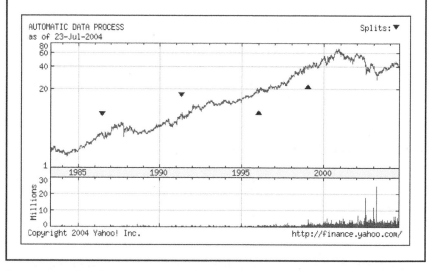

Source: Reproduced with permission of Yahoo! Inc. © 2004 by Yahoo! Inc. YAHOO! and the YAHOO! logo are trademarks of Yahoo! Inc.

Dover is a modern, behind-the-scenes conglomerate. Rarely mentioned in the media, it makes everything from gasoline-pump nozzles to automated printed circuit board assemblers to tractor trailers. They have shown consistent revenue and earnings increases throughout the 1990s, both internally and through acquisitions. Buffett bought shares in the first quarter of 2001 and kept adding to his position until early 2003, approximately around the time that the stock bottomed. Paul Tudor Jones, one of the greatest traders ever, once stated, "losers average losers." I think it is more a matter of "to each his own." Buffett clearly likes to buy good companies that are going through hard times and then average down as the stocks become cheaper. With Dover, Buffett had a company with so many years of consistent growth and earnings that he was confident, once the recession of 2001–2002 was over, that it would return to its old form. As of the end of 2003, when Buffett started selling his shares, Dover's book value was the highest it had ever been, even after the dip of 2002.

EXHIBIT 4.2 DOV

Year	Revenues	Net Income	Margin	Book/Share	ROE
3-Dec	4413.3	285.2	6.5	$13.52	10.7
2-Dec	4183.7	211.1	5	$11.83	7.2
1-Dec	4459.7	166.8	3.7	$12.44	9.9
Dec-00	5400.7	533.2	9.9	$12.02	21.3
Dec-99	4446.4	405.1	9.1	$10.06	45.6
Dec-98	3977.7	326.4	8.2	$8.67	19.8
Dec-97	4547.7	405.4	8.9	$7.65	23.8
Dec-96	4076.3	390.2	9.6	$6.62	26.2
Dec-95	3745.9	278.3	7.4	$5.40	22.7
Dec-94	3085.3	202.4	6.6	$4.39	20.3

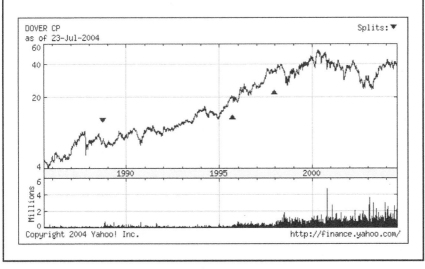

AMERICAN EXPRESS

Symbol: AXP (NYSE)

Date Purchased: 1991

American Express is the world's largest issuer of charge cards and traveler's checks. They also provide other financial services such as financial planning, investment advisory services, insurance, annuities, mutual funds, and so on.

EXHIBIT 4.3 AXP

Year	Revenues	Net Income	Margin	Book/Share	ROE
3-Dec	25866	3000	11.6	$11.93	19.6
2-Dec	23807	2671	11.2	$10.62	19.3
1-Dec	22582	1311	5.8	$9.04	10.9
Dec-00	23675	2810	11.9	$8.81	24
Dec-99	21278	2475	11.6	$7.52	24.5
Dec-98	19132	2141	11.2	$7.14	22.1
Dec-97	17760	1991	11.2	$6.84	20.8
Dec-96	16237	1901	11.7	$6.01	22.3
Dec-95	15841	1564	9.9	$5.53	19.5
Dec-94	14282	1380	9.7	$4.19	22.7

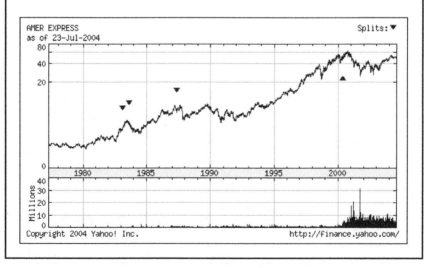

Source: Reproduced with permission of Yahoo! Inc. © 2004 by Yahoo! Inc. YAHOO! and the YAHOO! logo are trademarks of Yahoo! Inc.

AMERICAN STANDARD

Symbol: ASD (NYSE)

Another mega-conglomerate in Buffett's holdings, American Standard makes products ranging from kitchen equipment to air-conditioning systems to bathroom fixtures. When Buffett was rolling up furniture companies and carpet companies, he was also probably assuming that the

EXHIBIT 4.4 ASD

Year	Revenues	Net Income	Margin	Book/Share	ROE
3-Dec	8567.6	405.2	4.7	$3.27	56.8
2-Dec	7795.4	371	4.8	$1.05	161.4
1-Dec	7465.3	295	4	($0.42)	NA
Dec-00	7598.4	315.2	4.1	($1.88)	NA
Dec-99	7189.5	264.1	3.7	($2.34)	NA
Dec-98	6653.9	33.6	0.5	($3.34)	NA
Dec-97	6007.5	119.9	2	($2.82)	NA
Dec-96	5804.6	–46.7	–0.8	($1.61)	NA
Dec-95	5221.5	141.8	2.7	($1.69)	NA
Dec-94	4457.5	–77.7	–1.7	($4.36)	NA

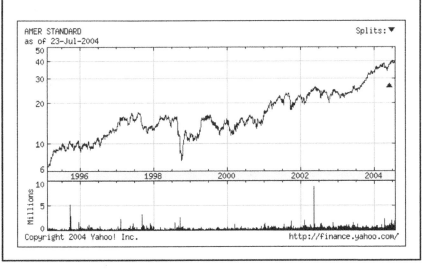

Source: Reproduced with permission of Yahoo! Inc. © 2004 by Yahoo! Inc. YAHOO! and the YAHOO! logo are trademarks of Yahoo! Inc.

housing bust would lead to more purchases in American Standard's domain. He first purchased American Standard stock in 2002.

H&R BLOCK

Symbol: HRB (NYSE)
Date Purchased: 2001

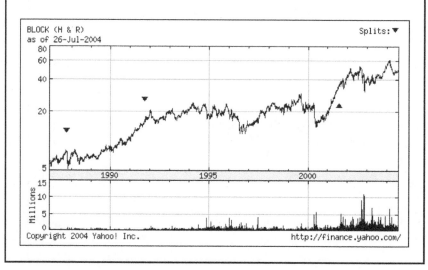

EXHIBIT 4.5   HRB

Year	Revenues	Net Income	Margin	Book/Share	ROE
4-Apr	3625.1	704.3	19.4	$10.96	37.1
3-Apr	3295.2	580.1	17.6	$9.29	34.9
2-Apr	2917.2	434.4	14.9	$7.56	31.7
1-Apr	2810.3	276.7	9.8	$6.39	23.6
Apr-00	2196.8	251.9	11.5	$6.22	20.7
Apr-99	1498.6	237.8	15.9	$5.44	20.3
Apr-98	1187.7	174.2	14.7	$6.27	29.2
Apr-97	1805.7	47.8	2.6	$4.80	4.8
Apr-96	764.6	125.1	16.4	$5.03	17
Apr-95	1233.8	107.3	8.7	$3.27	15.6

Source: Reproduced with permission of Yahoo! Inc. © 2004 by Yahoo! Inc. YAHOO! and the YAHOO! logo are trademarks of Yahoo! Inc.

Death and taxes are here to stay, but I would add to that by saying, "Death, taxes, and shaving." The purchase of H&R Block stock beginning in 2001 reminds me of another, larger Berkshire holding with Gillette. Every day, a billion people or more around the world are shaving. Similarly, every year, hundreds of millions of people pay taxes and H&R Block has the intangible brand that people know they can trust for cheap, easy, and money-saving tax advice. The stock dipped in 2000 along with the general market; Buffett, realizing that the fundamentals of the business had not changed at all but that the market was suddenly giving away stock at a cheaper price, began to buy.

COCA-COLA

Symbol: KO (NYSE)
Date Purchased: 1988

What can be said about this investment that hasn't already been said? Robert Hagstrom's summary of this investment, which appears in *The Warren Buffett Way*,[1] is excellent. Despite the steady and consistent revenues, earnings, and ROE of the 1990s, this was initially a turnaround play that Buffett bought at the tail end of the turnaround. In the 1970s, Coca-Cola was trying out new businesses from clothes to movies. Then, in the mid-1980s, the installation of CEO Roberto Goizueta got the company back on track. It was definitely not a Graham-Dodd play in the classic sense, whereby a company is bought for less than its net tangible assets. However, this is where the influence of Charlie Munger played a role. Buffett made an estimation of how to value the intangible of Coca-Cola's brand name. In effect, he was still trying to go the Graham-Dodd route but adding the intangible value of the brand name to the net tangible assets. How is it possible to determine the value of a brand name? To some extent, it can be done by looking at return on equity.

The beauty of capitalism is that money doesn't grow on trees. If there were such a tree, then everyone would instantly converge on that tree and pick all the money off until it were bare. High return on equity businesses are equivalent to such fictional trees—capitalism kicks in by provid-

---

[1]*The Warren Buffett Way*, Robert Hagstrom, John Wiley & Sons, Inc., 1993.

ing competition until the ROE decreases in response as margins go down. The mythology of the brand is what keeps entrepreneurs and potential competitors at bay and forces them to look toward other businesses and industries.

Interestingly, the rise of water as a marketable product (paying $5 a gallon for what you can get for free from your tap) is probably what has slowed Coke down a bit around the world. Buffett has repeatedly said that

EXHIBIT 4.6   KO

Year	Revenues	Net Income	Margin	Book/Share	ROE
3-Dec	21044	4347	20.7	$5.77	30.9
2-Dec	19564	3976	20.3	$4.78	33.7
1-Dec	20092	3979	19.8	$4.57	35
Dec-00	20458	2177	10.6	$3.75	23.4
Dec-99	19805	2431	12.3	$3.85	25.6
Dec-98	18813	3533	18.8	$3.41	42
Dec-97	18868	4129	21.9	$2.96	56.5
Dec-96	18546	3492	18.8	$2.48	56.7
Dec-95	18018	2986	16.6	$2.15	55.4
Dec-94	16172	2554	15.8	$2.05	48.8

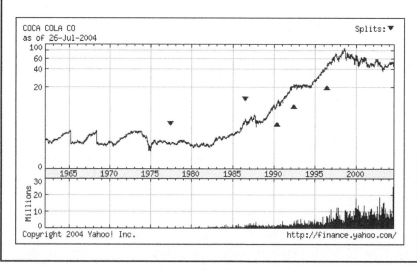

Source: Reproduced with permission of Yahoo! Inc. © 2004 by Yahoo! Inc. YAHOO! and the YAHOO! logo are trademarks of Yahoo! Inc.

this is one of his permanent holdings. And at 34% ROE, it is not a bad place to keep the billions Buffett has here. But he hasn't added to his position in a while; my guess is that he won't in the near future.

COSTCO WHOLESALE

Symbol: COST (NASDAQ)
Date Purchased: 2000

Buffett has always said that one of his biggest mistakes was not buying Wal-Mart. He thought the price was too high when he looked in the 1970s and kept waiting for the dip that never happened. When Munger encouraged Buffett to look at the Costco model (Munger is on the board of Costco), Buffett may have seen it as his second chance. Munger has always been a fan of the Costco model and said so at the Berkshire Hathaway 1999 annual meeting: "I'm such an admirer of the Costco culture and the Costco system that I'm not sure I'm totally rational. I love the place. That isn't so bad in life, to find a couple of things you love."

Costco is a great example of how Buffett approaches a stock purchase. He doesn't simply say, "This is a great company; I need to buy it." Buffett likes to play the mean-reversion game. When bad news affects a stock, people have a tendency to react in a strong fashion, and that reaction usually turns into an overreaction. When Costco missed analysts' earnings estimates by a penny on May 24, 2000, the stock fell 22%. At that point Buffett must have examined the news and asked himself: Are people irrationally selling this stock, or is this news serious? Perhaps Costco was growing too fast. Or maybe the margins were starting to get hit by increased competition from ex-Buffett mistake Sam's Club (owned by Wal-Mart).

We don't know for sure what Buffett looked at between May 24, 2000, when the shares sold off and September 30, 2000, by which point he had accumulated 24 million shares of the company. But presumably he wanted to see that the high-margin items (pharmacy, one-hour photo centers, optical) were still doing well. He probably wanted to make sure that management was still just as tight on their cost controls as they had always been. He definitely would have examined their inventory turnover to make sure they were still selling goods as quickly as before. Once he found a comfort level that the general market was being too aggressive on the sell side, he

EXHIBIT 4.7   COST

Year	Revenues	Net Income	Margin	Book/Share	ROE
3-Aug	42545.6	721	1.7	$14.34	11
2-Aug	38762.5	700	1.8	$12.51	12.3
1-Aug	34797	602.1	1.7	$10.92	12.3
Aug-00	32164.3	631.4	2	$9.48	14.9
Aug-99	27456	515.3	1.9	$7.98	14.6
Aug-98	24269.9	459.8	1.9	$6.82	15.5
Aug-97	21874.4	312.2	1.4	$5.78	12.6
Aug-96	19566.5	248.8	1.3	$4.53	14
Aug-95	17905.9	217.2	1.2	$3.92	14.2
Aug-94	16480.6	110.9	0.7	$3.87	4.2

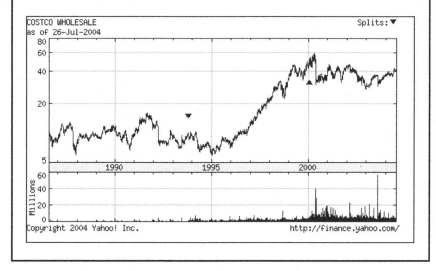

Source: Reproduced with permission of Yahoo! Inc. © 2004 by Yahoo! Inc. YAHOO! and the YAHOO! logo are trademarks of Yahoo! Inc.

began buying. Although we don't know his average cost, it was probably somewhat near where it was after the 2000 sell-off: in the low $30s. Currently the stock is slightly above $40.

FIRST DATA CORPORATION

Symbol: FDC (NYSE)
Date Purchased: 2002

First Data Corp. does credit card transaction processing for over 3 million merchants around the world. First Data also owns Western Union. Steady revenue growth in the 1990s was not enough to fight off the market contraction that occurred in mid-1998, and Buffett began to buy. He bought more in late 2002 when the stock dipped despite increases in revenues, earnings, and return on equity.

EXHIBIT 4.8   FDC

Year	Revenues	Net Income	Margin	Book/Share	ROE
3-Dec	8400.2	1394	16.6	$5.65	34.8
2-Dec	7636.2	1237.9	16.2	$5.52	29.8
1-Dec	6450.8	874.6	13.6	$4.63	24.8
Dec-00	5705.2	929.6	16.3	$4.74	24.9
Dec-99	5539.8	1199.7	21.7	$4.68	30.7
Dec-98	5117.6	465.7	9.1	$4.31	12.4
Dec-97	4978.5	356.7	7.2	$4.09	9.8
Dec-96	4934.1	636.5	12.9	$4.14	17.2
Dec-95	4081.2	−84.2	−2.1	$3.52	NA
Dec-94	1652.2	208.1	12.6	$2.30	20.5

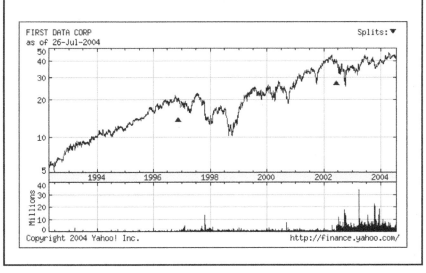

GANNETT CO. INC.

Symbol: GCI (NYSE)
Date Purchased: 1994

Gannet is the publisher of *USA Today* and others news publications. This is another of Buffett's permanent holdings and there are countless case studies of the investment, including ones in Robert Hagstrom's books, Mary Buffett's books, and of course, Andy Kilpatrick's *Of Permanent Value.*

EXHIBIT 4.9   GCI

Year	Revenues	Net Income	Margin	Book/Share	ROE
3-Dec	6711.1	1211.2	18	$30.92	14.4
2-Dec	6422.2	1160.1	18.1	$25.80	16.8
1-Dec	6344.2	831.2	13.1	$21.58	14.5
Dec-00	6222.3	971.9	15.6	$19.31	19.1
Dec-99	5260.2	919.4	17.5	$16.66	20.7
Dec-98	5121.3	999.9	19.5	$14.26	25.1
Dec-97	4729.5	712.7	15.1	$12.26	20.5
Dec-96	4421.1	624	14.1	$10.37	32.2
Dec-95	4006.7	477.3	11.9	$7.63	22.2
Dec-94	3824.5	465.4	12.2	$6.52	25.5

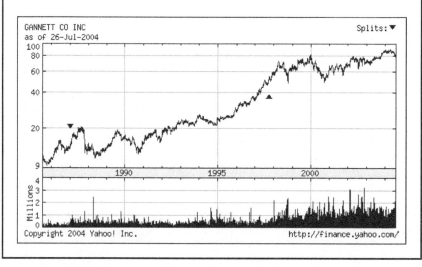

Source: Reproduced with permission of Yahoo! Inc. © 2004 by Yahoo! Inc. YAHOO! and the YAHOO! logo are trademarks of Yahoo! Inc.

GAP INCORPORATED

Symbol: GPS (NYSE)

Date Purchased: 2000

The Gap started having trouble in 2000 when decreased consumer spending, heavy expansion costs, and lower margins started affecting both profits and the stock price. The company had been making record revenues,

EXHIBIT 4.10   GPS

Year	Revenues	Net Income	Margin	Book/Share	ROE
4-Jan	15854	1030	6.5	$5.33	21.5
3-Jan	14454.7	477.5	3.3	$4.12	13.1
2-Jan	13847.9	−7.8	−0.1	$3.48	NA
1-Jan	13673.5	877.5	6.4	$3.43	30
Jan-00	11635.4	1127.1	9.7	$2.63	50.5
Jan-99	9054.5	824.5	9.1	$1.84	52.4
Jan-98	6507.8	533.9	8.2	$1.79	33.7
Jan-97	5284.4	452.9	8.6	$1.79	27.4
Jan-96	4395.3	354	8.1	$1.69	21.6
Jan-95	3722.9	320.2	8.6	$1.41	23.3

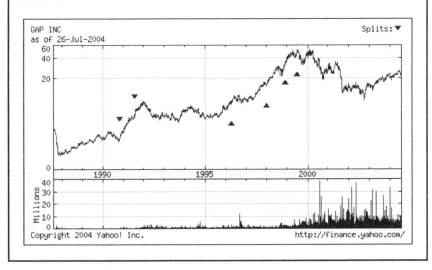

GAP INC
as of 26-Jul-2004

Splits: ▼

Copyright 2004 Yahoo! Inc.   http://finance.yahoo.com/

profits, and increases in same-store sales right up until 2000–2001. The fact that they had had a non–record-breaking year shouldn't be considered earth-shattering, and yet that is exactly how the market treated it. Buffett was perhaps impressed by its prior consistency and assumed that the strength of its brand, backed up by its prior high ROE would help the company stage a comeback. It proceeded to do exactly that by 2003 when its margins and ROE doubled and the book value reached a record high. Buffett began accumulating in 2000, continued his accumulation all through 2001 when the Gap was going through the worst of its troubles, and finally began selling in late 2003 when the shares began to rebound.

GILLETTE CO.

Symbol: G (NYSE)
Date Purchased: 1989

As will be covered more extensively in Chapter 7 on PIPEs, Buffett initially bought Gillette as a convertible preferred issue directly from the company where he was being paid a nine percent coupon. He later converted his holdings into common equity and has held for the duration.

HCA INC.

Symbol: HCA (NYSE)
Date Purchased: 2003

HCA is a hospital chain based in Nashville, Tennessee, owning almost 200 hospitals and over-80 surgery centers. When Berkshire's GEICO unit (where the investment decisions are made by Lou Simpson, Buffett's current #2 on the investment side of Berkshire Hathaway) began buying up shares of HCA in 2003, the hospital chain had just reported a 31% decline in profits. Again, Buffett/Berkshire rarely buys companies where the earnings are 100% consistent. No company, unless it is managing its earnings, is consistent forever. However, the market always makes the assumption that companies should and will have consistent earnings. Buffett, Simpson, Munger, Berkshire, and GEICO all wait for the usual earnings shortfall, the typical market overreaction (see the straight line in the HCA chart that occurred in mid-2003). Then they begin buying after thorough due diligence.

EXHIBIT 4.11 G

Year	Revenues	Net Income	Margin	Book/Share	ROE
3-Dec	9252	1375	14.9	$2.21	62.3
2-Dec	8453	1209	14.3	$2.16	53.8
1-Dec	8961	910	10.2	$2.02	42.6
Dec-00	9295	821	8.8	$1.83	20.4
Dec-99	9897	1260	12.7	$2.80	42.3
Dec-98	10056	1081	10.7	$4.04	24.2
Dec-97	10062	1427	14.2	$4.25	29.9
Dec-96	9697.7	948.7	9.8	$3.98	21.5
Dec-95	6794.7	823.5	12.1	$2.76	33.6
Dec-94	6070.2	698.3	11.5	$2.22	35.6

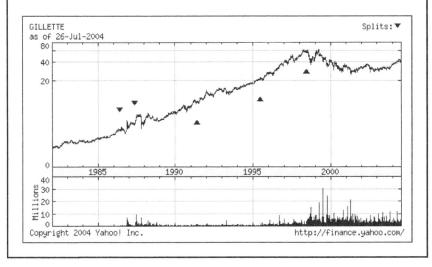

Source: Reproduced with permission of Yahoo! Inc. © 2004 by Yahoo! Inc. YAHOO! and the YAHOO! logo are trademarks of Yahoo! Inc.

In this case, the due diligence had to examine what had caused the earnings shortfall. Would it occur again? Specifically, in mid-2003, the company announced that the information system it had put together for the purpose of keeping track of its account receivables was not working too well. They dropped the system, taking a charge of $130 million, or 15 cents per share. They also increased their reserves for questionable receivables by $106 million, or 13 cents per share.

One factor that helped Buffett in his due diligence was that HCA had been in an accounting scandal before and had only a year earlier settled with the Department of Justice involving claims that they had overcharged the Medicare system. Part of the settlement involved the company's hiring auditing firms to conduct regular company-wide audits. The scandal also brought back prior CEO Tom Frist and his second-in-command, now CEO, Jack Bovende, who helped restore corporate governance and fiscal sanity

EXHIBIT 4.12   HCA

Year	Revenues	Net Income	Margin	Book/Share	ROE
3-Dec	21808	1332	6.1	$12.65	21.5
2-Dec	19729	833	4.2	$11.09	14.6
1-Dec	17953	903	5	$9.35	19
Dec-00	16670	219	1.3	$8.11	5
Dec-99	16657	657	3.9	$9.95	11.7
Dec-98	18681	532	2.8	$11.80	5
Dec-97	18819	182	NA	$11.30	NA
Dec-96	19909	1505	7.6	$12.82	17.5
Dec-95	17695	1064	6	$10.67	14.9
Dec-94	11132	745	6.7	$9.63	14.8

Source: Reproduced with permission of Yahoo! Inc. © 2004 by Yahoo! Inc. YAHOO! and the YAHOO! logo are trademarks of Yahoo! Inc.

to the company. With all of these eggs lined up, Simpson was probably confident that the write-offs were truly one-time events and that the company would get back on track, becoming profitable again.

IRON MOUNTAIN INC.

Symbol: IRM (NYSE)
Date Purchased: 2001

Buffett began buying up shares of Iron Mountain, the nation's largest document storage company, in late 2001, accumulating the bulk of his holdings in Q3 of 2002. This is another company that was consistently losing money but still had a strong enough model that Buffett decided to buy. During its growth phase, the company bought over 110 other companies involved in the same business. That, plus building new facilities for storage, kept earnings down but at the same time increased the company's moat over the competition. Once you have hundreds of thousands of your company's documents stored at an Iron Mountain facility, it is unlikely you are going to switch vendors. And with the complete accounting busts of Enron, WorldCom, Global Crossing, Tyco, and others in the 2001 and 2002, document storage became more important than ever.

Buffett began reducing his shares in 2003. Iron Mountain exemplifies the fact that debt, by itself, is not a bad thing, although it is usually considered so by many value investors. The very same value investors that are eager to see companies buy back shares and pay high dividends are usually loath to buy companies saddled with heavy debt. However, debt can be thought of as a type of equity whereby the company is forced to do a "share buyback" (an interest rate payment). That buyback can be more easily predicted than the "normal" share buyback. The end goal is that the debt gets reduced to zero, making the enterprise value per share that much higher than it was initially, even though no dividends have been paid or real shares bought back.

Debt is only a negative when it is used to buy growth and earnings to hide the fact that the organic business and model is faulty. For instance, WCOM used debt to fuel acquisitions that, in turn, hid the fact that the core company was not making any money. When WorldCom failed to buy Sprint, the jig was up and the only way to hide the lack of earnings was through massive accounting fraud. Because the addition of debt makes due diligence that much harder (and also, any debt at all always increases the risk of bankruptcy during hard

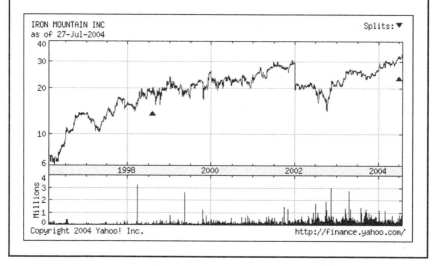

EXHIBIT 4.13 IRM

Year	Revenues	Net Income	Margin	Book/Share	ROE
3-Dec	1501.3	84.6	5.6	$8.31	7.9
2-Dec	1318.5	67	5.1	$7.41	7.2
1-Dec	1171.1	−32.2	−2.7	$7.01	NA
Dec-00	986.4	−24.9	−2.5	$7.42	NA
Dec-99	519.5	−1.1	−0.2	$6.10	NA
Dec-98	270.3	−11	−4.1	$1.50	NA
Dec-97	183.5	−9.2	−5	$1.46	NA

Source: Reproduced with permission of Yahoo! Inc. © 2004 by Yahoo! Inc. YAHOO! and the YAHOO! logo are trademarks of Yahoo! Inc.

times), value investors tend to shy away from companies with debt. It is important to note, however, that Buffett doesn't avoid these companies, provided that all the other characteristics of the business are positive.

M&T BANK CORPORATION

Symbol: MTB (NYSE)
Date Purchased: 1991

In the early 1990s, Buffett began scooping up banks when the banking industry was going through one of its worst periods ever. Buffett had been buying banks since the 1960s, and if there was any business other than insurance that he could be said to know well, it is certainly the banking industry. Buffett was familiar with M&T Bank, based in Buffalo, New York, by virtue of

EXHIBIT 4.14   MTB

Year	Revenues	Net Income	Margin	Book/Share	ROE
3-Dec	2957.7	573.9	19.4	$47.60	10
2-Dec	2354	485.1	20.6	$34.53	15.2
1-Dec	2579.3	378.1	14.7	$31.38	12.9
Dec-00	2097.5	286.2	13.6	$28.96	10.6
Dec-99	1761	265.6	15.1	$23.27	14.8
Dec-98	1622.4	208	12.8	$20.82	13
Dec-97	1258.1	176.2	14	$15.59	17.1
Dec-96	1167.6	151.1	12.9	$13.55	16.7
Dec-95	1077.7	131	12.2	$12.53	16.2
Dec-94	871	117.3	13.5	$10.30	17.2

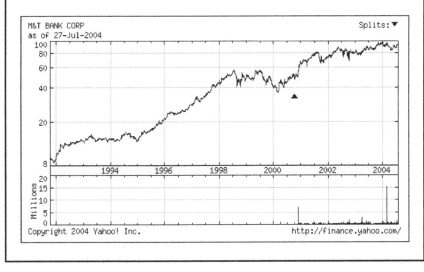

Source: Reproduced with permission of Yahoo! Inc. © 2004 by Yahoo! Inc. YAHOO! and the YAHOO! logo are trademarks of Yahoo! Inc.

his ownership stake in the *Buffalo News*. In fact, it was *News* publisher Stan Lipsey who introduced Buffett to Robert Wilmers, the CEO of M&T.

Interestingly, this was not a straight stock investment for Buffett. M&T needed some cash to make two acquisitions so Buffett made a PIPE investment in the company, a private investment in a public equity. Buffett lent them $40 million in exchange for a note that yielded nine percent a year and was convertible at anytime within five years into stock (pre-2001 split) of $78 per share, a 20% premium on where the stock was trading at that moment. In 1996, after collecting several years' worth of the nine percent coupons, Buffett converted his shares. His initial investment was $40 million and it is now worth well over $600 million.

The key issue when doing due diligence on a bank like M&T is whether or not the bank's risk-taking is excessive when lending money. A good shortcut to determining an answer to this is to look at insider ownership; then decide whether this is a shareholder-owned company or a company whose managers have less stake in the future results. Robert Wilmers, the CEO, owns 3.5 million shares of the company and, prior to the bank's acquisition of Allied Irish Banks in 2002, was the largest shareholder after Berkshire Hathaway. When the CEO of a bank owns the bulk its stock, he or she is much less inclined to take excessive risks with the balance sheet. Whereas Buffett intuitively grasped this, it was also the conclusion reached through empirical means by Seok Weon Lee, professor at Soonchunhyang University.[2]

MOODY'S CORPORATION

Symbol: MCO (NYSE)
Date Purchased: 1999–2000

When the firm Dun & Bradstreet spun off its Moody's division in 2000, Berkshire Hathaway became the largest shareholder. With the ballooning in corporate debt over the past two decades, Moody's and Standard & Poor's (the latter owned by McGraw-Hill) became the two behemoths in the space, both through the strength of their own brand names and SEC regulations that put

---

[2]"Insider Ownership and Risk-Taking Behaviour at Bank Holding Companies," Seok Weon Lee, *Journal of Business Finance & Accounting*, Volume 29, 2002.

EXHIBIT 4.15   MCO

Year	Revenues	Net Income	Margin	Book/Share	ROE
3-Dec	1246.6	363.9	29.2	($0.22)	
2-Dec	1023.3	288.9	28.2	($2.06)	
1-Dec	796.7	212.2	26.6	($1.97)	
Dec-00	602.3	158.5	26.3	($1.76)	
Dec-99	1971.8	256	13	($2.59)	
Dec-98	1934.5	246.4	12.7	($2.16)	

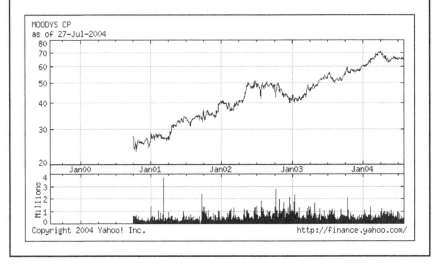

Source: Reproduced with permission of Yahoo! Inc. © 2004 by Yahoo! Inc. YAHOO! and the YAHOO! logo are trademarks of Yahoo! Inc.

them, along with Fitch, as the premier debt ratings agencies. With over $30 trillion in the debt out there having been assigned Moody's ratings, it is going to be hard to knock the company off its pedestal.

NIKE INC.

Symbol: NKE (NYSE)
Date Purchased: 1999

Nike, like Coca-Cola and Disney, is a classic "brand story" for Buffett. The world's largest seller of athletic footwear and apparel is held aloft by its strong brand and strong identification with athletic superstars like Michael Jordan and, more recently, Lebron James. Throughout the past three decades the company has had consistent earnings and ROE, so when the company slightly faltered in 1998 (and its stock along with it), Buffett became a buyer, making a bet that the strength of its brand backed up by the strong ROE

EXHIBIT 4.16   NKE

Year	Revenues	Net Income	Margin	Book/Share	ROE
4-May	12253.1	945.6	7.7	NA	NA
3-May	10697	740.1	6.9	$15.14	18.5
2-May	9893	668.3	6.8	$14.43	17.4
1-May	9488.8	589.7	6.2	$13.01	16.9
May-00	8995.1	579.1	6.4	$11.63	18.5
May-99	8776.9	451.4	5.1	$11.81	13.5
May-98	9553.1	399.6	4.2	$11.36	12.3
May-97	9186.5	795.8	8.7	$10.91	25.2
May-96	6470.6	553.2	8.5	$8.46	22.8
May-95	4760.8	399.7	8.4	$6.87	20.3

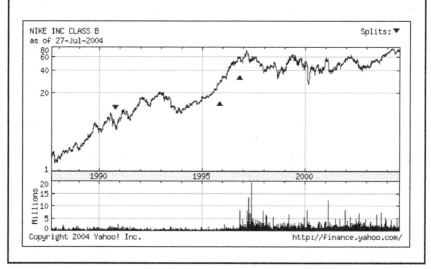

Source: Reproduced with permission of Yahoo! Inc. © 2004 by Yahoo! Inc. YAHOO! and the YAHOO! logo are trademarks of Yahoo! Inc.

would keep the company on top. In its latest report in 2004, Nike returned to its former ways, reporting its largest revenues, income, and margins ever.

OUTBACK STEAKHOUSE INC.

Symbol: OSI (NYSE)
Date Purchased: 2001

EXHIBIT 4.17   OSI

Year	Revenues	Net Income	Margin	Book/Share	ROE
3-Dec	2744.4	170.2	6.2	$13.82	16.6
2-Dec	2362.1	160.8	6.8	$13.88	15.3
1-Dec	2127.1	133.4	6.3	$12.25	14.2
Dec-00	1906	141.1	7.4	$10.54	17.5
Dec-99	1646	124.3	7.6	$8.95	17.9
Dec-98	1358.9	97.2	7.2	$7.37	17.8
Dec-97	1151.6	61.5	5.3	$5.90	14.1
Dec-96	937.4	71.6	7.6	$4.76	20.9
Dec-95	664	53.7	8.1	$3.77	21.1
Dec-94	451.9	39.3	8.7	$2.68	22.8

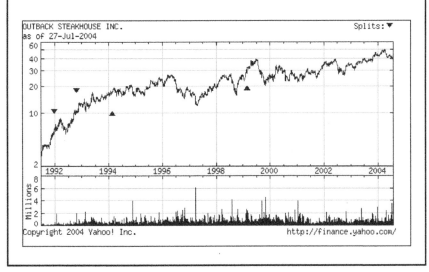

In 2001, for the first time in years, Outback Steakhouse reported earnings that were down from the prior year. The stock languished as a result and Buffett became a buyer. Once again, there are similarities between this stock and many of the other stocks reported in this chapter: consistent earnings, ROE, margins, and growth in Book/Share for years, followed by one downswing in earnings. The stock is published and Buffett is a buyer, knowing that at the very least he is buying a company that knows how to generate profits from its equity base, has a strong brand name, and knows how to generate consistent earnings. Note that despite the consistent earnings and the clear strength of the business, Buffett only started taking the dip in when the water got warm enough, that is, when the company experienced difficulties in its growth. The idea once again was that if a turnaround were in the works (as could be expected by the prior strength in ROE and the consistency of earnings), then that turnaround would be a catalyst for the shares.

SUNTRUST BANKS INC.

Symbol: STI (NYSE)

Growing earnings, consistent ROE, increasing book/share every year. But perhaps the most important aspect of this investment, one of Buffett's largest, is that SunTrust contains the only handwritten formula of the Coco-Cola syrup in a safe in Atlanta, Georgia. Buffett has to protect this investment!

WASHINGTON POST CO.

Symbol: WPO (NYSE)
Date Purchased: 1973

The purchase of Washington Post Co. has been detailed in countless books and articles about Buffett. Buffett loved the newspaper industry since he was a paperboy as a youth, and when he had the opportunity to buy WPO at 20% of book value, he seized it. The Washington Post probably is the best example of a "cigar butt" stock in the Graham-Dodd sense (a company trading well below book that is perhaps good to "pick up and take one more puff but that's it"). It then grew up to become a growing, permanent holding in the Berkshire stable.

Much has been written about Buffett's influence on the board of WPO and his effect on its corporate governance practices, but I think that

EXHIBIT 4.18   STI.

Year	Revenues	Net Income	Margin	Book/Share	ROE
3-Dec	7071.8	1332.3	18.8	$34.52	13.7
2-Dec	7526.9	1331.8	17.7	$31.04	15.2
1-Dec	8435.4	1369.2	16.2	$28.97	16.4
Dec-00	8619	1294.1	15	$27.81	15.7
Dec-99	7620.2	1124	14.8	$24.73	14.7
Dec-98	7392.1	971	13.1	$25.47	11.9
Dec-97	4584.9	667.3	14.6	$24.77	12.8
Dec-96	4064	616.6	15.2	$22.13	12.6
Dec-95	3740.3	565.5	15.1	$18.86	13.2
Dec-94	3252.3	522.7	16.1	$14.93	15.1

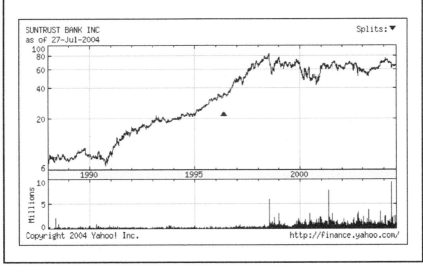

WPO has had just as much of an effect on Buffett. This was really Buffett's first major permanent holding. Even American Express, a great company that Buffett was able to buy in turnaround fashion in the mid-60s, did not notch in a permanent place until the 1990s. Without the success of WPO, Buffett may have never taken more aggressive chances with companies like Coca-Cola.

EXHIBIT 4.19   WPO

Year	Revenues	Net Income	Margin	Book/Share	ROE
33-Dec	2838.9	241.1	8.5	$217.45	11.6
2-Dec	2584.2	216.4	8.4	$193.18	11.8
1-Dec	2416.7	229.6	9.5	$177.30	13.6
Dec-00	2412.2	136.5	5.7	$156.55	9.2
Dec-99	2215.6	225.8	10.2	$144.91	16.5
Dec-98	2110.4	417.3	19.8	$157.35	26.3
Dec-97	1956.3	281.6	14.4	$117.37	23.8
Dec-96	1853.4	220.8	11.9	$121.25	16.7
Dec-95	1719.4	190.1	11.1	$107.61	16.1
Dec-94	1614	169.7	10.5	$101.08	15.1

Source: Reproduced with permission of Yahoo! Inc. © 2004 by Yahoo! Inc. YAHOO! and the YAHOO! logo are trademarks of Yahoo! Inc.

WELLS FARGO

Symbol: WFC (NYSE)

Date Purchased: 1990

Wells Fargo is another case study excellently covered in Hagstrom's books (and others') on Buffett. Suffice it to say, Buffett was a buyer when the market was cruelly punishing bank stocks and particularly California banks in the fallout of the Savings & Loan crisis.

EXHIBIT 4.20   WFC

Year	Revenues	Net Income	Margin	Book/Share	ROE
3-Dec	31800	6202	19.5	$20.17	18.1
2-Dec	28473	5710	20.1	$17.97	18.8
1-Dec	26891	3423	12.7	$16.01	12.6
Dec-00	27568	4026	14.6	$15.29	15.4
Dec-99	21795	3747	17.2	$13.44	17.1
Dec-98	20482	1950	9.5	$12.35	9.6
Dec-97	9659.7	1351	14	$9.01	19.8
Dec-96	8882.9	1153.9	13	$7.97	19.6
Dec-95	7582.3	956	12.6	$7.10	19.1
Dec-94	6032	800.4	13.3	$5.39	24

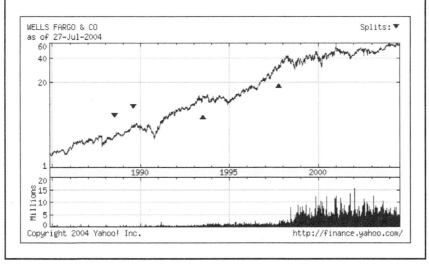

Source: Reproduced with permission of Yahoo! Inc. © 2004 by Yahoo! Inc. YAHOO! and the YAHOO! logo are trademarks of Yahoo! Inc.

CHAPTER 5

Merger Arbitrage Like Warren Buffett

Give a man a fish and he eats for a day. Teach him to arbitrage, and he will eat for a lifetime.

—Warren Buffett

We sometimes enter the arbitrage field when we have more money than ideas.

—Warren Buffett,
1985 Berkshire Hathaway annual report

Buffett went from a trader of Berkshire Hathaway's shares to a long-term investor as the result of an arbitrage gone bad. The company itself was trading for almost half its book value and was regularly buying back its shares through tender offers. Buffett would buy its stock, wait for the tender offer, and then sell the shares. This was almost a riskless arbitrage. He was buying stock for less than its liquidation value and the company was regularly offering to buy back shares at higher prices. It is this double-edged margin of safety (more than one possible exit strategy from the trade) that is the hallmark of a Buffett trade. In any case, it was this "out" that afforded Buffett the luxury of building a company worth more than $100 billion; the company CEO at that time, Jack Stanton, asked

Buffett at what price he would tender his shares. Buffett said 113⁄8 and then the company went ahead and tried to lowball him with a tender offer at 111⁄4. "Don't mess with Warren Buffett" is not necessarily a phrase whispered in the halls of Buffett's companies, and yet someone should have definitely advised Stanton against testing the great trader. Buffett ended up rejecting the tender offer, buying more shares, and outing Stanton—ultimately taking the CEO and chairmanship role for himself. We can only hope Stanton held onto any shares he might have had!

Early in his initial partnership, Buffett divided his investment activities into three buckets: generals, workouts, and controls. Generals were long-term value plays determined primarily by their discount to book value, although some qualitative standards were used as well (for example, when Buffett put much of his fund in American Express stock after the Salad Oil Scandal in 1964). Controls were usually "promoted" (or demoted, depending on your point of view) to Generals, where Buffett bought so much stock he ended up controlling the company. Usually, in the case of a "cigar-butt" stock, a stock that was so undervalued Buffett was able to buy shares at a significant discount to book value, Buffett didn't mind taking ownership in the company so he could control the liquidation in order to secure his ability to make money on the investment. He called these cigar-butt stocks because if you find a cigar-butt on the ground, it might be good for one more puff, but that's about it.

And, finally, there were the workouts. The following is from Buffett's letter to investors in 1963:

These are the securities with a timetable. They arise from corporate activity—sell-outs, mergers, reorganizations, spin-offs, etc. In this category we are not talking about rumors or "inside information" pertaining to such developments, but to publicly announced activities of this sort. We wait until we can read it in the paper. The risk pertains not primarily to general market behavior (although that is sometimes tied in to a degree), but instead to something upsetting the applecart so that the expected development does not materialize. Such killjoys could include anti-trust or other negative government action, stockholder disapproval, withholding of tax rulings, etc. The gross profits in many workouts appear quite small. A friend refers to this as getting the last nickel after the other fellow has made the first ninety-five cents. However, the predictability coupled with a short holding period produces quite decent annual rates of return. This category produces more steady absolute profits from year to year than generals do.

During any given year, 50 percent or more of Buffett's profits on the year could come from workout situations. Over the course of his 50 years of investing, Buffett has engaged in many forms of arbitrage, including merger arbitrage, relative value arbitrage, convertible arbitrage, fixed-income arbitrage, and other special situations that involved short-term trading unrelated to his usual bread and butter of stock picking. Does he still practice every form of arbitrage there is? No. In some cases, the sheer size of the amount of money Berkshire needs to put to work in a deal makes it inappropriate to attempt forms of investing where the capacity of the strategy is much smaller.

Later in this chapter we will examine Buffett's use of arbitrage and interview a "Buffett-like" manager who does merger arbitrage, John Orrico of The Arbitrage Fund.

What does it mean to be "Buffett-like"? In many cases, it is a comparison of apples and oranges. For instance, Warren Buffett seldom (if ever) engages in merger arbitrage these days. Nor is Berkshire Hathaway going around buying companies that are trading for less than their book value (usually these companies, if they exist, are too small for him). That said, there are many managers out there who have successfully applied Buffett's approach to investing in their own methods. This approach primarily consists of an *obsession with "margin of safety."* Buffett once said, "In the last chapter of *The Intelligent Investor*, [Graham] said the three most important words of investing: 'margin of safety.' I think those ideas, 100 years from now, will still be regarded as the three cornerstones of sound investing."

So what does "margin of safety" mean? In the basic Graham-Dodd analysis for a stock, it means "buying a stock that is trading at two-thirds of its liquidation value." However, even Buffett quickly moved beyond that understanding of the phrase in the early 1960s when he began focusing on more qualitative aspects of a stock such as brand value, earnings growth, and so on. It is probably easier to figure out what "margin of safety" is *not* when it comes to investing. It is not:

- Buying a stock because it closed above its 200-day moving average.
- Shorting a stock because "a 200 P/E is ridiculous!"
- Buying calls in a stock on takeover rumors.

In other words, the margin of safety will help prevent you from getting into a situation where the risk cannot be quantified or understood in terms of the size of the potential loss.

MERGER ARBITRAGE: WHAT IS IT?

The classic arbitrage took place frequently in the early 1900s. Securities and London might, for more than a few microseconds, trade at one price on the London Stock Exchange and then a different price on the New York Stock Exchange simply because information did not flow as quickly between the two exchanges as they do today. The complete lack of information flow severely disrupted the plans of an efficient market god. Computers and now the Internet have replaced the telegraph as the bridge toward bringing about a global marketplace, where severe information disconnects like the ones Baruch exploited no longer exists. When an arbitrage exists between any two assets, computer models often immediately pinpoint the spread and billions of dollars instantly go to work toward making that spread converge. The question now is, *Do opportunities continue to exist?* In the Berkshire Hathaway 1999 annual meeting, Buffett stated that techniques like arbitrage would still enable an investor to make more than 50 percent a year.

The first example of arbitrage to examine is risk arbitrage, which we will more accurately call merger arbitrage. The reason it is often called risk arbitrage is that the word "arbitrage" often implies there is no risk. How can there be risk if you are selling gold for $401 in London and buying it back for $400 in New York simultaneously? But with merger arbitrage enough risks exist such that a spread is created between the two assets involved that supposedly anticipate and define that risk.

A potential merger arbitrage situation is created when any merger is announced in which the target is a public company. Often the target company trades for less than the amount offered for that company. A trade exists where you can buy the target company shares and sell them when they reach the price specified in the deal. For instance, if company XYZ announces it is acquiring company ABC for $15/share in cash and company ABC is trading at $14, then you can buy shares in ABC with the idea that those same shares will be sold to XYZ when the deal closes at $15/share.

Why would there be risks to a merger? Why wouldn't the target company trade immediately at the price at which it was being acquired? There are at least four types of "deal risks" that can prevent a deal from closing:

1. **Due diligence risk.** After the deal is agreed upon there is usually a due diligence "out," meaning the acquirer can back out of a deal (usually after paying a breakup fee).

2. **Regulatory risk.** For instance, the GE/Honeywell merger was blocked by antitrust concerns from European regulators.

3. **Another acquirer can step in.** Particularly in a hostile takeover situation, a "white knight" might become involved. This would most likely be great for those who are long the target's shares, but in a stock deal, arbitrageurs who are short the acquirer's shares as a hedge will lose money.

4. **Interest rate risk.** If a deal is going to take a year to close and the spread between the target company and its acquisition price is four percent and interest rates are five, then an arbitrageur would rather sit tight in bonds unless the spread of the deal got wider.

Typically when a potential merger is announced, the stock of the target runs up, settling down near the level of the deal price. The spread between the price it trades at and the eventual deal price is dependent on the risks described above and how much the market, particularly the group of arbitrageurs who are stepping in to make money on the spread, value those risks. In an all-stock deal, the stock of the acquirer will also most likely come down as arbitrageurs short the stock to hedge their risk. The amount of risk an arbitrageur takes in the deal is usually related to the amount the stock ran up the day the deal was announced. If news of the deal had been leaked in the days prior to the deal being announced, then an arbitrageur must include that increase when taking into account the size of the risk.

In each type of merger, there are different methods of assessing the value of the deal for an arbitrageur and the value of the spread. Some types of mergers are:

Cash Deal

Company X offers cash to buy the shares of Company Y. In this situation an arbitrage exists, as in the previous example, when X trades below the price being offered. The arbitrageur buys shares in X and holds until the price converges. The value of the deal to an arbitrageur is measured roughly by this formula:

$$V = P ((D - T) / T)$$

where   V = the expected value of the deal if the deal works out
        P = the probability the deal will be completed
        D = the price the target stock will be if the deal works out (the deal price)
        T = the price of the target stock when the arbitrageur acquires it

Example
If XYZ is being acquired for $11/share in cash, it is a small, friendly takeover, you feel it has 100 chance of completion, and it trades at $10, then

$$V = 1 \times (11 - 10) / 10 = 10\%.$$

This doesn't present the full picture, but it's a start. Next, the arbitrageur must consider the likelihood that the deal takes place within a certain number of days (let's call it x) and then the annualized value (AV) of the deal can be calculated as:

$$AV = V \times (365 / x)$$

To continue our example, if the deal is estimated to take a year, then the annualized value of the deal to an arbitrageur considering it would be

$$10 \times (365 / 365) = 10\%$$

If this annualized return is better than the returns the arbitrageur can make on any other deal, then he or she would begin considering it.

All-Stock Deal

Company X offers to buy Company Y for Z number of shares. For instance, on April 2, 2003, First Data Corporation announced it was going to buy Concord EFS by paying 0.40 shares of each First Data stock for each share of Concord EFS stock. First Data was trading at 34.68 at the time of the merger and Concord EFS had close to 500 million shares, valuing the deal at approximately $7 billion. Even though the deal placed the value of Concord EFS shares at 13.87, CE shares immediately traded from a range of 9–10 to a range of 11–12 over the next several weeks. Why was there such a big discount?

The regulatory risk played a large part. The combination of Concord EFS and First Data would create the world's largest debt-transaction processor and the Justice Department was going to definitely have regulatory issues. This could potentially cause the deal not to happen but at the very least it would slow the deal down, increasing the risk that there were better deals out there for arbitrageurs to enter. In January 2004, First Data reached a settlement with the Justice Department to avoid antitrust issues and on February 26, 2004, the deal closed.

In an all-stock deal, the problem of just going long the target stock (in other words, buying the stock of the company being acquired) is that the acquirer's shares might go down, in which case the deal price also goes down (because the target's stock is pegged in a fixed ratio to the acquirer's stock).

Various Other Types of Deals, Including:

- Mixture of cash and stock.
- Mixture of cash, stock, and debt.
- Stock deals where there is a collar, meaning the ratio changes upwards if the stock of the acquirer falls below a certain price.
- In a hostile takeover, the formula for calculating value would be similar to the example, but the risks of a deal falling through would be much greater, as well as the risk that another acquirer would step in.

The formulas about determining the value of a deal are only a starting point. And even with those formulas there is a big, gaping hole: how to assess the probability that a deal will close and, if so, how to estimate the time needed for it to close. With most clear-cut, systematic strategies, a fair amount of discretion and reevaluation must take place. On top of this reevaluation and decision making is also deciding how much capital to put to work. Ideally, you would have more than 100 of capital at work, using leverage, in many uncorrelated merger arbitrage opportunities—uncorrelated so that the success of one is not dependent at all on the success of the others.

How does an arbitrage opportunity become uncorrelated with other opportunities?

- Different industries.
- Different sizes.
- Different countries.
- Different type of deal (for example, some deals in a merger arbitrage portfolio might be all-cash, others might be a combination of cash and stock, all-stock, stock and debt, and so on).

When taking into account whether you should use leverage, it is also important to take into account the interest rate you are paying on that leverage. The lower the interest rate, the longer the possible time frame to deal completion is allowed, depending on the initial spread after a deal is announced.

Part of the decision-making process is the hedging method. In the basic stock-for-stock deal, you short the acquirer and buys the target. However, what if the acquirer's shares are difficult to short? In order to short, you need to find shares of the acquirer to borrow (the brokerage firm you trade through will tell you if shares are "borrowable" for shorting) in order to sell them in the shorting process. Because there is a lot of money invested in merger arbitrage funds, it quickly becomes impossible to find shares to borrow. All of the arbitrage funds have borrowed them already. Here are two possible solutions:

1. Don't short as much as you should, thereby adding to the risk of the deal but placing a bullish bias on the result.
2. Most of the price movement in a stock is strongly correlated to the prices of the market in general and even more so with prices of stocks in its sector. You can short a basket of stocks in the sector or index exchange traded funds (ETFs) and futures. This leaves you with stock-specific risk, meaning that the company could suddenly fall apart with-

out affecting any of the other companies in its sector. The beauty of doing this is that the "upside risk" of the hedge is now negligible. In other words, if the deal falls through, the acquiring stock will shoot upwards as the hedgers in the deal depart from their short positions, but the shares of other stocks in the sector will not go up as much.

Merger arbitrage funds often have access to sophisticated resources ranging from analyst reports to computers to constant evaluations of the spreads, probabilities, and so on. However, the average trader can certainly take advantage of the Internet resources out there to compete on an almost equal, if not more advantageous, playing field (due to the lower amount of money that he or she needs to put to work to have a successful annual return). My favorite Internet source for merger arbitrage data is at *thedeal.com*. Exhibit 5.1 shows a snapshot of the type of information that thedeal.com provides to the aspiring arbitrageur.

Thedeal.com does all of the basic calculating for you, in terms of figuring out the spread, the annualized return, and even the estimated date that the deal is expected to close (all of this information is not shown in Exhibit 5.1, but it is available on the Web site). The big question now is, *What deals should you do?* We saw in the first case mentioned above that Warren Buffett likes to give himself more than one way out. In the Berkshire Hathaway example, when Berkshire came in with a tender offer Buffett was unhappy with, he was also content to simply buy up the shares and ride it out a little longer.

In his 1988 letter to Berkshire Hathaway shareholders, Buffett attributes much of the success of the 1987 portfolio to arbitrage—and this in a market that had suffered through the 1987 crash. In the letter, he describes how he evaluates the risk in an arbitrage situation, and then goes through the specifics of the Arcata 1981 deal in which buyout firm KKR was involved.

To evaluate arbitrage situations you must answer four questions: (1) How likely is it that the promised event will indeed occur? (2) How long will your money be tied up? (3) What chance is there that something still better will transpire—a competing takeover bid, for example? and (4) What will happen if the event does not take place because of anti-trust action, financing glitches, etc.?

EXHIBIT 5.1 Arbitrage Situations as of Market Close on January 9, 2004

Target	Acquirer	$	Spread w/ dividends	%	Change from previous day	Annualized return %	Exp. close
Abington Bancorp Inc.	Seacoast Financial Services Corp.	-0.13	-0.13	-0.32	0.04	-1.10	4/30
AdvancePCS	Caremark Rx Inc.	1.08	1.08	2.14	0.05	9.50	3/31
Allegiant Bancorp Inc.	National City Corp.	-0.35	-0.24	-0.87	-0.4	-3.90	3/31
Amersham plc	General Electric Co.	2.14	2.14	2.98	0.45	13.30	3/31
Applied Molecular	Eli Lilly and Co. Evolution Inc.	0.18	0.18	1.01	0.13	5.60	3/15
Ashanti Goldfields Co. Ltd.	AngloGold Ltd.	0.90	0.90	6.80	0.01	37.60	3/15
Bank of Bermuda Ltd.	HSBC Holdings plc	0.00	0.00	0.00	0.05	0.00	2/25
Barnes & Noble.com	Barnes & Noble Inc.	0.02	0.02	0.83	0.13	6.00	2/28
BioReliance Corp.	Invitrogen Corp.	0.00	0.00	0.00	0.10	0.00	2/5
Business Bank of California	UnionBanCal Corp.	0.43	0.43	1.43	-0.01	22.70	2/1
CB Bancshares Inc.	Central Pacific Financial	5.19	5.55	8.74	0.00	18.40	6/30
CCBT Financial Corp.	Banknorth Group Inc.	0.43	0.62	1.83	0.00	4.70	5/31
Cima Labs Inc.	Cephalon Inc.	0.95	0.95	3.80	-0.02	9.70	5/31
Cinar Corp.	TD Capital	-0.01	-0.01	-0.28	N/A	-2.60	2/17
Coastal Bancorp Inc.	Hibernia Corp.	0.28	0.64	1.55	0.00	5.10	4/30
Cole National Corp.	Luxottica Group SpA	-0.53	-0.53	-2.63	0.03	N/A	N/A
Concerto Software Inc.	Melita International Ltd.	-0.06	-0.06	-0.50	0.01	-30.30	1/15
Concord EFS Inc.	First Data Corp.	0.16	0.16	1.07	-0.02	5.90	3/15
Connecticut Bancshares Inc.	New Haven Savings Bank	0.39	0.39	0.76	-0.13	7.50	2/15
Denison International Corp.	Parker hannifin Corp.	0.04	0.04	0.17	-0.03	4.70	1/22
Dial Corp.	Henkel KGaA	0.26	0.26	0.91	-0.01	4.10	3/31
Dreyer's Grand Ice Cream Inc.	Nestle SA	5.25	5.73	7.37	0.06	3.66	1/13/06

Company	Acquirer					Date
Duane Reade Inc.	Oak Hill Capital Partners LP	0.19	0.19	1.13	-0.09	2.88	5/31
Esperion Therapeutics Inc.	Pfizer Inc.	0.44	0.44	1.27	-0.02	4.15	4/30
First Essex Bancorp Inc.	Sovereign Bancorp Inc.	-0.31	-0.39	-0.65	0.24	-8.50	2/6
FirstFed America Bancorp Inc.	Webster Financial Corp.	0.01	0.01	0.05	-0.03	0.30	3/15
FleetBoston Financial Corp.	Bank of America Corp.	1.07	1.07	2.52	0.09	8.20	4/30
Franklin Financial Corp.	Fifth Third Bancorp	0.48	0.48	1.57	-0.20	4.00	5/31
FTD Inc.	Leonard Green & Partners	0.20	0.20	0.81	0.00	8.00	2/15
GA Financial Inc.	First Commonwealth Financ	0.33	0.33	0.95	0.28	2.40	5/31
Garden Fresh Restaurant Corp.	Centre Partners Management	0.30	0.30	1.87	-0.01	13.90	2/27
GlobespanVirata Inc.	Conexant Systems Inc.	0.07	0.07	1.05	-0.01	4.70	3/31
Gucci Group NV	Pinault-Printemps-Redoute	-0.08	-0.08	-0.09	0.11	-0.30	4/30
Gundle/SLT Environmental Inc.	Code Hennessy & Simmons	0.25	0.25	1.37	-0.04	6.10	3/31
Holly Corp.	Frontier Oil Corp.	0.08	0.08	0.29	0.28	N/A	N/A
Igen International Inc.	Roche Holding Ltd.	-13.58	-13.58	-22.32	-0.35	-370.40	1/31
John Hancock Financial Services	Manulife Financial Corp.	0.59	0.59	1.49	0.01	6.70	3/31
Manufacturers' Services Ltd.	Celestica Inc.	0.15	0.15	2.26	0.05	37.40	1/31
Mid Atlantic Medical Services I	UnitedHealth Group Inc.	0.39	0.39	0.60	-0.04	3.30	3/15
MONY Group Inc.	Axa Financial Inc.	-0.35	-0.35	-1.12	0.09	-8.10	2/28
Moore Wallace Inc.	RR Donnelley and Sons Co.	0.24	0.24	1.24	0.05	10.10	2/23
New Focus Inc.	Bookham Technology plc	0.10	0.10	1.87	-0.02	-76.00	12/31
Newhall Land and Farming Co.	LNR Property Corp.	0.14	0.14	0.35	-0.04	2.50	2/28
OneSource Information Services	ValueAct Capital Partners LP	0.11	0.11	1.17	-0.06	8.60	2/28
Patriot Bank Corp.	Susquehanna Bancshares Inc.	0.24	0.24	0.84	0.29	2.20	5/31
PeopleSoft Inc.	Oracle Corp.	-3.17	-3.17	-13.98	-0.50	N/A	N/A
PetroCorp Inc.	Unit Corp.	0.39	0.39	2.87	-0.02	47.50	1/31
Pinnacor Inc.	MarketWatch.com Inc.	0.01	0.01	0.51	-0.01	8.50	1/31

EXHIBIT 5.1 (continued)

Target	Acquirer	$	Spread w/ dividends	%	Change from previous day	Annualized return %	Exp. close
Plains Resources Inc.	Vulcan Capital	-1.85	-1.85	-11.49	-0.17	-29.30	5/31
Progress Financial Corp.	FleetBoston Financial Corp.	0.10	0.10	0.33	0.27	5.40	1/31
Republic Bancshares Inc.	BB&T Corp.	0.23	0.23	0.74	-0.18	1.90	5/31
Resource Bankshares Corp.	Fulton Financial Corp.	0.32	0.32	1.05	-0.31	4.70	3/31
Right Management = Consultants	Manpower Inc.	0.22	0.22	1.19	0.18	36.10	1/21
Sicor Inc.	Teva Pharmaceutical Indust	0.32	0.32	1.16	-0.12	19.20	1/31
SoundView Technology Group	Charles Schwab Corp.	0.02	0.02	0.13	-0.02	N/A	1/9
Southern Financial Bancorp = Inc.	Provident Bankshares Corp.	0.61	0.61	1.43	-0.05	4.70	4/30
Staten Island Bancorp Inc.	Independence Community B	0.41	0.41	1.86	-0.35	6.10	4/30
Systems & Computer Technology	SunGard Data Systems Inc.	0.07	0.07	0.43	0.00	2.40	3/15
Titan Corp.	Lockheed Martin Corp.	0.19	0.19	0.87	-0.08	3.90	3/31
Travelers Property Casualty Corp.	St. Paul Cos.	0.98	0.98	5.74	0.09	14.70	5/31
Travelers Property Casualty Corp	St. Paul Cos.1.01	1.01	5.93	0.09	15.10	5/31	
Troy Financial Corp.	First Niagara Financial	-0.27	-0.27	-0.77	-0.68	-70.70	1/13
Trust Co. of New Jersey	North Fork Bancorp	0.64	0.34	0.83	-0.39	2.10	5/31
UniSource Energy Corp.	KKR, J.P. Morgan, Wacho	0.60	0.60	2.43	-0.03	5.10	6/30
WellPoint Health Networks Inc.	Anthem Inc.	1.96	1.96	2.06	-0.08	6.70	4/30

N/A = not available

Spreads, including deals with collars that are not yet in the pricing period, are calculated using stock figures available at market close. The final terms for deals with collars may be different. When estimations for pricing periods are not available, the spread is determined by the acquirer's share price at the market close. The close date is estimated. Spreads do not include dividend payments that have not been announced.

Source: The Deal website, http://www.thedeal.com, January 8, 2004.

Arcata Corp., one of our more serendipitous arbitrage experiences, illustrates the twists and turns of the business. On September 28, 1981, the directors of Arcata agreed in principle to sell the company to Kohlberg, Kravis, Roberts & Co. (KKR), then and now a major leveraged-buy out firm. Arcata was in the printing and forest products businesses and had one other thing going for it: In 1978 the U.S. government had taken title to 10,700 acres of Arcata timber, primarily old-growth redwood, to expand Redwood National Park. The government had paid $97.9 million, in several installments, for this acreage, a sum Arcata was contesting as grossly inadequate. The parties also disputed the interest rate that should apply to the period between the taking of the property and final payment for it. The enabling legislation stipulated six percent simple interest; Arcata argued for a much higher and compounded rate.

Buying a company with a highly speculative, large-sized claim in litigation creates a negotiating problem, whether the claim is on behalf of or against the company. To solve this problem, KKR offered $37.00 per Arcata share plus two-thirds of any additional amounts paid by the government for the redwood lands.

Appraising this arbitrage opportunity, we had to ask ourselves whether KKR would consummate the transaction since, among other things, its offer was contingent upon its obtaining "satisfactory financing." A clause of this kind is always dangerous for the seller: It offers an easy exit for a suitor whose ardor fades between proposal and marriage. However, we were not particularly worried about this possibility because KKR's past record for closing had been good.

We also had to ask ourselves what would happen if the KKR deal did fall through, and here we also felt reasonably comfortable: Arcata's management and directors had been shopping the company for some time and were clearly determined to sell. If KKR went away, Arcata would likely find another buyer, though of course, the price might be lower.

Finally, we had to ask ourselves what the redwood claim might be worth. Your Chairman, who can't tell an elm from an oak, had no trouble with that one: He coolly evaluated the claim at somewhere between zero and a whole lot.

We started buying Arcata stock, then around $33.50, on September 30 and in eight weeks purchased about 400,000 shares, or five percent of the company. The initial announcement said that the $37.00 would be paid in January 1982. Therefore, if everything had gone perfectly, we would have achieved an annual rate of return of about 40 percent—not counting the redwood claim, which would have been frosting.

All did not go perfectly. In December it was announced that the closing would be delayed a bit. Nevertheless, a definitive agreement was signed on January 4. Encouraged, we raised our stake, buying at around $38.00 per share and increasing our holdings to 655,000 shares, or over seven percent of the company. Our willingness to pay up—even though the closing had been postponed—reflected our leaning toward "a whole lot" rather than "zero" for the redwoods.

Then, on February 25 the lenders said they were taking a "second look" at financing terms "in view of the severely depressed housing industry and its impact on Arcata's outlook." The stockholders' meeting was postponed again, to April. An Arcata spokesman said he "did not think the fate of the acquisition itself was imperiled." When arbitrageurs hear such reassurances, their minds flash to the old saying: "He lied like a finance minister on the eve of devaluation."

On March 12 KKR said its earlier deal wouldn't work, first cutting its offer to $33.50, then two days later raising it to $35.00. On March 15, however, the directors turned this bid down and accepted another group's offer of $37.50 plus one-half of any redwood recovery. The shareholders OKed the deal, and the $37.50 was paid on June 4.

We received $24.6 million versus our cost of $22.9 million; our average holding period was close to six months. Considering the trouble this transaction encountered, our 15 percent annual rate of return excluding any value for the redwood claim was more than satisfactory.

But the best was yet to come. The trial judge appointed two commissions, one to look at the timber's value, the other to consider the interest rate questions. In January 1987, the first commission said the redwoods were worth $275.7 million and the second commission recommended a compounded, blended rate of return working out to about 14 percent.

In August 1987 the judge upheld these conclusions, which meant a net amount of about $600 million would be due Arcata. The gov-

ernment then appealed. In 1988, though, before this appeal was heard, the claim was settled for $519 million. Consequently, we received an additional $29.48 per share, or about $19.3 million. We will get another $800,000 or so in 1989."

Another example of arbitrage, similar to the example at the beginning of this chapter, occurred in July 1992 when General Dynamics made a tender offer for 20 percent of its stock. The price would be determined by Dutch auction at prices ranging from $65.37 to $72.25 per share. Buffett began buying shares in anticipation of tendering them. But once he started buying them, he decided that he liked the fundamentals of the company and chose to hold onto the shares instead, quadrupling his investment. Again this is an example where he could have taken the safe money of the arbitrage, but he had the extra "out" for himself by knowing after studying the fundamentals that he could hold onto the shares and ride the investment.

In his 1963 letter to investors in his partnership, Buffett presented the details of a very straightforward merger arbitrage situation in Texas National Petroleum (TNP). Buffett mentions that he had heard rumors that TNP was going to be acquired by Union Oil of California, but he did not act on those rumors and in fact reported, "I never act on such information." And there is no need to, when profits can be straightforward once the deal is announced.

A deal was announced and Buffett determined what he would do with each category of security that TNP had:

- TNP had debentures yielding 6.5 percent that would be called once the deal was done.
- Common stock for which Union Oil was going to pay $7.42 per share.
- Warrants.

Buffett was able to acquire each class of security in the six months leading up to the merger at a reasonable spread between his buy price and the acquiring price. In particular, on the debentures, he was also able to get a nice 6.5 percent interest rate while he was waiting.

Additionally, Buffett noted that:

- "Risk of stockholder approval was nil" since the deal was negotiated by the controlling shareholders.
- There were no anti-trust problems or legal problems.

Buffett therefore had a high degree of comfort that the deal would be done. The only issue on the timing was that TNP needed a tax ruling by the IRS. The ruling took slightly longer than expected by about two months, and Buffett's return on the entire investment when it concluded was an annualized return of approximately 21 percent. The longer time span allowed Buffett to get more payments on the bonds.

His comment on this, which applies to most arbitrage situations, is that "(1) the deals take longer than originally projected and (2) the payouts tend to average a little better than estimates." He also notes that "I definitely feel some borrowed money is warranted against a portfolio of workouts, but feel it is a very dangerous practice against generals."

THE BIG QUESTION IS: DOES MERGER ARBITRAGE WORK IN GENERAL?

There are three directions in which we can look to determine an answer to this question. The first is academia, where studies have been done on every merger announcement over the past twenty years to determine what the results would have been had one blindly played each situation possible. The second is the results of hedge funds and mutual funds devoted only to merger arbitrage. The third is statements by Warren Buffett, who has engaged in merger arbitrage for almost fifty years. Each of these directions has problems in determining a complete answer, but perhaps the aggregation of the answers will give us insight.

On the academic side, perhaps the most comprehensive study has been done by Mark Mitchell and Todd Pulvino.[1] I categorize them as "academic," but both of these professors have been active in actually trading merger arbitrage deals, having become partners in AQR Capital's Merger Arbitrage fund. In their paper, "Characteristics of Risk and Return in Risk Arbitrage," they analyze every merger from 1963 to 1998 and blindly play the spread that existed on the day after the announcement in every case. Altogether they studied the results of 4,750 mergers. The results are roughly summarized in Exhibit 5.2.

---

[1]"Characteristics of Risk and Return in Risk Arbitrage," Mark Mitchell and Todd Pulvino, *Journal of Finance*, vol LVI, No. 6, Dec. 2001.

EXHIBIT 5.2 Risk Arbitrage Returns

Year	Value-weighted Risk Arbitrage (VWRA) Return	Risk Arbitrage Index Manager (RAIM) Return	CRSP Value-weighted Average Return	Risk-free Rate of Return	$ Value of Announced Deals/Total Market Value
1963	14.51%	6.64%	20.89%	3.13%	0.40%
1964	10.27%	4.44%	16.30%	3.48%	0.35%
1965	9.09%	3.30%	14.38%	3.94%	0.47%
1966	11.46%	−4.03%	−8.68%	4.69%	0.69%
1967	14.45%	9.06%	28.56%	4.05%	1.16%
1968	−8.65%	−2.88%	14.17%	4.75%	1.72%
1969	22.10%	3.18%	−10.84%	6.49%	1.10%
1970	14.18%	5.70%	0.08%	6.17%	0.30%
1971	19.93%	5.79%	16.20%	4.15%	0.15%
1972	16.65%	3.52%	17.34%	3.93%	0.13%
1973	20.38%	−7.45%	−18.77%	7.17%	0.39%
1974	12.95%	12.93%	−27.86%	7.97%	0.42%
1975	12.83%	12.29%	37.37%	5.63%	0.29%
1976	19.93%	19.20%	26.77%	4.91%	0.36%
1977	28.56%	8.27%	−2.98%	5.25%	0.72%
1978	20.40%	18.03%	8.54%	7.41%	0.93%
1979	17.15%	13.85%	24.40%	10.42%	0.82%
1980	29.30%	38.54%	33.23%	11.33%	0.47%
1981	38.44%	35.15%	−3.97%	14.50%	0.68%
1982	38.41%	31.99%	20.42%	10.38%	0.42%
1983	17.35%	12.67%	22.70%	8.86%	0.45%
1984	21.45%	8.13%	3.28%	9.62%	0.63%
1985	15.65%	15.00%	31.46%	7.38%	0.50%
1986	13.32%	20.61%	15.60%	5.93%	0.68%
1987	13.81%	3.81%	1.76%	5.17%	0.63%
1988	27.23%	27.63%	17.62%	6.50%	0.61%
1989	6.83%	5.36%	28.44%	8.16%	0.32%
1990	6.69%	4.38%	−6.02%	7.53%	0.11%
1991	18.19%	12.13%	33.59%	5.32%	0.07%
1992	9.12%	4.48%	9.03%	3.36%	0.07%
1993	14.16%	12.31%	11.49%	2.90%	0.09%
1994	17.07%	12.58%	−0.62%	3.98%	0.12%
1995	12.57%	10.96%	35.73%	5.47%	0.11%
1996	11.32%	15.39%	21.26%	5.14%	0.06%
1997	9.48%	11.64%	30.46%	5.11%	0.06%
1998	12.64%	4.09%	22.49%	4.70%	0.06%
Compound annual rate of return	16.05%	10.64%	12.24%	6.22%	
Annual standard deviation of returns	9.29%	7.74%	15.08%	0.73%	
Sharpe ratio (annual)	1.06	0.57	0.40	0.0	

Source: Mark Mitchell and Todd Pulino, "Characteristics of Risk and Return in Risk Arbitrage," *Journal of Finance* 56, Issue 6, December 2001, Table II, pp. 2151. Reprinted by permission from Blackwell Publishers Journal Rights, Email: JournalRights@oxon.blackwellpublishing.com.

The Value-Weighted Risk Arbitrage (VWRA) return in the exhibit refers to the return that would be generated if you were to value each merger by its size. The Risk Arbitrage Index Manager (RAIM) return represents what would happen if you played each merger subject to more realistic constraints—for instance, only limiting each position to 10 percent of your portfolio and also restricting yourself to deals involving more liquid securities. The results demonstrate that even if you blindly play every single merger that exists you can still obtain a slight risk-adjusted premium to the market. The spread between the risk-free return and the value-weighted return is 10 percent in the value-weighted index and four percent in the RAIM index.

While I think this study demonstrates that merger arbitrage is a decent strategy, it also is very conservative for the following two reasons:

1. An arbitrageur won't blindly do every deal, but will instead use a variety of factors to limit the risk in a deal.
2. An arbitrage fund may use leverage to attempt to get the risk-adjusted returns multiplied by the leverage factor.

Also interesting is the fact that the VWRA portfolio in the above table returns more than the index, which does not take into account the size of the deal. This suggests that the larger the companies involved, the more likely it is for a deal to succeed.

Eliezer Fich and Irina Stefanescu,[2] who are both from the University of North Carolina, confirm this by demonstrating that when an acquirer is in the S&P 500 Index the risk arbitrage portfolio returns are 85 percent higher than when the buyer is not in the Index.

Perhaps most interesting is to look at the results of the Crédit Suisse-First Boston (CSFB) hedge fund sub index devoted to merger arbitrage. Exhibit 5.3 shows the summary tables.

Since inception, the merger arbitrage index has underperformed the CSFB Hedge Fund Index (8.39 versus 10.59 percent), but the standard deviation has been much less (4.48 and 15.85 percent), making the equity curve much smoother.

---

[2]"Expanding the Limits of Merger Arbitrage" by Eliezer Fich and Irina Stefanescu, University of North Carolina working paper, 2003.

EXHIBIT 5.3 CSFB Merger Arbitrage Index

Monthly Performance

	Jan	Feb	Mar	Apr	May	Jun	Jul	Aug	Sep	Oct	Nov	Dec	Year	S&P 500 Total Return	MSCI World $
2003	-0.39%	-0.71%	-0.27%	1.52%	2.56%	0.75%	0.48%	1.16%	0.95%	1.21%	0.42%	N/A	7.90%	22.27%	25.84%
2002	0.29%	-1.22%	1.00%	0.88%	0.03%	-1.17%	-2.73%	-1.23%	-0.56%	0.52%	0.21%	0.53%	-3.46%	-22.10%	-19.54%
2001	1.91%	1.49%	0.33%	0.50%	1.31%	-0.43%	0.68%	1.01%	-2.65%	-0.01%	0.81%	0.67%	5.68%	-11.89%	-16.52%
2000	0.15%	3.52%	0.05%	1.81%	0.68%	1.43%	1.58%	1.57%	1.01%	0.35%	0.28%	1.39%	14.69%	-9.10%	-12.92%
1999	-1.51%	-1.37%	2.56%	3.39%	2.47%	1.22%	0.16%	0.80%	2.16%	1.75%	0.52%	0.47%	13.23%	21.04%	25.34%
1998	-0.54%	3.81%	2.38%	1.64%	0.23%	-0.53%	-0.37%	-6.15%	-0.65%	2.41%	2.04%	1.55%	5.58%	28.58%	24.80%
1997	1.28%	0.22%	-0.42%	-1.67%	1.31%	2.39%	1.21%	0.57%	1.48%	0.02%	1.09%	2.01%	9.84%	33.36%	16.23%
1996	1.02%	1.57%	0.63%	2.00%	1.09%	0.28%	1.05%	1.23%	2.15%	0.45%	0.45%	1.12%	13.81%	22.96%	14.00%
1995	1.61%	1.88%	0.63%	-0.45%	0.61%	2.07%	1.56%	0.60%	1.14%	0.16%	1.68%	-0.16%	11.90%	37.58%	21.32%
1994	0.57%	-0.44%	1.86%	-0.96%	0.25%	0.18%	0.57%	1.69%	0.38%	0.20%	0.61%	0.26%	5.25%	1.32%	5.58%

EXHIBIT 5.3   Risk Arbitrage Index

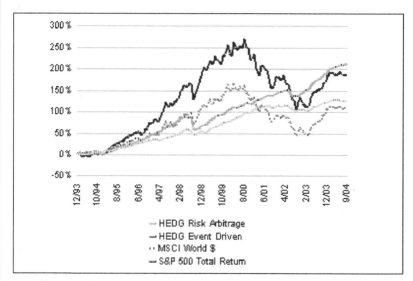

Cumulative Performance

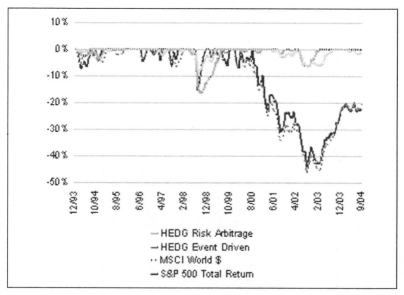

Draw Down Graph

EXHIBIT 5.3   *(continued)*

Net Performance	HEDG Risk Arbitrage	S&P 500 Total Return	MSCI World $
1 Month	0.42%	0.88%	1.55%
3 Months	2.60%	5.46%	8.28%
6 Months	5.08%	10.80%	14.90%
1 Year	8.47%	15.09%	19.76%
2 Years	4.87%	−3.92%	1.90%
3 Years	11.62%	−15.66%	−14.10%
3 yr Avg	**3.73%**	**−5.52%**	**−4.94%**
5 years	45.19%	−2.34%	−3.23%
5 yr Avg	**7.74%**	**−0.47%**	**−0.65%**
Since Inception	122.25%	171.39%	95.38%
Incep Avg Annl	**8.39%**	**10.59%**	**6.99%**

Statistics	HEDG Risk Arbitrage	S&P 500 Total Return	MSCI World $
Avg Month	0.68%	0.95%	0.65%
Best Month	3.81%	9.78%	9.06%
Worst Month	−6.15%	−14.46%	−13.32%
Mth Std Dev	1.29%	4.58%	4.24%
Mth Std Dev, Ann'd	**4.48%**	**15.85%**	**14.70%**
Beta(vs S&P 500)	**0.13**	**0.97**	**0.86**
Sharpe	**0.95**	**0.41**	**0.19**

Correlations	HEDG Risk Arbitrage	S&P 500 Total Return	MSCI World $
Dow	0.44	0.93	0.89
MSCI World $	0.45	0.94	1.00
MSCI EAFE $	0.43	0.77	0.94
S&P 500 Total Return	0.44	1.00	0.94
NASDAQ	0.39	0.80	0.79

Index data begins January 1994. Sharpe ratio calculated using a rolling 90-Day T-bill rate

None of this takes into account Warren Buffett's own studies on the possible results of merger arbitrage. In his 1987 letter he writes: "Though we've never made an exact calculation, I believe that overall we have averaged annual pre-tax returns of at least 25 percent from arbitrage."

Although the academic studies as well as the practical results demonstrated by the hedge fund index show that merger arbitrage is a viable risk-adjusted strategy, the one problem both of those studies and approaches have is that they have to trade every year, and in almost every situation. Buffett, not being specifically an arbitrageur, can wait for the situations that he feels afford an extra level of safety. This leads to one of the biggest aspects of Buffett's career that I admire: He writes his own rules. Many hedge funds out there (and this is definitely the case for almost all mutual funds) are obligated to tell their investors their monthly results. These monthly results can be like a straitjacket. The second the results begin to dip or become volatile, there is always the risk that the investor can pull out. It is this desperation for smoothness to the equity curve that compels many hedge funds to be extremely risk-averse and not always take advantage of every opportunity available to them, even when the odds are greatly in their favor. Buffett clearly stated to his investors, "I'm open for business one day a year," and that was that. Once a year he could tell investors how he was doing, and if they didn't like it, so be it.

Modern hedge funds also abhor "style drift," the propensity to switch styles midstream; a fund will not go from value to growth stock-picking, or suddenly start day-trading futures after having advertised itself as a biotech investor. The primary reason for this is that the primary allocators to hedge funds or fund-of-funds have very specific mathematical models for how to allocate and diversify their own portfolio. If they invested in you because they thought you were a merger arbitrage fund, then you had better remain a merger arbitrage fund. Buffett didn't care for any of that. He did what he wanted to do, and told investors their results when he felt like it. Power to him.

HOW TO ARBITRAGE LIKE WARREN BUFFETT

Buffett mentions in his 1988 letter the four conditions that an arbitrageur must ask, in addition to the obvious question. *What is the spread?* They are:

1. What can cause the deal to fail?
2. What is the time it will take for the deal to occur?
3. What other opportunities might be available?
4. What are you going to do if the deal does not go through?

It is this fourth question and the way he phrases it that most intrigues me. The question is not "What is your downside risk?" as is most often asked in textbooks on arbitrageurs, but, *What are you going to do if the deal is not completed?* This emphasizes the importance of having a backup plan, an extra exit in case the deal does not go through.

Also, before making a trade, it is possible to eliminate the cases that statistically offer more risk.

- Buy deals in which an S&P 500 company is the bidder.
- Buy deals in which the targeted company is trading for less than book.
- Don't do a deal when it is a hostile takeover (it is less likely to be completed).
- Try to do deals in which you are bullish on the fundamentals of the underlying company or its sector.
- Buy a deal in which there are multiple bidders.

Some examples of having an "out" in an arbitrage trade are when the targeted company also happens to be trading below its liquidation price. Deals like that do not happen very often, but occasionally they do. A recent example from the penny stock world was when Liberty Media-controlled Open TV (OPTV) was making a bid for IATV in mid-2002. IATV was burning a lot of money, but also happened to be trading at a market cap well below the cash it had in the bank and with no debt. It had approximately $1/share cash in the bank and the deal was priced at approximately $1.10 in OPTV stock. Because OPTV was itself a penny stock, trading around $2, there were no shares around to borrow; the spread was therefore enormous. In addition, on several occasions the deal was postponed and Liberty Media, run by John Malone, was notorious for changing deal terms at the last minute. IATV traded down as low as $0.50 before finally consummating the deal in March 2003. It was a roller coaster ride for the arbitrageur, but the ride was worth it, and the consolation if the deal did not work out was the solid $1/share in cash that the company had left in its coffers.

As Buffett has said, "I'd rather have a lumpy 15 percent than a smooth 12 percent." That said, it usually doesn't get any smoother than a portfolio of merger arbitrage situations.

The next section is an interview with John Orrico, a merger arbitrage specialist who strives to take as many risks as possible out of the trade before making the trade. The Arbitrage Fund is a mutual fund that focuses on merger arbitrage situation.

INTERVIEW WITH JOHN ORRICO OF THE ARBITRAGE FUND

JA: Can you give us some personal background?

JO: When I got out of Georgetown, I went to Morgan Stanley and worked in corporate finance for two years and institutional equity for two years. From the mid-'80s to the mid-'90s, after Morgan Stanley, I held a variety of positions in trading, institutional equity, as an analyst and as a portfolio manager.

JA: When you say trading, that's primarily...

JO: At Morgan Stanley, I was at the Institutional Equity Desk. I was on the over-the-counter desk and actually making markets on stocks there. When I went to Instinet, when that firm was still in its infancy, I ran the Institutional Equity Desk there, but we didn't commit capital so there was no principal trading involved. It was really more agency brokerage. Then, you know, Instinet got bought out by Reuters...and I wanted to get to the buy side. So, I took a couple of steps back to do that, among other things. And I've worked as an analyst for a while at one firm. I got a job as an assistant portfolio manager at another firm.

JA: What kind of portfolios do you normally pick?

JO: When I worked as a portfolio manager for the U.S. investment arm of a Japanese life insurer, they were clearly just long-only portfolios, bonds, and stocks. The hedge fund was pretty much a rapid-trading hedge fund (when I had some experience working for a small hedge fund), but again, long and short strategies, but primarily looking for trading ideas.

JA: So like something that would pop on earnings?

JO: Exactly—special situations, deep-value type of situations.

JA: How did that work out overall?

JO: Unless you're a great stock picker or you really want a balanced portfolio in terms of the long-short strategy, I think those strategies are really kind of victim to the ups and downs of the market. It's easy to make money if you're a long-only type of trader when the markets are rising. It's, of course, much more difficult in flat, volatile, or down markets.

I just think it's a lot harder than it seems to a lot of people, and I can speak for myself and say that early in my career I had no clue. When I look back, I really had no knowledge of the type of hedging techniques and strategies that are or were out there and available. It's really about getting in front of the right people, working for the right people, getting into the right shop where you can learn a lot of those things, whether it's on the buy side or the sell side.

A lot of people do run funds, limited partnerships and trading vehicles. But I think the number of people who do it really well consistently over time is quite limited. That's just my own feeling after having seen it all and knowing a lot of people in this industry.

My history prior to going to work for Martin Gruss at Gruss & Company, which is a private family trust where I learned a skill set around merger arb[itrage], was really as a kind of a trader, a money manager with kind of a long focus.

I then went to work for the Gruss family; for their family private accounts, they have been utilizing merger arb and event-driven strategies for decades. So I went into a shop that really had a history with this particular strategy and knew what they were doing, where I could learn.

JA: What was your initial attraction to those strategies?

JO: I really didn't know when I first went there. When I walked in the door, it wasn't to go work with the merger arb team; it was to work on a team that was running the internal hedge fund there, a long-short kind of fund. But after getting introduced to the merger team and their strategies, it became clear to me that the merger arb and event-driven strategies—whatever you want to call it, although they do talk about event-driven as inclusive of merger arb—really force you not only to understand the underlying companies that you're involved with but also to take a directional bet. You can still take a directional bet if you have a strong feeling one way or the other, and that comes into the way you hedge and into the strategies you develop around your position.

So what attracted me to it? The very analytical and quantitative skills that come into play are very important in that strategy in terms of analyzing the underlying assets that you're investing in or selling short. You need to understand the situation and be able to follow the strategic rationale behind each event. And you can describe many of these events as binary, or events that are not predicated on overall directional moves in the marketplace.

JA: Can you give an example of one situation in which you might have taken a directional bet?

JO: Back in the late '90s, when Conrail put itself up for sale, we had two of the largest railroads in the country bidding for this property, which had no peers, couldn't be replicated, and most likely would never be for sale again. In that particular case, our analysis told us that this bidding war between the two interested parties was likely to continue, driving the asset price much higher than what we thought might be its intrinsic or fundamental value. That doesn't mean that there is no risk, but it means there might be a way for us to increase our exposure to that particular deal.

The option markets are very liquid, and typically with a lot of the bigger situations, there are ways to hedge yourself. The outcome may take a couple of months to unfold, but when we're playing a situation in which we think prices will go higher amid more aggressive bidding, we will buy some stock, marry a put to it, and just go to sleep. It may be an out-of-the-money put, but as long as we can measure our downside, in a general sense, that's how we view our business. We want to be able to understand what our downside looks like. In some cases, our upside is well-defined; in other cases, it's not.

That's what attracted me to merger arb. It's a much more interesting strategy than just taking a bet on a stock. You can always take bets on stocks, and we can always figure out ways to hedge ourselves. However, in the context of a deal or how a deal will be viewed by the Street—whether it's a merger, a takeover, or a hostile bid— there are always other ways to look at the event as it unfolds and other ways to play it.

There may be an event unfolding that we're quite bearish on, where we don't like the probable outcome; even if the deal goes through, we may not like the combined entity. We may think it's too overleveraged. We may think the market may not like it. We think the shareholders may vote it down. So it doesn't mean we're always betting on a successful conclusion. We can anticipate a successful conclusion, but anticipate share prices going lower.

Every deal has its own twists and turns, and there's always a different way to look at any particular deal. But as long as we can get a sense for what our downside is, that allows us to continue to run a business day in and day out and always be around to play another day.

JA: In the Conrail example, do you think that Conrail initially was trading below its own intrinsic value or your calculation of intrinsic value?

JO: I guess the question is, *Were we looking at the stock before the internal decision was made at Conrail to put itself up for sale?* In that case, those shares trade based on the fundamentals of that particular industry, relative to their peer group. But as an entity that had some governmental oversight and some government control to a certain extent, once we understood that transaction was given a green light—meaning that the sale of that asset was going to be allowed to go forward by the regulators—then it puts a whole different light on what underlying value might be. Then you're talking about the types of synergies that a potential buyer will be able to extract from that particular asset. That could increase by some factor related to the synergy that the new buyer brings in. How much traffic can the new buyer run over those rails that it's now shipping in expensively by truck or by air?

Once we understand the rationale of the deal, then we're able to examine what the benefits are and what benefits will accrue to the buyer or the entity on a pro forma basis. It puts a whole new evaluation on the deal. In this particular case, it's a one-of-a-kind asset. There aren't going to be any more rails into the Northeast or into the ports of New York, Philadelphia, or Boston. Once this thing is off the market or not available to other buyers, that's it. It will never come up for sale again. So if you're a strategic buyer and that asset could be strategic to your firm's overall growth, you're probably going to pay more than what it's worth because it can't be replicated.

So that's a special kind of situation, and that doesn't always happen. Look at a deal that's taking place today, such as Pfizer's deal to

buy Esperion Therapeutics, a company that doesn't have any products on the market—just in development—and Pfizer is willing to pay
almost $2 billion for this asset. You have to ask yourself: What does
Esperion control, what has it developed, or what potentially does it
have in the way of technology that makes it that desirable?

If it's that desirable to Pfizer, does it mean that other players are
aware of this technology or this drug pipeline and may be interested
as well? Or is it just more valuable to Pfizer than anyone else because
Pfizer has such a big stake in this particular segment of the health
care industry already?

Here we're talking about cardiovascular disease and the drugs that
have to do with controlling cholesterol levels in the body. Pfizer has a
big platform that's already dominant in the field. This particular company has new technologies on the horizon and new products in the
pipeline, and a lot of people in the industry think it can be quite valuable.
Does it ensure Pfizer's success in this field into the next decade? Does
it give them a platform by which they can then extend the patent life on
their current drug portfolios? I mean, what's it really worth to Pfizer?

It's hard because then this asset is worth different values to different players. To a player that wants to get into the market and
doesn't have a presence in cardiovascular treatment, maybe this is a
springboard into that, avoiding the startup costs related to doing it
on your own. For Pfizer, which is looking to extend its current platform and develop the new technologies it may feel are needed to
ensure it remains No. 1 in the field, it needs to pay top dollar for this
and keep it out of anyone else's hands.

Who knows what it's worth to any one particular buyer unless
you understand how that buyer is positioned, how it competes, how it
would potentially compete with or without this particular deal and
how the regulators are going to look at it? It gets complicated because
as much as you try to put yourself in the shoes of the buyer, it's hard.
You'll never know everything they know. You'll never know what's in
their product pipeline or what's on their drawing boards. So we can
guess a lot. We can try to understand by talking to the companies, by
talking to analysts, by talking to other players in the field about what
makes this asset so attractive to a particular player and really try to
build our own models around what we learn.

JA: Why is it so necessary to know what's on the mind of the buyer? You
know they want to buy the company, and at that point, let's say there's

a regulatory risk or a risk that the deal is not going to go through. How does knowing what is on the mind of the buyer help you deal with those and other risks?

JO: Well, for instance, in the biotech sector, a buyer is also concerned about how the trials are going. When do the new benchmarks or results come out? During the course of the next three months, we may hear some significant news on some of these drugs in development that may torpedo a deal if they find that the endpoints were not met.

Look at First Data's deal to buy Concorde, which ran into some regulatory problems. The potential for regulatory problems is always on our minds. What's also on our minds, though, was that these were related to Concorde's economic performance. For the duration of this deal, many Concorde contracts with some of its largest banking customers come up for renewal, and many of those customers may not renew their business relationships with Concorde in terms of debit and credit card processing.

How much of Concorde's business could bleed to the loss of renewals or the loss of new business before First Data says the economics of this deal don't make sense anymore? That was a concern because there's always a disruption to the target's underlying business: concern among customers, concern among employees, you may lose some top salespeople when you're going through a potential transaction. Caremark, which is in a whole other field in terms of pharmaceutical delivery, is buying Advance PCS, which just lost a large contract to a competitor. And we know it has other contracts up for renewal.

So we ask ourselves what the merger agreement says with regard to business losses. In Caremark's merger agreement, it does not have to go through with this deal if revenues exceeding a certain percentage of Advance's business disappear between now and the close. They can weigh that condition and go through with the deal anyway, but these merger agreements contain numerous conditions not only on the regulatory side but also on how much business it's willing to divest in order to meet regulatory requirements. Clearly that's usually carved out.

Also, what are the economic requirements? Are there revenue targets, EBITDA [earnings before interest, taxes, depreciation, and amortization] targets, earnings targets? Many of the merger agreements today have conditions such as those. Say you have a deal that's been negotiated based on a particular value; let's say $30 in stock is going to be distributed at close. Well, if the acquirer shares fall from $30 to $15, it goes from a one-to-one exchange to a two-for-one exchange. Some companies will not go through with a deal if their share prices fall to a level such that they have to issue significantly more shares. What was an accreted transaction then turns into a diluted transaction. But again, you have to ask yourself why the acquirer's shares fell from $30 to $15. Does that open the door for another buyer to step in?

Every deal has its own twists and turns, and it really forces us to examine the quality of the companies that are involved. When I say "quality," I'm talking about their earnings consistency, the quality of earnings, the transparency of their accounting, and the type of management that runs the company. What do the balance sheets look like? What are the peer-group valuations relative to these two companies, and what is their competitive position within the industry? What factors could impact any of those issues? And that's just the basics. That's just to get comfortable with where we are in the deal before we invest in it.

It's much easier with larger companies and larger deals. Everybody knows Bank One and J.P. Morgan; you have 50 analysts following the two companies. But in some of the smaller deals, like in the health care technology field, software and hardware, it gets a little more complicated. We're not experts in any one particular industry; we're basically generalists.

Over the course of my career, I've been involved in a couple of hundred financial deals or dozens of HMO deals. You start to see things again and again, and you begin to know what to look for. Having a history helps because typically you've seen the merger agreements and the language before. You can get an early heads-up when something doesn't look or smell right, or something is done differently.

JA: Is there any type of deal you won't do, like for instance the Bank One-J.P. Morgan deal? Where would your edge or your margin of safety be in that deal if you were to play it? (A deal had just been announced at the time of the interview.)

JO: I don't believe we have an edge when it comes to a deal that size, which is well covered by the Street and by the arb desks. If there is an edge to be had, it's going to come from taking an independent view of the deal from a valuation and earnings standpoint, taking a look at what, for instance, the new management team from Bank One will bring to this combined entity and what it will do in terms of valuation overall in terms of P/E multiples. We'll look at how it will sit with the analysts on the Street; we know that there will be a number of upgrades as a result of this deal.

At the end of the day, after we do all our work and look at the numbers, the pro formas, valuations and peer-group valuations, we'll talk to the analysts and get a feel from the company how quickly cost cuts can take place. When all of our analyses are done, we may think that J.P. Morgan is an undervalued stock now, whereas that wasn't the case before. Our edge is bringing our experience and analysis to bear in a situation and maybe coming up with a way to look at this deal that other people don't.

That might mean to be hedged instead of selling J.P. Morgan short. We're going to pay some premiums for those puts. We may end up setting up J.P. Morgan-Bank One not at, let's say, a five percent annualized rate of return, but using puts, we're going to set it up at a worst-case—1.5 percent to 2 percent—annualized rate of return. When I say worst case, I mean our puts get an exercise and we put our short on 2.5 points lower than where it is.

But the upside is that we're going to give J.P. Morgan room to run. The stock opened up on the morning after the deal announcement. It closed at $39 and change, opened at $39.70, and traded down following that open, basically closing unchanged on the day. The stock is above that level since, but we have never witnessed a bank deal of that size where the acquiring bank traded up.

JA: What happened on the morning after that announcement? Did everybody in your firm get in early and start crunching the numbers?

JO: We actually saw the announcement the previous night, so we had some opportunity to crunch numbers, take a look at the pro formas, see what the analysts had to say, and attend a conference call and watch the press. We did get a head start, but we came in at 8 AM the next day like we normally do. Some of my analysts are here earlier. They were watching J.P. Morgan initially trade down 50 cents at $38.70 and then begin to trade up. From 8 to 9, it went from $38.70 to $40 and a quarter as we got some bullish comments. Maybe the market was acting better overall. People liked the deal. Everyone likes Jamie Dimon. Who knows why, but it traded up significantly, and we had never seen a bank financial deal move up that much.

We actually shorted a little bit of stock in J.P. Morgan early, before the open as it moved up, without buying Bank One, because we thought we had a $62 billion deal here. If 10 percent of that deal is held by the arb, a significant amount of short selling will have to take place in J.P. Morgan over the next few weeks into the duration of the deal.

You get the pre-opening kind of euphoria around the deal, but our history tells us this stock will most likely, at some point during the day, trade lower than its prior close. Sure enough, every share that we sold in the morning was a great sale. We were really able to set that up—not at the spread at which it was trading at any one time—but at probably a level two to three times that.

JA: At that time, at the open, did you start buying Bank One shares as well?

JO: We waited for the short sellers to come in. We waited for the arb community to come and put some pressure on J.P. Morgan. While we could have bought Bank One at the open and set it up at a decent spread based on where we had sold J.P. Morgan, we waited. I think on that day, Bank One opened at $51.20, and relative to J.P. Morgan, it had about a 75- or 85-cent spread. We waited, and J.P. Morgan came down, during the course of the day, a dollar from its opening price. Then we began to buy Bank One, and we set it up at a much more attractive spread. But that's more of a trading opportunity that doesn't always present itself.

JA: What do you do when a deal is announced and by the time you start shorting, there are no shares left to borrow?

JO: We'll go to a prime broker and get them to commit to us the number of shares early. And in some cases, we can lock those shares up. Even if we don't sell short on that particular day, we can lock up. We have to pay a fee for it. But we can say we want to get a borrow at 100,000 shares and commit to that for 30 days. So they'll charge us even though we don't actually effect the short sale. We may never affect the short sale, and that's the price we pay to be able to have that stock available to us.

In some cases, we may have a problem maintaining our short position. But clearly if we're working with our prime broker and they know what they're doing, they're going to borrow shares for us, and they're going to lock up shares for us that they consider to be a good borrow and on not a short-term basis.

If we have a concern that it's a very difficult-to-borrow name, and let's say they identify a certain amount of stock and one of their clients is willing to lend it on the borrow, we'll sometimes lock those shares up and actually enter into an agreement to maintain that short position, to maintain that borrow through the duration of the deal. Instead of earning a rebate, we end up paying a fee, and we'll agree to pay that for a period of 90 days, 120 days, or whatever. If we think the deal will last 120 days, we'll lock up the shares for 120 days.

So there are ways to protect yourself, to protect your borrow and not get caught having to go into the marketplace and buy the shares because the borrow became too tight. So that's not typically a problem for us.

JA: What types of deals do you find to be safer, such as large-cap, small-cap, all cash, stock-for-stock?

JO: There's no rhyme or reason. The better we understand the companies, the higher the comfort level we have with the way we think that deal will play out. But across the board, some big deals are going to run into antitrust, regulatory problems, or they're going to take longer to close. The longer it takes to close something, the more technology changes and the more the economy changes. Some utility deal that's announced today could close in 12 to 15 months. I don't know what's going to happen in the utility sector between now and then, so it's tough to go out that far in any deal.

So timing is a factor. The quicker the deal, the more certainty we have that the deal will get done. Fewer things will happen along the way to interrupt it. The higher the quality of the companies, the larger the bet we're willing to take.

So it's all about managing your risk. If I have a stronger comfort level with the intrinsic value of a target, I might take a bigger position, knowing that even if the deal were to break, my downside is limited. I may have more risk in a deal break of my short position going against me significantly. Another buyer may come in and make a bid for the acquirer, or maybe the acquirer's shares become severely depressed during the duration of the deal. If it were to walk away from the deal, maybe those shares will bounce back up to where they were prior to the deal.

We're always examining where our risk lies. Is it on the target's shares or on the acquirer's shares? If it's a cash deal, I only have one side to worry about. But I may have financing to worry about at that point. Maybe it's a cash deal, with a condition on financing.

JA: How did you fare during the 2002 market? How did you survive that?

JO: We survived by always anticipating the worst. We were nimble and small. We were in and out of deals in a heartbeat. If we got wind of bad news, we were out and we could get back into it the next day. There was so much volatility in the market in general that if we were quick and nimble enough in watching our positions, we could trade in and out of positions.

Arbs[arbitrageurs] aren't always willing to stick their necks out and keep buying more and more, especially when there's a lot of volatility in the marketplace. If we see a spread go out from a $1 to $2, it's not going to be just a knee-jerk reaction to put some more into the portfolio. People want to know why it's out at $2. Maybe it's out just because of fundamental sellers of the target shares; there are not enough buyers among the arb community to absorb that selling. It also could be that there are no more short notes, no more borrowing capability of the acquirer's shares, so arbs can't put any more of it on because we can't get a borrow.

Spreads go all over the place for a number of reasons, especially in a volatile market. Is it an opportunity or a warning? That's the tough part: trying to figure out if a widening spread is indicative of a problem or a potential opportunity coming your way.

We tried to put stuff on when it widened and take it off when it narrowed, and we did that with enough frequency and stayed out of trouble. A lot of the deals were structured with pricing mechanisms, so as the acquirer's shares fell, we needed to have a greater short position. We needed to sell more to get their value. Or, you may have a static fixed ratio on an exchange. Maybe the acquirer's shares are between, let's say, $40 and $60, but they then fall below $40. You may be getting a different type of consideration on the deal. You may have to short more.

So we try to anticipate that, and in 2001, 2002, and 2003, we tried to be a little bit proactive in the way we hedged. If we anticipate the worst case—the market looks heavy, and fundamentals aren't really improving—the arbs are going to have to keep shorting more stock as it drops, so let's get out in front of that selling and short early. Let's buy some puts early so we have an opportunity to exercise those puts, establish a short position if the shares do fall, and then leg in on the long side. We always wanted to be prepared for the downside in the 2001 and 2002 and even in the 2003 market. That insurance—putting structure in collars around your acquirer's shares by buying puts, selling calls, whatever—will typically cost you money.

When you have as much volatility as we did in 2001 and 2002, it helped protect us. It gave us an additional hedge, and it allowed us to set up some deals at extremely wide rates of return. In 2003, it probably cost us a couple of percent because we were so cautious.

JA: Do you find that when an acquiring stock is starting to get near its floor—the bottom of the collar—there's a magnet effect?

JO: When the acquirer's shares begin to trade down toward the bottom of the collar, people worry that if it breaks through that, the deal could suddenly be off and we're also going to have to short more stock. You're going to see arbs panicking.

Northrop fell through the bottom of its collar in one day. It traded between $105 and $130, which was the collar for six months of the TRW deal. Then, before that deal was closed, in the pricing period now, the stock opened down 15 points one day. Now it not only opened down 15 points, but it opened below the collar. So you had to be short that much more, and many arbs were prepared for it.

We kind of structured the deal. We put a collar on the shares; we bought the 95 put and we sold the 125 call to pay for it. Our risk came if it went well north of 125 because we're going to be short the 125 early. It didn't come to that. It broke through the bottom of the collar. We had our puts on, and we were set. We didn't lose money there. It actually gave us a chance to buy more TRW cheap.

We hate to be in a position where we're panicking with the rest of the Street. To the extent we can anticipate that or maybe be a little bit prepared, we're going to try to do that. It doesn't always work, but that's what we try to do.

JA: It seems like as soon as a deal is announced, the entire merger arbitrage community gets in and the spreads go down to almost nothing very quickly. It sounds like you're able to overcome that by trading around the initial position like you did with J.P. Morgan and Bank One, but is that possible in general?

JO: In today's environment, spreads are really tight, and they typically get very tight very quickly. So how do we add value as managers in this space? We've got to look to add value by understanding what's actually happening in the transaction. If we want to take a directional bet, if we want to find another way to hedge other than by shorting stock, it's about being able to look at other ways to play the deal, waiting for the right opportunity, just being patient. But it means you've got to monitor these things every day. On that one day when something gets out of whack because the market sells off or a fundamental seller comes in and knocks the spread open, you've got to be there. You've got to be ready to act, and you can't do that if you're not following the deal from day one or at least being on top of what's going on. It's tough to do that when you don't have a position to begin with.

We have to add value by watching these spreads and deals constantly and by just sitting there waiting to pounce. This environment is really tough. With interest rates as low as they are, we have a lot of money in the space that has a low cost of capital. So they're able to put on deals with a very low rate of return and still make money. That won't always be the case.

We've been through other cycles where it looks like spreads were lousy and then within a couple of years, they were back to pretty wide levels. We're very opportunistic. We're not just playing. If the spreads aren't there, then we're going to pass.

JA: Do you ever use leverage to attempt to increase your returns?

JO: The Arbitrage Fund, which is a public mutual fund, doesn't utilize leverage. Many players out there do utilize leverage, but we don't.

JA: Is that because of restrictions on mutual funds?

JO: Well, there are some restrictions in terms of our ability to leverage. But primarily, it's because we don't think it's a good practice. In a hedge fund or a privately managed account, if the clients are comfortable with that and we think that leverage makes sense, then we'll take a look at it. We just don't do it in the public mutual fund.

JA: Do you put most of your own personal money into the fund?

JO: Yes. Virtually all of my net worth is tied up in this business.

JA: In 1998, Warren Buffett said that essentially, through using arbitrage, he feels it's possible to make 50 percent a year. This was roughly the quote. Do you think that statement still holds?

JO: Well, back in '98 and '99, the environment was one in which the spreads available in the marketplace, following deals, were mirroring the types of valuations that you were seeing in general in the marketplace. Market caps were inflated. Deal values were inflated. It was a buoyant, frothy market, and spreads reflected that.

There were a number of reasons why spreads reflected that, but it was primarily because of the risks associated with the stocks you were buying back then. If you were involved in a deal between Tellabs and Ciena or JDS and Uniphase, these were multibillion-dollar deals with stock prices in the hundreds of dollars. And we know what happened in 2000 and 2001 when these stock prices came in to something representing fair value. They plummeted by 90 percent, 80 percent, or more.

So, there were opportunities in '98 and '99, at the peak of the market in terms of valuation, to capture some enormous spreads. Those spreads were really, really out of whack. The market capital of those deals was far greater than the dollars pursuing merger arbitrage strategies at the time. Through the use of leverage, you could probably get a 30 percent, 40 percent, maybe even a 50 percent rate of return. But the risk you had to assume back in those days was enormous.

JA: Since starting your firm, what would you say is the worst trade you have entered into?

JO: It's been in those deals that have fallen apart due to fundamental problems on the part of the target company.

JA: What's a specific one?

JO: Well, we could talk about Cardinal Health making an acquisition of Syncor International. The deal was announced in June 2002, and I think the deal was scheduled to close in the mid-November time frame. In the first week of November 2002, the companies announced that the auditors, as part of their due diligence, had uncovered that bribes were paid out of the foreign subsidiaries of Syncor. So the deal was on hold.

That's the kind of deal where you're caught completely off-balance by some type of fraudulent activity on the part of the insiders of the target company. That leads to the transaction being put on hold pending an investigation, due diligence, legal settlements, what have you. In this case, while it was a short-term pickup for us in terms of impact on the portfolio, that deal eventually did close, and we were able to position ourselves to make money on this deal and to also increase our position.

JA: So you didn't unwind your position when you heard that news?

JO: No, because by the time we heard the news, the stocks weren't even trading. The stocks will then open up reflecting a worst-case scenario.

At that point, we go back to fundamental analysis. What is this company worth on a worst-case basis? If we're looking at a problem in the foreign subsidiaries and the wrongdoing has been limited to those foreign subsidiaries, then what's the value of the rest of the company, assuming we take a value of zero for those foreign subsidiaries and assuming that there's some kind of penalty or fine that's will result out of that wrongdoing? And we try to put a valuation on this company.

Ultimately we felt the two companies were committed to doing the deal, regardless of the wrongdoing that took place. The wrongdoing and the dollars involved were small relative to the overall size of the deal. So our job at that point was to determine if Cardinal was going to go forward with this deal and whether it would change the terms. How would it possibly change those terms, and when would this deal close?

Now we're going to have a new merger agreement and a new shareholder vote. There may be other issues that come into play. So you have a number of variables that you try to define, such as the extent of the wrongdoing, the fines involved, the extent of the investigation in terms of timing, and how the Justice Department, Securities and Exchange Commission and Cardinal Health will view the merger. You're looking at an opportunity for Cardinal to lower the price, substantially perhaps.

So we take all that in[to] consideration, all with an eye toward valuation. Ultimately we have to understand what we're owning. And we felt pretty comfortable, based on what the companies told us— through their press release, on the phone, by talking to Cardinal Health, by speaking to lawyers—that the incidents involving foreign bribes had been confined to the Asian subsidiaries. That being the case, it made our job a lot easier.

The more typical deals that fall apart are those in which the target company fails to meet its earnings or revenue estimates. That's going to happen now and again in many deals. But sometimes a company substantially underperforms, and a lot of times it's due to the fact that there's a deal on the table. There's a lot of disruption involved when a company is being bought out. Some customers will sit back and wait to see what happens. After the deal closes, employees may quit. Certain facets of the business may begin to suffer because of the disruptions associated with a corporate transaction.

Most companies and most partners to a deal will account for that ahead of time. They anticipate there may be some slowdown on the part of customers. There may be some interruption in terms of overall business because of a deal. But during the recessionary environment of 2001 and 2002, there were quite a few companies whose businesses just fell off a cliff because of the industries they operated in—telecom, technology, software, hardware. Some of those deals ran into big trouble.

JA: When will you actually not do a deal? Let's say a deal is announced. When would you look at it and say, "Ah, we're not going to get involved in that. That's too hairy."

JO: When we don't have any confidence in the buyer, number one. Also, when we don't have confidence that the financing—if there's financing involved—will be successfully obtained. When we view the target's business as being severely impaired and having a strong likelihood of not being able to go it as a stand-alone company. So for the most part, we're going to avoid certain distressed situations where we think our risk far outweighs the spread we could capture through setting the deal up.

JA: What's an example that you didn't play right from the get-go?

JO: Well, there are a lot of small, tiny deals that we don't play. We look at them, but they're too illiquid; there's not enough of a spread there. And they're too numerous for me to name.

But some of the higher-profile deals may have a lot of potential risk for regulatory problems, such as Nestle's and Dreyer's. We didn't play that deal for nine months. We played in the last inning, after some turbulence came into the deal, once it began to become problematic due to antitrust issues.

There are going to be deals and opportunities that we miss. But we've got to have a comfort level that what we're looking at makes sense from a risk-reward standpoint.

JA: Do you ever give preference to all-cash deals or all-stock deals? Or is there any type of deal that statistically you've found works out more than other types?

JO: Not really. We tend to play wherever the deals are. The ratio of cash to stock deals is going to change. And there are many deals in which we're involved that have a component of cash and stock in the consideration. But no, there's no preference on our part.

JA: Do you ever play relative value deals, like for instance, the Palm/3Com arbitrage that occurred when Palm was spun off?

JO: We'll look at spin-offs. I guess our presence in those types of transactions is going to be dictated by the valuation work we do. Deals for those types of transactions are a little tougher because you don't really have a defined return laid out for you. But we'll look at any type of corporate transaction if there's an opportunity.

JA: Can the average investor do this? You have a full staff and have been doing this for many years. Can a retail investor make money playing the merger arbitrage game?

JO: Yes, but on a very limited basis, I think. Certain deals will be conducive for individuals to get involved with. It may be a cash deal; it may be a straightforward stock-for-stock deal where they want to continue to own the shares that they acquire. Those individuals need the capability within their brokerage accounts to sell short, but they are unlikely able to capture a rebate on those short proceeds.

Can they analyze the deals and be kept abreast of the regulatory issues that come during the duration of the deal? You know, it's tough to do that on more than a limited basis if you're an individual watching positions in your account. You can pick and choose and then be very selective about how you play.

A firm like ours has a much broader mandate in terms of the deals we play and our presence across a wide variety of deals, with a wide differentiation in terms of the types of deals, the risks associated with the deals, and the duration of those deals.

It's just like any other type of portfolio. Some people feel they can manage their own. But they may not be as well diversified as a mutual fund that focuses on the same sector. And we stay pretty well hedged in the portfolio, and that may not be the case for individual investors, who may decide that they like the combined entity and they're just going to stay long and not hedge. In that case, they're not really doing merger arbitrage; they're not really capturing a defined rate of return. They're just basically owning an acquirer's shares at a slight discount for when the deal will get done.

I think there are people who are probably qualified to do it individually, but they are few and far between. They probably come out of this business and are basically managing their own portfolios going forward.

But it's hard because there are so many moving pieces. If we have 50 or 60 deals on in the portfolio, we're watching another 50 or 60. Within those deals, there are all different terms: the tenures, the durations, the players, the issues, the risks. So there are a lot of things to watch.

CHAPTER 6

Relative Value Arbitrage

A nother type of arbitrage that both Buffett and his mentor Ben Graham specialized in was "relative value" arbitrage. This became a bread-and-butter part of Buffett's "workout" strategy. The idea of the relative value arbitrage is to buy an asset when it is convertible into other assets that have more value than it does.

The most prominent example of the past few years is the case of Palm Computing and 3Com. Palm was a division of 3Com when 3Com decided to spin off Palm's shares to the public. On the first day of trading, Palm shares shot up so much that the stake that 3Com held in Palm was actually worth more than the market cap of 3Com. The market was effectively valuing 3Com's ongoing business at less than zero—business that had been around for thirty years and was immensely profitable. We will discuss this example in more detail later.

Another example is from Benjamin Graham's first steps in this arena. In 1915, when Graham was working for Newburger, Loeb, & Company, he stumbled upon the following relative value arbitrage: Guggenheim Exploration Company. The Guggenheim family, now known for its art museum in Manhattan, made most of its fortune by buying and developing mining properties. The Guggenheim Exploration Company was a holding company for many of the family's mining properties. On September 1, 1915, the company

EXHIBIT 6.1   Guggenheim Exploration Company Value on September 1, 1915

1 share of Guggenheim Exploration Company would equal:	
.7277 share Kennecott Copper @ $52.50 =	$38.20
.1172 share Chino Copper @ $46.00 =	$5.39
.0833 share American Smelting @ $81.75 =	$6.81
.1850 share Ray Consolidated Copper @ $22.88 =	$4.23
Other assets =	$21.60
Total:	$76.23

decided to dissolve and distribute the shares it held in other companies to its shareholders. On that day it was trading for $68.88. Graham added up the value of its holdings and came up with the table shown in Exhibit 6.1.

So Graham figured that buying one share of Guggenheim would net him an arbitraged profit of $7.35. He bought up Guggenheim and sold short shares in the corresponding companies, locking in his profit.

Another example occurred in the 1920s when DuPont, capitalizing on the cash it earned in its wartime successes, bought a large block of shares in General Motors. The market at that time, though, discounted DuPont's other businesses in the same way the market later discounted 3Com's business and valued DuPont shares only at the value of its GM shares, valuing DuPont's other businesses at zero. Graham was able to buy Dupont and short GM to capitalize on this spread.

One can say "But all of this was 80 years ago—how can such an obvious example of information arbitrage (the idea that information is not received equally by all market participants) exist now, with the existence of the Internet, analysts, computers to analyze these situations, etc.?" And yet, we see from the first example—PALM and 3Com—that the situation was even more extreme.

Buffett first dabbled in relative value arbitrage when he was working for Graham at the firm Graham-Newman. An amusing story about this is that Graham at first refused to hire Buffett because Buffett wasn't Jewish. Graham felt that Jews couldn't get jobs at the mostly Waspish Wall Street, so he sought to counterbalance this by only hiring Jews. Buffett, not to be dissuaded, kept sending Graham ideas for stocks until Graham finally hired him. Graham called his results in arbitrage "Jewish Treasury Bills."

When Buffett first came to Graham-Newman, he was 24 years old and raring to go. In the 1988 Berkshire Hathaway letter to investors, he discusses his first foray into arbitrage when he was working for Graham. Rockwood & Company was a modestly profitable maker of chocolate products that was sitting on an enormous supply of cocoa. In 1954 there was a shortage, and the price rocketed up. The company did not want to sell the cocoa outright because there would have been a tax consequence. A young investor by the name of Jay Pritzker helped Rockwood & Company to use the 1954 tax code to its advantage. He pointed out a provision that said it could distribute the cocoa to shareholders without incurring the almost 50 percent tax liability if it were part of a restructuring that reduced the scope of its cocoa business.

The company then offered to repurchase its shares in exchange for cocoa (as opposed to dollars). Buffett would buy shares on the open market, sell the shares to the company in exchange for cocoa, and then sell the cocoa for a nice profit. His only risk was that the price of cocoa would fall below the level he was paying for the shares. Since he would attempt to do these sales as simultaneously as possible, his risk was negligible.

So, again, that was then and this is now. Clearly such spreads wouldn't exist right now, right? But then again, let's look at the PALM-3Com example.

March 2, 2000, only eight days before the Nasdaq's all-time peak (as of this writing in January 2004), Palm went public. Initially scheduled to go public in a range of $14 to $16 per share, demand was so great that the shares priced at $38 per share. This translated to a huge cash bonanza for the company. On the first day of trading the shares opened at $150, immediately traded as high as $165, before finally settling down and ending the day at $95.06. At this point only four percent of the company was available to the trading public. 3Com (Nasdaq: COMS) still owned 95 percent of the company and was preparing to distribute 1.5 shares of PALM for every one share of COMS. If the only value of COMS had been its share of PALM, that would value each share of COMS at 1.5×95.06. In addition, COMS had approximately $10 per share in cash and it had zero debt, not to mention that COMS had an ongoing *profitable* business.

So one would think that COMS now would be trading...where? At least $152 / share (the value of PALM plus the value of its cash). Or maybe $177 per share, since at least one analyst thought that its non-PALM assets

EXHIBIT 6.2   Stub Value, 3Com

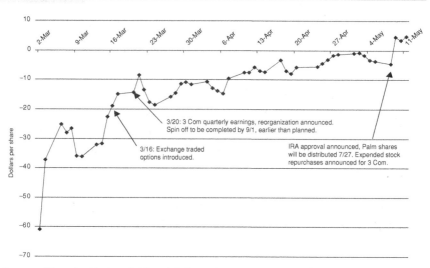

Source: "Can the Market Add and Subtract? Mispricing in Tech Stock Carve-outs."
by Owen A. Lamont and Richard H. Thaler (National Bureau of Economic Research
and University of Chicago), *Journal of Political Economy*, Volume III, Number 2,
April 2003. Published by the University of Chicago.

were worth approximately $35. However, on the day of the IPO, COMS
shares ended up at $81. This implied a spread of at least $60 between the
value of the PALM shares and the value of the COMS shares, even if one
valued all of COMS' other assets (cash in the bank plus a profitable business) at zero (see Exhibit 6.2).

The stub value (the market-implied value of the 3Com assets minus its
PALM shares) converged to zero, and finally above zero, by September of
2000 when 3Com finally spun out the shares to shareholders. This would
have been an immensely profitable arbitrage. The difficulty in implement-
ing it would have been in finding shares of PALM to short. Recent IPOs are
often difficult to short.

An example of such a trade where investors lost an immense amount
of money occurred in early 2003 in Japan with the Eifuku fund. A similar
situation to the PALM/COMS spread occurred when Nippon Telephone
became severely undervalued compared to its DoCoMo subsidiary. The

Eifuku fund made a massive leveraged bet that the spread would close. Instead, the spread widened and within seven days the fund lost over 90 percent of its value, closing down when Goldman Sachs took control and closed all of its positions.

A similar situation occurred with Long-Term Capital Management (LCTM) and Royal Dutch Shell. Royal Dutch, which traded on the NYSE and Shell, which traded on the London stock exchange, were actually the same company, formed in 1907 by a merger between Royal Dutch and Shell Transport. The split between the two was 60/40 and should have traded accordingly (the value of Royal Dutch shares trading on the NYSE should be 1.5 times the value of the Shell shares trading on the LSE. Instead, the disparity is often much more.

Richard Thaler provides Exhibit 6.3, which shows the disparity between the way the shares traded and the way they should have traded (the 60/40 split).

EXHIBIT 6.3 Royal Dutch Shell Pricing Disparity

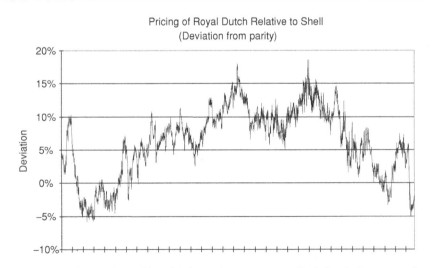

Source: "Can the Market Add and Subtract? Mispricing in Tech Stock Carve-outs." by Owen A. Lamont and Richard H. Thaler (National Bureau of Economic Research and University of Chicago), *Journal of Political Economy*, Volume III, Number 2, April 2003. Published by the University of Chicago.

In August 1998 this disparity reached an all-time high, precisely when Long-Term Capital Management was hanging on by a thread to this position as well as many other arbitrage positions that were experiencing a similar widening.

It is interesting that at this time, when LTCM was on the brink of losing its $3 billion fund, Buffett offered to pay approximately $100 million to take charge of its portfolio. They turned him down, but Buffett was definitely sniffing around for a good cause.

Are we wasting our time, then? Do these situations happen on a regular basis and, if they do happen, is it unusual for the results to pay off? Mark Mitchell, Todd Pulvino, and Erik Stafford[1] examine every situation between 1985 and 2000 in which the market capitalization of a company traded for less than the sum of its parts.

They note that there are two types of risk in this strategy. The first is fundamental risk, the risk that the shares of the two securities might never converge. The parent company, for instance, can go bankrupt, having used the value of shares in the spin-off as collateral before finally collapsing. The other type of risk to the arbitrageur is financial risk, the risk that the securities might converge, but first they might diverge in such a way that substantial losses by the arbitrageur are incurred, as happened in the LTCM and Eifuku cases above.

Mitchell, Pulvino, and Stafford walk through the example of Creative Computers and Ubid. Ubid was an eBay-like auction site started by Creative Computers. Creative spun out 20 percent of Ubid to the public on December 4, 1998. Like all good dot-com stocks at that time, Ubid shares began trading in a frenzy and at the end of the first day of trading after the IPO, UBID shares were trading at a market capitalization of $439 million, making the 80 percent that Creative Computers still held in UBID worth approximately $80 million more than the entire market capitalization of Creative. The authors go on to assume that an arbitrageur would have waited four days before trying to play the spread due to the lack of short-

---

[1]"Limited Arbitrage in Equity Markets," by Mark Mitchell, Todd Pulvino, and Erik Stafford, *Journal of Finance*, April 2001.

EXHIBIT 6.4   Creative Computers/UBID Arbitrage

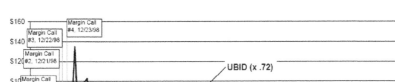

Source: Mark Mitchell, Todd Pulvino, and Erik Stafford, "Limited Arbitrage in Equity Markets," *Journal of Finance* 57, Issue 2, April 2002, Figure I, pp. 568. Reprinted by permission from Blackwell Publishers Journal Rights, Email: JournalRights@oxon.blackwellpublishing.com.

able shares in Ubid immediately after the IPO. On the fourth day, the value of the stub value had increased from −$80 million to −$28 million.

Attempting to capitalize on this spread, an arbitrageur would have shorted 0.72 shares of UBID for every one share of Creative Computers. Assuming that Creative was going to spin out the shares to shareholders within six months of the IPO, the return to the arbitrageur would have been approximately 45 percent.

However, within a few weeks the value of the stub would have decreased from −$28 million to less than −$700 million. The losses sustained by an arbitrageur would have been close to 100 percent assuming the arbitrageur met all of the margin calls, as detailed in Exhibit 6.4. Although the prices eventually did converge, the roller coaster was too painful for any investor to handle.

The authors assume that all margin calls are met, they assume transaction costs and they also limit the initial investment in any one deal to 20 percent of total equity. Additionally, they assume short rebates of three

EXHIBIT 6.5

Year	Pure Negative Stub Value Portfolio
1986	9.5%
1987	44.4%
1988	17.5%
1989	−0.3%
1990	29.3%
1991	17.6%
1992	6.4%
1993	55.6%
1994	2.5%
1995	2.1%
1996	41.1%
1997	20.5%
1998	−14.2%
1999	15.7%
2000	77.4%
Mean	22.0%
Std	24.8%
Sharpe Ratio	0.676

Source: Mark Mitchell, Todd Pulvino, and Erik Stafford, "Limited Arbitrage in Equity Markets," *Journal of Finance* 57, Issue 2, April 2002, Figure VI, pp. 575. Reprinted by permission from Blackwell Publishers Journal Rights, Email: JournalRights@oxon.blackwellpublishing.com.

percent a year, where the cash they make from selling the shares they borrow yields interest. Exhibit 6.5 demonstrates their results.

The strategy of playing the spread between a parent and subsidiary resulted in an average return of 22 percent per year between 1986 and 2000.

CHAPTER 7

PIPEs and High Yield

O bviously, not every technique that Buffett has used to trade can be used by the average investor or trader. Some of the techniques he used in the 1960s and 1950s, like driving around putting up signs for people to sell him shares in specific "cigar-butt" companies, do not apply to today's Internet-driven world. What is important is to identify the common thread that drives each of his investment decisions: the quest for a margin of safety in each trading strategy. Again, this is not "margin of safety" in the Graham-Dodd sense of buying a company at two-thirds its liquidation value, but the idea of making a trade or investment where you have multiple reasons, hopefully uncorrelated reasons, to believe that the investment will not lose money.

For example, in Chapter 5 I discussed the Arcata deal where KKR had an offer to buy the company. Buffett was buying shares of Arcata because he believed the deal would be consummated. However, the key is that Buffett also went through the exercise of asking, "If this deal never happens, can I get out of these shares with a profit?" At that point, he also analyzed the liquidation value of the company and determined that the exit, while probably slightly longer off, would still result in a profitable trade for him. In other words, he had an "out," a back door exit available to him just in case the front door exit he had planned for did not work. It is this that sums up Buffett's margin of safety in every case.

The use of private investments in public equities (PIPES) is a technique that Buffett often exploits to get his hoped-for margin of safety, but this is not necessarily a technique available to the average investor.

A public company typically goes the PIPE route when other avenues for raising capital are closed off. Normally, a public company that needs to raise money either does a secondary offering or a debt offering. In other words, the company can hire an investment bank like Goldman Sachs or Morgan Stanley. They put together an offering memorandum explaining the risks and the possible benefits in investing in their company, and then they go on the road, meeting investors who might be interested in their offering. Typically, a secondary offering is at a slight discount to wherever the stock is then trading, in order to give the secondary investors an added advantage to purchasing the secondary instead of simply buying the shares on the open market.

Additionally, the common stock of a company usually suffers in both a secondary stock offering and a debt offering. When there is a secondary, current shareholders of the company know that they are about to be diluted and that each stock is therefore worth less. Both Dalia Marciukaityte[1] and Mikkelson and Partch[2] conclude that immediately after a secondary offering, the stock price tends to decline. Perhaps shareholders are worried about the effects of dilution. Or perhaps shareholders wonder why management chose this time to sell off common stock. In other words, did management view the stock as overvalued, so, like any investor with enormous information about a company's prospects, it made an investment decision?

Similarly, after a debt offering, common stock tends to sell off, as well as many of the recipients of the new debt now hedge their bets by shorting the stock.

Additionally, the costs of a secondary are not trivial. The bank takes its fees, which could be as high as six or seven percent. In addition, the SEC requires various filings to register the shares in advance (which also

---

[1]"Investor Behavior and the Timing of Secondary Equity Offerings," Dalia Marciukaityte, Louisiana Tech University working paper, 2002.
[2]"Study Price Effects of Secondary Distribution," Mikkelson & Partch (JFE, 1985).

telegraphs to the public at large that a secondary is looming, causing perhaps an initial selloff in shares).

For these reasons, many companies opt to go immediately into the PIPE route, selling shares directly to private investors without having to take the secondary route. In many cases this avoids the costs associated with hiring an investment bank to manage a secondary offering. Also, smaller companies or companies deeply in distress may not be able to hire an investment bank to take them through the ropes of a secondary.

The typical PIPE comes in one of two flavors: common stock (with a warrants kicker) or debt (usually convertible).

A common stock PIPE might work as follows: Company XYZ is trading at $10 a share and needs to raise $4 million. It sells 500,000 shares at $8 a share (a 20 percent discount) and for every 10 shares of stock an investor buys, he or she also receives four warrants with a strike price of $12 a share (40 percent warrant coverage at a 20 percent premium strike price). Typically, the shares cannot be sold immediately, but only after a waiting period, usually anywhere from three months to one year. The investor in such a PIPE can justify his margin of safety in two primary ways:

1. **The 20 percent discount.** If not specified in the agreement, a PIPE investor can hedge his shares by immediately shorting at $10, locking in the $2 spread (since he owns at $8). However, usually the PIPE agreement will specifically state that no hedging is allowed. Also, the shares might not be liquid enough for such a hedge.

2. **With luck, the share purchaser was attracted to other aspects of the deal beyond the 20 percent discount**. If the company is a legitimate investment, then the buyer of the PIPE shares just received a great bargain compared to the common stock holder. If the stock goes up, not only does the PIPE investor benefit from the 20 percent discount, but also the warrants.

From January 1, 2004 to May 1, 2004, there were 436 examples of PIPE deals involving common stock, according to PrivateRaise.com. These deals added up to $5.1 billion in investments. Most (298) of these deals were on companies with a market capitalization less than $100 million. So they were mostly micro-cap companies.

For example, on April 29, 2004, Capital Title Group (NasdaqSC: CTGI) announced it raised $10.1 million at an average price of $3.60 a share. The day before, the stock had closed at $4.20. Additionally, the purchasers of the $2.8 million shares at $3.60 were granted warrants that gave them the right to buy at any point over the next five years 889,252 shares of common stock at an exercise price of $4.00 per share.

The other type of PIPE deal is a private offering of debt that later converts to equity. This can take a wide variety of forms, but it usually involves a fairly high interest rate and an attractive conversion price that is somewhere near where the stock is currently trading. If the debt-holder never converts, then he or she benefits from the high yield. If the stock goes up, the debt-holder can benefit by converting to common stock at a much lower stock price and reaping the benefits of the capital gain.

Convertible PIPEs became notorious in the late 1990s when many technology companies, desperate for cash as the bubble began to burst, offered what became known as "death spiral convertibles" or "toxic convertibles." These were debt offerings that converted whenever the debt-holder wanted, at whatever the stock happened to be trading at, no matter how low. The result was that many investors in these PIPEs would immediately begin shorting the stock as soon as they took hold of the convertible, in order to drive down the price of the stock as low as possible. While this was usually a rare and unpleasant form of PIPE, which ultimately resulted in bankruptcies and lawsuits, this practice gave the PIPE offering a bad name.

Although Buffett has never engaged in these death-spiral convertibles or anything remotely close, he has been an active investor in distressed companies through the use of PIPES. In some cases, as with Salomon and Champion, Buffett has been approached by management to be a "white knight" so that the company could avoid the grasp of an unwelcome suitor. Such knighthood carried its cost for the company and Buffett was often granted favorable terms through the use of a PIPE.

In other cases, Buffett has been an investor in distressed companies, usually securing generous terms with companies in dire straits. In addition to the terms of the offering, Buffett would often achieve his margin of safety by having the offering backed up by significant assets, as in the case of Williams Co., which we will examine later.

GILLETTE, JULY 1989

There has been a lot of analysis of Buffett's core holdings in companies such as Gillette and Coca-Cola. These are great brands, they have consistent earnings, and their stock prices have gone up enormously since Buffett bought them. In hindsight they seem like no-brainers. Why didn't everyone buy these stocks?

Things were definitely not so simple in the late 1980s when Buffett decided to purchase a stake in Gillette. The company, founded in 1923 by King Gillette, was being stalked by disposable blade inventor Bic. Gillette was surprised by the strength of public demand for the low-margin disposable razors, which quickly grabbed up to 50 percent of the razor market. Although return on equity was incredibly stable and the company was still growing, Gillette was no longer achieving a growth rate attractive enough for institutions. In addition, the stock price was faltering. Sales were growing at a meager one percent a year. In addition, the company had to increase its debt load to fight off four different takeover attempts. This is not normally thought of as the typical Buffett investment.

In July 1989, Buffett contacted the CEO, Colman Mockler, and worked out an arrangement whereby he received $600 million in convertible preferred stock yielding 8.75 percent a year for ten years and convertible into common stock at a conversion price of $50 a share. The stock was then trading at $40, but had been rising pretty steadily in the 1980s until about a year or so earlier, when it had flattened out along with its sales and margins (see Exhibit 7.1).

In February 1991, Buffett was able to convert into common stock when Gillette was trading at $73 per share, for a 45 percent profit on his original investment, not counting dividends. Much has been written on Gillette's value to Buffett as an equity investment over the years, but it is interesting to note that it did not start that way. However, the PIPE that Buffett did enabled him to essentially have a free ride on Gillette. The one thing that Buffett knew, based on the company's 60-year earnings history, was that Gillette would not go out of business. In other words, he was going to get his 8.75 percent yield no matter how badly margins got squeezed by disposable razors. He also knew that given the strong brand of Gillette, it would take a lot longer than ten years, the life of the bond, for anyone to knock Gillette off its pedestal, even if it were attacked on all sides.

EXHIBIT 7.1   Gillette: 1982–2004

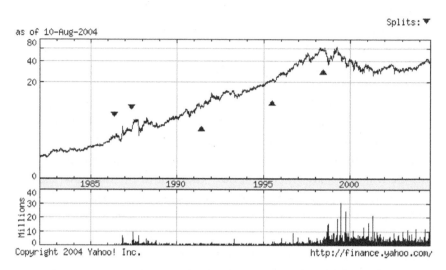

Source: Reproduced with permission of Yahoo! Inc. © 2004 by Yahoo! Inc. YAHOO! and the YAHOO! logo are trademarks of Yahoo! Inc.

In other words, Buffett had a free ticket to watch the show in the cut-throat razor-blade business while getting his 8.75 percent coupon no matter what. He could simply wait for the right moment, should it come, to convert at an enormous profit. He did exactly that. For a detailed analysis of Gillette as an equity investment at the time that Buffett did his conversion, I highly recommend Hagstrom's book, *The Warren Buffett Way*.

SALOMON INCORPORATED

Salomon is another company that definitely did not fit Buffett's style. Investment banks are subject to the whims of their times, and very few banks achieve the type of moat status that Buffett covets. Also, investment banks go in and out of favor depending on the market. If the market is down, mergers and acquisitions (M&A) are less frequent; alternately, IPOs are less frequent, and investment banks earn less money in fees. During those periods, investment banks are dependent on their proprietary trading, which Salomon at that time was well known for—particularly their bond trading group as made famous by Michael Lewis in his classic book, *Liar's Poker*.[3]

However, despite Salomon's acumen as a money-raiser or as a trading operation, these were not revenues or earnings that could be considered predictable. Nevertheless, Buffett had worked with John Gutfreund, the CEO of Salomon, in the past (most particularly when Buffett took over Geico in 1976). When corporate raider Ron Perelman was stalking the company, Gutfreund called Buffett and made a deal.

In 1987, Buffett bought $700 million worth of convertible preferred stock paying a nine percent annual dividend. The preferred would be redeemed over a five-year period beginning in October 1995. Meanwhile, the preferred stock could also be converted into common stock at a price of $38 per share, with the common at that moment trading at $33. If the stock went up from $33, Buffett would be very happy because he would get the full appreciation of any price move above $38.

However, the market crashed a month after Buffett did the PIPE, causing Salomon stock to sink to $16. Was Buffett worried? Not at all. As far as he was concerned, at that point he had a very solid bond paying nine percent per annum. In other words, he had a free ride on the company.

The story would have a pleasant ending if that was all there was to it. However, the Salomon preferred stock almost became Buffett's most costly mistake ever: On August 16, 1991, Salomon announced, with the stock just pennies from Buffett's $38 strike price, that the company had violated U.S. Treasury rules involving the government bond auctions and that all of the top officers were resigning.

What happened afterward has been written about in numerous places. Lowenstein[4] and Hagstrom[5] document the incident thoroughly. Buffett basically took control of the company and cleaned house. He fired everyone involved with the scandal, pleaded successfully with the government

[3]*Liar's Poker*, Michael Lewis, Penguin Books, 1990.

[4]*Buffett: The Making of an American Capitalist*, Roger Lowenstein, Random House, 1995.

[5]*The Warren Buffett Way*, by Robert G. Hagstrom, John Wiley & Sons, 1994.

to be mild in any penal suspensions of trading activity, and guided the company back on course.

Suffice it to say, Buffett made money on his investment, both in his steady nine percent annual return on the dividend, and from the eventual conversion of portions of his preferred stock into common once Salomon eventually traded above the conversion price of $38 in 1993. Again, this is an example where if it were not for the PIPE investment, it is unlikely that Buffett would have been a buyer of common stock shares of Salomon in 1987. But the PIPE allowed him to get a free ride while at the same time getting a very respectable dividend. This provided a considerable margin of safety, making up for the fact that the economics of the business might not have fit Buffett's sweet spot.

CHAMPION INTERNATIONAL

Another similar PIPE deal was Buffett's 1989 arrangement with Champion International; he bought $300 million worth of convertible preferreds paying a 9.25 percent interest rate and convertible into common stock at $38 per share when it was trading at $30.

The company had almost nothing going for it. Return on equity was a meager seven percent. The company had a very erratic earnings history and no real growth to speak of. That said, there were several million acres of timber on the books that nobody knew how to value. Buffett knew that during the 10-year holding period of the bonds he would get his 9.25 percent interest rate. In the worst-case scenario, the company could just sell off more timber to pay the coupon. On top of that, timber was a useful hedge against inflation. And, finally, if the company had a turnaround or was able to liquidate the timber, then the shares would substantially appreciate. Buffett was able to cash out his converted shares at a profit within five years.

All of these PIPE deals from the late 1980s were interesting in that they are often used (particularly Gillette) to describe the features Buffett looks for in an equity investment. It is true that they each became equity investments once Buffett converted his shares, but he essentially got a "free look"—or a "lottery ticket" as Roger Lowenstein describes it in his biography of Buffett. Buffett was able to enjoy the benefits of the bond, which required a different level of due diligence than doing an equity investment, and then ride the capital gains later as the stocks all went up—even though in the case of Salomon, he became perilously close to losing his investment. In the October 1997 edition of *Fortune*, Buffett said about the Salomon investment, "I'd say we hit a scratch single, but not before the count got to 0 and 2."

At the time of these transactions Buffett and the companies involved were criticized; the complaint was that Buffett was getting a sweetheart deal at the time unavailable to other investors. This criticism is true and the action is hard to defend. However, the rationale was that Buffett's playing the role of "white knight" saved the shareholders from whatever horror would have resulted had the company been taken over by hostile raiders or incapable management. And Buffett's abilities in a clutch situation were certainly demonstrated when he saved Salomon from almost certain bankruptcy during its 1991 troubles.

In the post-bubble downturn of 2000–2002, Buffett again engaged in several PIPE transactions.

LEVEL THREE COMMUNICATIONS

Level Three Communications (Figure 7.2) was a surprise investment. Just as an aside, it reminded me of the Fischer-Spassky chess match in 1972. Bobby Fischer was a rather eccentric chess grandmaster who became the first post-war American to challenge the Russians in the world championship. He also was notorious for *only* liking one first move: moving his king pawn two squares. Anyone who prepared for Fischer only needed to study this move, because he had stated repeatedly that this is the only first move worth playing. Hence, it came as an unbelievable shock when he played his queen pawn as the opening move in the middle of the match.

Buffett pulled a similar maneuver in July of 2002 when he made a private investment in Level Three Communications, a provider of broadband services. Level Three was a bubble stock founded by Buffett's good friend and Berkshire director, Walter Scott. In early 2000, Level Three shares were worth over $100 per share.

It was around this time that Buffett was getting the most criticism for not investing in technology. He was getting grief on two levels:

EXHIBIT 7.2   Level 3 Communications Inc

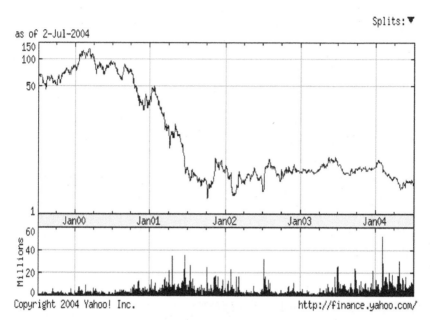

Source: Reproduced with permission of Yahoo! Inc. © 2004 by Yahoo! Inc. YAHOO! and the YAHOO! logo are trademarks of Yahoo! Inc.

1. Many investors were patting themselves on the backs for beating out the "world's greatest investor" when they loaded up the boat on tech stocks in 1999 and 2000. Buffett certainly missed an incredible move up in the Nasdaq during this period.

2. Was Buffett going a little too far in not investing in technology? Was he ignoring the American dream of constant exploration and conquest, now expanding not only in land and industry, but also through the cyber-depths of the Internet?

To Buffett's credit, he remained consistent and stuck to his investment philosophy of waiting for a margin of safety. For Buffett, buying Level Three on the open market at $100 a share did not give him his margin of safety. But on July 8, 2002, when it was announced that Buffett, along with several other investors, had bought $500 million of Level Three convertible preferred in a private placement, things were different.

For one thing, Level Three was now trading at $2.89, a greater than 95 percent fall from its peak. Second, the preferred was going to pay a nine percent dividend and was going to be redeemed within 10 years. Buffett felt that the company had sufficient assets to at least pay him his coupon over the next several years. It had $1.5 billion in cash and a 20,000-mile network that could always be sold off in a worst-case scenario. Finally, the shares were convertible at a very reasonable $3.41/share.

The news of Buffett's investment was surprising enough to send the shares up to $4.26 per share the day the deal was announced, putting Buffett's shares already 50 percent in the money. By the time Buffett had liquidated 95 percent of his investment in November 2003 he had made 95 percent on his money. As of this writing in October 2004 the shares of Level Three are back down to $3.71.

Note that these were not distressed bonds that Buffett was snapping up at a discount, an activity in which other investors and traders often engage. This investment in Level Three was specifically a deal engineered in part by Buffett's friend and partner, Walter Scott, who was running the show at Level Three. Again, this is not a criticism of the approach. Buffett has built his career on the fact that opportunities come knocking on his door rather than the other way around. However, it makes the challenge of trading or investing like Buffet that much more difficult.

Buffett would not have bought common stock shares of Level Three without having that dividend kicker to give him his free ride—not even at the low price of $2.89. And once he did convert to common stock, he was mostly a seller rather than a holder. Nor was there any way to buy the distressed debt of LVLT at that time; the company did not have any debt with those specific terms, nor was its debt as distressed as that of many of its peers due to its strong balance sheet (an aspect that I'm sure gave Buffett his margin of safety in the investment).

WILLIAMS COMPANIES

Williams Companies was another recipient of PIPE financing by Buffett. In March 2002, the entire energy industry was in a death spiral due to the collapse of Enron. Energy companies were all being quarantined by the banks in a vicious epidemic of "Enronitis." In other words, all of the energy companies were having difficulty getting financing and were quickly selling off assets to stave off bankruptcy. It was at this time that Buffett entered the picture through his Mid-American Pipeline subsidiary.

In March 2002, he purchased $275 million of convertible preferred stock directly from Williams. The preferred paid a 9.875 percent dividend per year and was convertible into stock at $18 per share. The stock instantly jumped from between $16 and $17 to over $20. However, this rise was short-lived as the company continued to report losses and the stock eventually slid below one dollar. At this time (August 2002), Buffett participated in a group loan to Williams for another $1.17 billion, this time secured by substantially all of Williams' oil and gas assets.

Less than one year later, Williams was back on its feet enough (and the banks were starting to do energy financing again) so that it was able to redeem both of these loans at a nice profit for Buffett (see Exhibit 7.3).

While it is difficult, if not impossible, for the average investor to find himself or herself a group of good PIPE deals to enter into, there are several key lessons to take away from this chapter:

- When examining Buffett's past equity holdings, it is always worthwhile to understand how he came to hold those equities and what was involved in the investment decision. It is one thing if he bought common stock on the open market. It is another if he was able to convert to those shares after enjoying several years of nine percent dividends at low risk.
- Buffett looks at the notion of margin of safety not only in the fundamentals of the underlying equity, but in the structure of the transaction itself. Not every investor can do this, of course, but it is important to realize that having more than one "back door" in a strategy is an important exercise. Always ask yourself what your recourse will be if your initial plan for a stock purchase or a trade of any sort does not work out.
- While it might not be possible to get the specific PIPE deals that Buffett has gotten, it is interesting to note that Buffett took the two absolute worst industries, broadband telecom and independent power producers, and plowed money into them. He did this not with common stocks, but into more senior levels of the capital structure. If an investor did

EXHIBIT 7.3 Williams COS

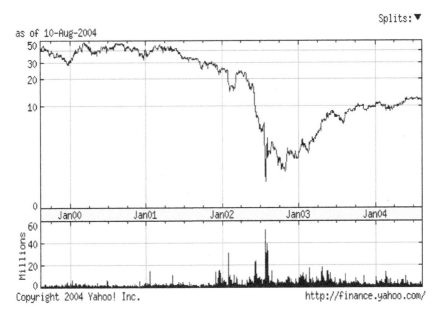

Source: Reproduced with permission of Yahoo! Inc. © 2004 by Yahoo! Inc. YAHOO! and the YAHOO! logo are trademarks of Yahoo! Inc.

not have access to PIPEs but did buy senior-level bonds in a basket of telecom and energy companies during these periods, he or she would have done very well.

CHAPTER 8

Junk

W hen businesses need to raise money, they can do so in two ways (assuming that raising money through profits is not possible). They can sell off equity (for instance, in an IPO or a secondary offering, or a PIPE transaction), or they can borrow money by selling bonds. The interest rate on the bond is determined by a variety of factors, the most important two being what the federally imposed discount rate is and what rating the ratings agencies such as Moody's and Standard & Poor's have assigned the company.

The discount rate is important for the following reason: If I can get a yield of, say, five percent from treasuries and I know this is risk-free unless the government defaults, then a corporation with presumably more risk than the U.S. government better be paying me substantially more than five percent for me to take on that risk.

The rating from the ratings agencies is also fairly important. Moody's and Standard & Poor's, in general, do enough due diligence on every company in order to determine the relative safety between the bonds of different corporations. If a company is rated AAA (for example, Berkshire Hathaway), then I have a high degree of comfort that I will be paid back if I loan them money. (Hence, when Berkshire Hathaway issued its SQUARZ bonds in May 2002, it actually had a negative yield. The yield was a function of the historic lows on federal interest rates, the extreme safety of

Berkshire as determined by the ratings agencies, and the fact that the bond was actually a convertible, so it had extra features other than the yield. This bond is the first, and at the time of this writing, the only, example of a bond with a negative yield). If a company is rated in junk territory, B– or below, then the interest rate needs to be high enough to compensate the bond-holder for that additional risk.

Although bonds are rated by the agencies, once they are issued, the market sets the price and yield. As with any other securities, the twin forces of greed and fear in the bond market will often send prices to one extreme or other. In 2002, for instance, after the bankruptcy of Enron, many of its bonds went straight to zero. As a result, many investors had no idea what shoe would drop next and ended up selling the corporate bonds of many energy companies en masse, even somewhat stable ones. Similarly, when the prices of Internet stocks were falling up to 99 percent, the bonds also were in a freefall and some corporate debt was yielding up to 20 percent or more.

When Buffett analyzes junk bonds, he doesn't care as much if the company has a stable and consistent ROE or earnings. All he wants to know is, *Can the company generate enough cash to pay him back?*

In the 2002 annual Berkshire Hathaway letter, Buffett comments:

> *[Junk bonds] are not, we should emphasize, suitable investments for the general public, because too often these securities live up to their name. We have never purchased a newly issued junk bond, which is the only kind most investors are urged to buy. When losses occur in this field, furthermore, they are often disastrous: Many issues end up a small fraction of their original offering price and some become entirely worthless.*

There are a couple of interesting points in these four sentences. First, "often these securities live up to their name." In other words, the market is usually efficient. If the market is telling us that these bonds are junk, then chances are they are junk. This is not to say that they will not pay their exorbitant yields, but the risk is commensurate with the payoff and there is no additional margin of safety.

Furthermore, the fact that Buffett has never purchased a newly issued junk bond is telling. Many people do purchase such issues. In fact, Wall Street would almost cease to exist if people stopped purchasing such issues. But Buffett has determined there is essentially zero edge to buying into an issue that Wall Street right from the start is labeling as "distressed" enough to be paying a junk rate yet in demand enough that many investors are clamoring to pay those rates. Chances are, he figures, the rates are not high enough at the moment of issuance and he would prefer to wait.

However, Buffett goes on to say in the same annual letter: "Despite these dangers, we periodically find a few—a *very* few—junk securities that are interesting to us. And, so far, our 50-year experience in distressed debt has proven rewarding." There is an important reason why it is only the "very few" that appeal to Buffett. A bond, unlike a growing company, has a maximum value it can return to the investor: the face value plus all of the coupons of the bond. A business, on the other hand, can keep growing forever—there is no cap on the maximum return of a business. Nevertheless, in extreme cases, the returns of a bond can exceed the hoped-for returns, in the short-term, of even the best businesses.

For instance, in 1983, the Washington Public Power Supply System (WPPSS) was involved in five building projects. Two of these, Projects 4 and 5, were building nuclear reactors. It was these projects that turned into a $2.25 billion default for WPPSS when it had to abandon the projects after a state ruling that threw into question who would pay for the energy that is produced if it is no longer needed. However, although Projects 1, 2, and 3 had "material differences in the obligors, promises, and properties underlying the two categories of bonds, the problems of Projects 4 and 5 have cast a major cloud over Projects 1, 2, and 3" (from the Berkshire Hathaway 1984 annual letter). This cloud sent the bonds issued to pay for these projects down to 40 cents on the dollar and yielding an average of 16 percent. Buffett bought $139 million of the bonds.

The question was: Is the potential reward worth the risk inherent in buying $139 million of the bonds? Buffett knew that there is a ceiling to the amount he could get back: the coupons plus the initial face value of the bonds. Buffett also realized that these bonds might be worth zero if he did not analyze the risks of the defaults on Projects 4 and 5 carefully enough. Would it be better, for instance, for him to buy a business for $139 million? However, he states:

> *In the case of WPPSS, the "business" contractually earns $22.7 million after tax (via the interest paid on the bonds), and those earnings are available to us currently in cash. We are unable to buy operating*

businesses with economics close to these. Only a relatively few busi-nesses earn the 16.3 percent after tax on unleveraged capital that our WPPSS investment does and those businesses, when available for purchase, sell at large premiums to that capital.

Viewing the investment in the context of "Should I buy a bond or an operating business?" allows the investor to avoid many mistakes that bond investors have made in the past. Buffett points out the example of AAA tax-exempt bonds in 1946:

In effect, the buyer of those bonds at that time bought a 'business' that earned about one percent on "book value" (and that, moreover, could never earn a dime more than one percent on book), and paid 100 cents on the dollar for that abominable business. This was during a period of substantial post-war growth when businesses were earning up to 15 percent on their book value.

Additionally, in that 1984 letter to Berkshire shareholders, Buffett stated another interesting factor in his decision on the WPPSS bonds. He noted that these bonds were not long-term, and the risk of runaway infla-tion in the future makes him hesitant to ever purchase a long-term bond. This theme remained with Buffett until the present day, when the fear of inflation has even compelled him to make, for the first time ever, substan-tial investments in foreign currencies.

There is a similarity between the WPPSS bonds and the next junk bonds that Buffett mentions in his annual letters: The RJR Nabisco bonds. In both cases, the sell-off on the bonds was not directly related to faltering economics in the business.

RJR Nabisco was the target in the famous takeover engineered by leveraged-buyout shop KKR and made famous in the book and subsequent movie, "Barbarians at the Gates." In order to pay for the takeover, KKR had to issue junk bonds backed up by RJR's cash flow. If KKR had made a mis-take in how they valued the cash flows prior to the takeover, or the busi-ness faltered for whatever reason, then the potential for full payment on those junk bonds could become suspect.

However, RJR was performing fine as a business. The real issue was the blowup in general of the high-yield market. With the demise of Michael

Milken and Drexel, the credibility of all high-yield bonds came into question. And for good reason. As Buffett noted in the 1990 letter to Berkshire Hathaway shareholders:

> *In some cases, so much debt was issued that even highly favorable business results could not produce the funds to service it. One particularly egregious "kill-'em-at-birth" case a few years back involved the purchase of a mature television station in Tampa, bought with so much debt that the interest on it exceeded the station's* gross revenues. *Even if you assume that all labor, programs, and services were donated rather than purchased, this capital structure required revenues to explode—or else the station was doomed to go broke.*

With issuances like that, which were being quickly bought up and devoured by savings and loans institutions that would soon be bankrupt, it is no wonder that investors decided to throw out the baby with the bathwater and sell off all high-yield instruments they could find in their portfolios.

This explains the sell-off in RJR bonds. Buffett, having dealt with KKR before (see the Arcata example in Chapter 5 on merger arbitrage), determined that the cash flows on RJR were sufficient to pay off the bonds and bought up to $440 million of the bonds during late 1989. In 1991 RJR announced that it was retiring the bonds and paid off the full face value of the bonds, rendering Berkshire a healthy profit of $150 million.

As seen in Chapter 7, Buffett's interest in high yield extended to not only purchasing discounted bonds on the open market, but buying them in the form of convertible preferreds directly from the company. This gave him the added one-two punch of getting not only the benefits of the high yield, but removing the problem of having the ceiling on his potential return by allowing him to convert into equity at a later date.

In the tech and energy company sell-off of 2001 and 2002, Buffett again dipped into the high-yield market on several occasions.

For instance, in late 2002, Buffett began buying up debt in telecom company Nextel. Nextel's stock had fallen 95 percent from its peak in 2000 to its low in 2002; in 2002, it was even flirting with possible bankruptcy. In response, it used cash flow to retire up to $3.2 billion in debt and slashed 5,300 jobs in an attempt to cut costs. For 2002, Nextel posted a $1.4 billion profit, its first profit in 15 years. However, the combination of the recession and Nextel's prior problems still had the rating agencies ranking the company's debt as junk. In this environment, when interest rates were also being cut down to 50-year lows, Buffett was able to buy up $500 million of Nextel's bonds.

In early 2003, the markets were reeling in anticipation of the war in Iraq and the uncertainty that would come with it. At the same time, Buffett was coolly buying $100 million worth of Amazon.com bonds yielding 10 percent in anticipation that they would be called back by the company within a month—with the $1.3 billion in cash and marketable securities that the company had on hand. The company did redeem the bonds, giving Buffett a 22 percent annualized return for his efforts at relatively low risk.

CHAPTER 9

Warren Buffett's Personal Holdings

M ost people think of Warren Buffett and Berkshire Hathaway as the same entity. And this is not unreasonable. The fortunes of both have been inextricably linked since Buffett took financial control of the company in 1965 and became the full-time chairman and CEO in 1968. However, Buffett does occasionally make stock trades outside of the context of his role as chief asset allocator of Berkshire. These are particularly interesting to look at for three reasons:

1. At Berkshire he has to be able to allocate over $30 billion. Many good investments or trades are not appropriate for a cash portfolio of this size simply because they are too small. Buffett probably takes the best of these small investments and does them for his own portfolio when they are not appropriate for the Berkshire portfolio.

2. At Berkshire, Buffett has more often than not gone the Fisher/Munger route of "paying up" for good, growing companies that might be trading higher than book value, or in some cases, higher than their intrinsic value. Many of these investments have worked out quite well (Coca-Cola and Gillette come to mind, and more recently Petrochina), but they are not the classic Graham-Dodd investments that Buffett was

schooled on. In his personal portfolio, Buffett has more often gone back to his roots and picked companies that were trading below book or even liquidating their assets. These are cigar butts that Buffett felt obligated to pick up off the ground and smoke one more time.

3. The picks in his personal portfolio are more reminiscent of the types of trades he would do in his hedge fund. He did work-out situations that in many years resulted in up to 50 percent of the profits or more for that year.

For all of these trades, it is impossible to know the full details of the trade; Buffett never talks about them and is only obligated to file his ownership when it exceeds five percent of the company. However, we can still pick through the filings and the news reports on the companies and try to examine what happened, when, and why.

LASER MORTGAGE

Laser Mortgage was a mortgage-backed real estate investment trust (REIT) that quickly got into trouble in 1999 and 2000 when interest rates spiked up. They used heavy leverage and made very concentrated bets that backfired horribly when mortgage lenders defaulted on them, causing them to mark down book value significantly. Because of these defaults and markdowns, investors lost faith in management's ability to correctly value its portfolio and the stock soon plunged below book. In October 2000 the management threw up its hands and announced it was looking into a possible liquidation of its portfolio and ultimate distribution of proceeds to the shareholders.

Buffett began acquiring stock most likely in early 2000 when the stock was trading around $4 and book value was around $4.51. On April 13, 2001, Buffett filed a Schedule 13G filing with the SEC stating that he owned 979,000 shares, or about 6.98 percent of the company.

On April 25, 2001, the Laser Mortgage board of directors approved the liquidation and dissolution of the company, immediately approving an initial distribution of $3.00 per share. In 2003, they made another distribution of $0.50 and on July 5, 2004, they made a final distribution of 0.86 and closed the doors.

JDN REALTY

JDN Realty was a REIT (real estate investment trust) that owned 15 million square feet of shopping centers. For each shopping center the company attempted to anchor the shopping center with a "value" tenant such as Walmart or Lowe's, who were its two biggest tenants. The company reported steady results until 1999 when they announced they had to restate their prior five years' worth of earnings. The management team was hiding executive compensation by not properly reporting related party transactions detailing up to $5 million. The stock crashed from high to low over 50 percent and the lawsuits started flying.

However, the value of JDN's real estate did not change at all. Both Walmart and Lowe's reaffirmed that they were going to remain tenants of JDN properties. When the company began trading below its book value, in stepped Buffett. His first filing was in April 2000, when he reported that he owned 1.7 million shares. This was followed by a later filing in February of 2001 where he announced he was up to 2.5 million shares. In Q1 of 2003, JDN merged with DDR Realty for $13 per share.

TANGER FACTORY OUTLET CENTERS

Without getting into the discussion of whether the Internet created a bubble, the technology certainly consumed the public imagination in a way not seen since the advent of the printing press. REITs involved in the development of shopping malls were particularly hurt because of the belief that shopping would soon be dead except through e-commerce.

Tanger develops factory outlet centers, and shares were decreasing in direct proportion to the Internet index increases. People assumed that factory outlets were no longer necessary since they could now buy everything they needed from the comfort of their living room. The millennia-old technique of trying on clothes before buying them was deemed no longer nec-

EXHIBIT 9.1   Tanger, 1993–2004

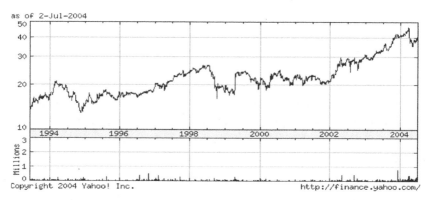

Source: Reproduced with permission of Yahoo! Inc. © 2004 by Yahoo! Inc. YAHOO!
and the YAHOO! logo are trademarks of Yahoo! Inc.

essary. By March of 1999, the company was trading at a 27 percent discount
to its net asset value, much lower than that of its peers. Additionally, the
company was yielding a 12 percent dividend and steadily increasing the dividend. And it wasn't in danger of overdeveloping like many REITs do during boom times, since Tanger pre-leases every space before it begins the
development of a new strip mall.

In April of 1999 Buffett bought five percent of the company, eventually
increasing his stake to more than 13 percent by 2000 and then reducing his
stake to below five percent by mid-2001. When Buffett first bought the
stock, it was trading at almost 40 percent from its high just a few months
earlier, even though business was better than ever (see Exhibit 9.1).

Around the same time that Buffett bought Tanger he also bought a five
percent stake in Town and Country Trust, a developer of office buildings.

HRPT PROPERTIES TRUST

On December, 2001, Buffett filed with the SEC that he had bought 5.1 percent of HRPT for his personal portfolio. I think the graphic in Exhibit 9.2
describes it best.

EXHIBIT 9.2   HRPT Property Trust

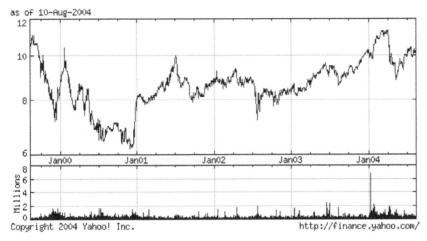

as of 10-Aug-2004

Source: Reproduced with permission of Yahoo! Inc. © 2004 by Yahoo! Inc. YAHOO! and the YAHOO! logo are trademarks of Yahoo! Inc.

It looks like Buffett filed right when the stock hit its five-year low point. Right before the announcement, HRP, which was a developer of office building space, announced that it was going to be receiving shares of Five Star Quality Care through its ownership in Senior Housing Properties Trust which was distributing the shares of Five Star. HRP, in turn, was going to distribute the shares to its shareholders. In addition to HRPTs' having a steady income and dividend—plus a divesting of unstable healthcare properties—Buffett probably calculated an arbitrage involving the Five Star shares. Within two months he had collected his Five Star shares, and then promptly reduced his stake to 1.77 percent.

BURNHAM PACIFIC PROPERTIES

Throughout 1999 and 2000 Burnham Pacific, an owner of shopping malls, was consistently selling off its stores at a premium to the value of those stores recorded in the books. With the company trading at a discount to net asset value, otherwise known as NAV, and a poison pill adopted to ward off a hostile takeover, shareholders were getting restless (and suing). Finally, at the end of 2000, shareholders approved a complete liquidation plan.

Buffett bought over five percent of the liquidating company in December, 2001, and enjoyed the benefits of its final six months of liquidating properties for more than they were initially valued at.

MGI PROPERTIES

Buffett first bought shares of MGI Properties in October 1998 when he filed with the SEC disclosing a five percent stake. Later this stake was raised to 8.3 percent and then 13.5 percent.

In June 1998, the company disclosed that it was liquidating all of its assets and distributing the proceeds to shareholders. The liquidation value was estimated at $33 and the stock at the time was trading around $20. We don't know what Buffett's acquisition price was, but it is fair to say he believed in the liquidation value and assumed he was getting a decent arbitrage between the price he was acquiring and the eventual liquidation value. Around 1998–1999 when Buffett was making many of his REIT purchases, reports were appearing in the media that seemed to suggest that these REIT purchases were part of a bigger macro statement on REITs in general. However, this was definitely not the case. In most of the situations, Buffett was buying purely for the liquidation value and the ensuing arbitrage.

BELL INDUSTRIES

Bell has been around for 50 years in a variety of businesses. It is a mini-conglomerate that began a transition to the IT services business in the late 1990s and began selling off its other businesses. In 1999 it sold the precision metalcraft division, an electronics distribution division, and its graphics imaging business. On December 13, 1999, Buffett filed with the SEC that he owned 5.93 percent of the shares. We don't know the exact reasons for his filing; perhaps he assumed that there would be more liquidations and more distributions of the results of those sales.

EXHIBIT 9.3   Bell Industries

as of 9-Jul-2004

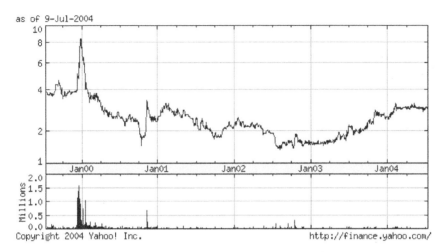

Copyright 2004 Yahoo! Inc.   http://finance.yahoo.com/

Source: Reproduced with permission of Yahoo! Inc. © 2004 by Yahoo! Inc. YAHOO! and the YAHOO! logo are trademarks of Yahoo! Inc.

Buffett sold his shares within two months when the stock spiked upwards, probably because he had bought them—not a bad investment technique, if you can manage it. In Exhibit 9.3 you can see the spike in volume that occurred on the left-hand side precisely when he announced his holdings.

Another type of arbitrage that Buffett has engaged in with his personal portfolio is closed-end fund arbitrage. A closed-end fund (something that Buffett's detractors often accuse Berkshire Hathaway of being) is a fund whose shares trade on the stock exchange like any other company. Unlike an open-end fund, a closed-end fund has a fixed number of shares and no longer accepts inflows or outflows of money.

In the next chapter on closed-end fund arbitrage, we examine another example from Buffett's personal portfolio with Baker Fentress.

Although 99 percent of Buffett's net worth is in Berkshire Hathaway stock, it is interesting to see him dart in and out of stocks through the years, using Graham-Dodd principles and snatching profits where he can.

It is worthwhile to note here the holdings of the Buffett Foundation, although its portfolio is not quite the same as his personal portfolio, which Buffett seems to actively manage. Exhibit 9.4 shows the holdings as of June 30, 2003, as filed in the Foundation's 990-PF filing.

EXHIBIT 9.4   Buffett Foundation Holdings as of June 30, 2003 Filing

Investments	# Shares	Cost	Market Value
Dover	800	3,134.07	23,968.00
Dow Jones	100	4,044.56	4,303.00
Dun & Bradstreet	50	595.26	2,055.00
Edison International	100	1,862.42	1,643.00
Energizer	3	27.28	94.20
Entertaiment Properties	100	1,383.00	2,875.00
Exelon Corp	100	4,588.74	5,981.00
Federal Express	200	5,588.05	12,406.00
Fed National Mortagage Assn	1,200	3,529.42	80,928.00
First Energy	66	3,188.74	2,537.70
First Industrial Realty Trust	100	2,346.54	3,160.00
Five Star Quality Care	1	7.26	1.51
Fleetwood Enterpnses Inc	100	479.16	740.00
Florsheim	16	588.33	0.00
Fortune Brands	400	3,061.70	20,880.00
FPL Group Inc	100	5,491.28	6,685.00
Franklin Covey	100	2,251.76	175.00
Friedmans	100	1,882.77	1,137.00
Furniture Brands Intl	100	1,709.54	2,610.00
Gabelli Equity Trust	183	1,691.15	1,367.01
Gabelli Global Multimedia Trust	18	144.00	139.50
Gabelli Utility Trust	18	165.29	172.98
Gallaher Group	400	1,784.30	15,640.00
Gannett	200	4,861.95	15,362.00
GATX	400	3,035.00	6,540.00
GC Companies	20	254.88	3.18
General Dynamics	400	4,208.03	29,000.00
General Electric	1,200	4,095.85	34,416.00
Gilden Activewear Inc	100	1,474.54	2,632.00
Gillette Co	800	2,723.16	25,488.00
Glimcher Realty Trust	100	1,562.76	2,240.00
Golden West Financial Corp	600	3,960.00	48,006.00
Graham-Field	210	1,237.90	0.63
Haverty Furniture	200	1,229.49	3,500.00
HCA Inc	100	3,285.43	3,204.00
Hershey Foods	1,200	5,535.50	83,592.00
Highwoods Properties	100	2,356.15	2,230.00
Hollinger	105	1,119.15	300.00
Hollinger International	100	1,450.98	1,077.00
HomeFed Corp	950	135.47	2,612.50
Horace Mann Educators	200	3,461.38	326.00
Hospitality Properties Trust	100	1,992.38	3,125.00
H&R Block	200	3,239.60	8,650.00
HRPT Properties Trust	100	729.48	920.00
Insignia/ESG Holdings	1	2.19	11.11
Insweb Corp	16	2,378.36	76.00
International Business Machines	400	11,630.90	33,000.00
International Flavors&Fragrances	300	10,466.65	9,579.00
International Paper	70	2,214.10	2,501.10
IStar Financial	115	2,909.45	4,197.60
Laser Mortgage Mgmt	100	374.27	80.50
Leucadia National	1,200	1,487.91	44,544.00

EXHIBIT 9.4   *(continued)*

Investments	# Shares	Cost	Market Value
Level (3)	100	1,596.66	670.00
Liberty Property Trust	100	3,000.55	3,460.00
Liz Claiborne	200	3,513.00	7,050.00
LNR PPTY	100	1,868.79	3,740.00
Loews Corp	3,000	8,635.50	141,870.00
Aetna Inc	100	3,475.00	6,020.00
Alleghany Corp	136	2,111.68	25,975.00
Allied Domecq PLC	25	964.25	567.25
Allstate	184	2,170.64	6,559.60
Altria	2,400	4,783.50	109,056.00
Amazon com Inc	100	856.49	3,632.00
American Express	612	2,636.76	25,587.72
American Financial	200	1,400.50	4,560.00
American International Group	2,370	13,202.00	13,077.66
AMLI Residential Pptys Trust	100	2,072.62	2,355.00
Anheuser Busch	2,400	5,835.03	122,520.00
AOL Time Warner	1,470	2,928.27	23,652.30
Archer Daniels Midland	413	2,104.40	5,315.31
Argonaut Group	30	300.00	369.90
Associated Estates Realty	100	1,282.78	657.00
Atlantic American	200	2,635.60	494.00
Banc One	100	2,572.13	3,718.00
Bear Steams	199	1,610.77	14,411.58
Bedford PPTY Inv	100	1,703.16	2,840.00
WR Berkley	49	135.00	2,582.30
Boeing	200	10,969.61	6,864.00
Bombardier	200	1,525.83	972.00
Burnham Pac PPTYS Inc	100	315.71	59.90
CAE Inc	200	841.50	1,146.00
Campbell Soup	1,600	5,095.40	39,200.00
Camden Property Trust	100	2,716.56	3,495.00
Car Wax	125	831.49	3,768.75
Champion Enterprises Inc	100	222.53	518.00
Chelsea Property Group	200	2,991.64	8,062.00
Chubb Corp	600	3,894.42	36,000.00
Circuit City Stores	400	1,675.26	3,520.00
Citicasters	100	998.50	3,000.00
Citigroup	2,737	7,884.84	117,143.60
Claires Stores	100	2,034.40	2,536.00
Coca Cola Bottling Co Cons	200	5,413.91	10,920.00
Coca Cola CO	2,400	4,918.50	111,384.00
Coca Cola Ent	300	1,573.50	5,445.00
Coca Cola Femsa	300	3,423.86	6,450.00
Colonial Properties Tr	100	3,254.21	3,519.00
Commercial Net Lease Realty	100	1,110.76	1,724.00
Compania Cervercerias Unidas	100	2,909.00	1,609.00
Conseco	100	542.00	1,800.00
Consolidated Tomoka Land	100	1,346.45	2,512.00
Converse	33	1,635.34	0.00
Cornerstone Realty	100	998.24	731.00
Costco	26,575	200,324.55	972,645.00

EXHIBIT 9.4   Buffett Foundation Holdings as of June 30, 2003 Filing *(continued)*

Investments	#Shares	Cost	Market Value
Cott Corp QUE	200	2,144.01	4,138.00
Countrywide Credit Ind	200	5,660.44	13,914.00
Cousins Properties	100	2,529.38	2,790.00
Crown American Realty Trust	100	644.50	1,074.00
Curtiss Wright Class B	6	56.38	373.80
Daily Journal Go	100	700.00	2,440.00
Danielson Holdings	101	1,941.40	161.60
Dempster Industries	50	5,000.00	1.00
Developers Diversified Realty	103	3,393.61	2,929.32
Disney	1,200	12,015.15	23,700.00
Thomson Corp	167	1,582.00	7,478.26
Tiffany & Co	1,200	4,026.76	39,216.00
Timberland	400	2,145.59	21,144.00
Torchmark	3,653	30,296.86	136,074.25
Town&Country Trust SBI	100	1,529.77	2,325.00
Travelers Class A	117	166.74	1,860.30
Travelers Class B	242	369.69	3,816 34
21st Century Insurance Group	80	377.50	1,144.00
Union Pacific	100	3,879.49	5,802.00
United Dominion Realty Trust	100	1,011.36	1,722 00
Unitrin	94	828.75	2,549.28
US Air Group	100	5,359.10	0.00
US Bancorp	379	3,906.36	9,285.50
US Industries	7	5.00	20.00
UST Inc	100	3,192.75	3,503.00
Valhi, Inc	115	76.73	1,106.30
Viacom. Inc	80	653.20	3,496.00
Viacom Non-Voling	80	240.00	3,492.80
Vornado	10	68.00	6.50
Vornado Realty Trust	200	3,738.69	8,720.00
WalMart Stores	800	4,017.75	42,936.00
Washington Federal	133	2,149.06	3,074.00
Washington Post Co	10	1,994.19	7,329.00
Wells Fargo & Co	1,660	8,648.96	83,664.00
Wendy's Intl	100	2,225.67	2,897.00
Whitehall Jewellers	150	2,133.60	1,360.50
White Mountains Insurance	100	2,742.50	39,500.00
Williams Co	100	1,655.05	790.00
Yum	180	258.21	5,320.00
Zale Corp	100	1,247.77	4,000.00
Zenith National Insurance Co	110	2,730.00	3,135.00
		762,729.50	3,736,207.91

CHAPTER 10

Closed-End Fund Arbitrage

A closed-end fund is a publicly traded investment fund. The managers of the fund raise money by going public on an exchange and then using the proceeds of the offering to make investments. The managers typically charge a fee—for instance, two percent of assets annually and 20 percent of annual profits. This is different from a mutual fund where the investors purchase shares in the fund directly from the fund itself. A mutual fund always values itself based on its net asset value (NAV), which represents the fund's total assets minus its total liabilities. For example, if XYZ Fund has $100 million in stocks and no debt, then its NAV is $100 million. When mutual fund investors want to redeem their shares, they are able to sell their shares back to the mutual fund at the NAV price. A closed-end fund investor sells his shares on the open market, so the shares may or may not trade at NAV.

Closed-end funds can invest in anything from bonds to illiquid stocks to private equity investments. At the time of this writing, many private equity firms such as KKR or Apollo are starting up business development companies, which are a form of closed-end fund.

Typically, a fund begins trading at a premium to its net asset value. Then, over time, a discount sets in so that the closed-end fund is trading at a lower price than that suggested by the net asset value. There are many reasons a discount results:

- **Closed-end funds are not popular investments.** Many people do not even know they exist. After its initial IPO release, a closed-end fund might languish and the shares slowly drift down, out of nothing but ignorance.
- **Poor performance frightens off investors.** If a closed-end fund begins to underperform its indices, investors will begin to not trust the managers and sell the shares accordingly despite the discount to NAV.
- **The NAV might include capital gains that have yet to be taxed.** The shares will properly reflect this tax liability by trading at a discount.
- **There are too many illiquid or hard-to-value securities in the portfolio.** For instance, many private equity firms will not be able to properly evaluate their portfolio and this will cause investors to take a more conservative approach when evaluating the NAV.

The benefits of investing in a closed-end fund are that they often pay high dividends. In addition, many of the funds trade at a discount to the NAV. Closed-end funds typically dividend out all or most of their profits, much like REITs.

There are then two reasons for investing in a closed-end fund that is trading at a steep discount to its NAV:

1. **The discount will potentially narrow.** For instance, if an activist buys many shares and then liquidates the fund, the discount will instantly narrow.
2. **The high dividend that one gets at a discount.**

Baker Fentress, now BKF Capital Group, was one of the oldest closed-end funds. In 1923, they bought Consolidated Naval Stores, which later became Consolidated-Tomoka Land Company. Consolidated owned 16,000 acres of real estate in Daytona Beach, Florida, and, 76 years after Baker first bought it, was one of the primary pieces of value that Baker owned. At the time, in May 1999, Baker was trading at a 26 percent discount to its net asset value, an extreme discount compared with its peers. At that point, they announced a partial liquidation plan and a distribution to shareholders. Shortly after this announcement, in August 1999, Buffett filed with the SEC that he owned more than five percent of the company. It also appears that he never reduced his holding so he may have continued to hold onto his shares of Baker Fentress (now BKF Capital Group) after its partial liquidation. See Exhibit 10.1.

EXHIBIT 10.1   BKF Capital Group Inc. from June 1999 to July 2004

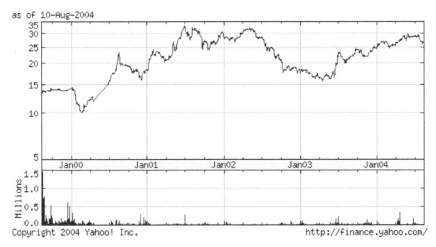

Although closed-end funds usually trade at a discount, the discount normally stays consistent and seldom varies. Dominic Gasbarro and J. Kenton Zumwalt of Murdoch University, along with Richard Johnson from Colorado State University, discuss that while the discount remains, it does tend to mean-revert.[1] In other words, if the discount quickly gets larger, it has a tendency to snap back to historical norms. In their paper, they even use Baker Fentress as an example.

However, discounts in closed-end funds do not necessarily eventually narrow (unless they hit an extreme as just described). In the 2004 paper by Sean Masaki Flynn of Vassar College, the author discusses that blindly playing a portfolio of going long discounted funds and going short funds trading at a premium is not a successful strategy and often offers negative returns.[2] At the end of this chapter I interview two hedge fund managers, Zeke Ashton and Mohnish Pabrai, who specifically play this strategy and discuss how the average retail investor can get an edge.

---

[1]"Evidence on the Mean-Reverting Tendencies of Closed-End Fund Discounts" by Dominic Gasbarro, J. Kenton Zumwalt, and Richard Johnson, *The Financial Review* Volume 38, 2003.

[2]"Arbitrage in Closed-End Funds: New Evidence," Sean Masaki Flynn, Vasser College Dept of Economics working paper, 2004.

Buffett, as usual, did not simply play a blind closed-end fund arbitrage strategy but always had an "out." There are not many examples, but the Buffett strategy in the closed-end fund world was:

1. Find funds trading at a discount to the NAV.

2. The components by themselves were deep value situations that were also possibly hard to value (as in the Baker Fentress example), thus suggesting why the discount was larger than it should have been.

3. Look for a catalyst that would get the funds trading closer to the NAV.

    a. One possible catalyst would be if there were a change in management where the new management had ideas about stock-picking closer to Buffett's.

    b. Another catalyst would be if there were a possible liquidation that would get fund assets distributed to shareholders at prices closer to the NAV.

    c. A third catalyst would be if Buffett (or Munger, in the case of the Fund of Letters described below) were planning to take control of the fund in order to initiate either "a" (since he would be the manager) or "b," or both.

Two other examples of Buffett taking advantage of severe discounts in NAV occurred in the 1970s. In the first instance, Buffett and Munger began buying up shares of the "Fund of Letters." The Fund of Letters had its start in the go-go 1960s, precisely when Buffett was winding down his partnership because of a dearth of opportunities in the stock market. The booming economy of that time period plus the rise of the notion of conglomerates fueled the fire of speculation. Gerry Tsai with his Manhattan Fund and Fred Carr with his Enterprise Fund were among the "market wizards" of the day, with Carr racking up gains of 177 percent in 1967 and 44 percent in 1968, while the S&P 500 went up "only" 25 percent and 11 percent, respectively. Carr started the closed-end fund Source Capital in 1968 to take advantage of the public's demand for this type of speculation.

The strategy was to simply keep the money moving and go from one hot story to the next, hence the term "go-go." This was momentum investing at its finest, only seen again in the late 1990s when anything with "dot-com" in it attracted the momentum dollars. When the market for go-go investing fell apart in the early 1970s, Carr and his funds were greatly discredited and investors fled. Source Capital, which had an NAV of $18 per share, was trading at a 50 percent discount of $9 per share when Blue Chips Stamps, controlled by Buffett and Charlie Munger, began accumulating shares.

They eventually owned 20 percent of the fund and Munger took a place on the board of directors. After Carr left, Source Capital became a haven of value investing under the leadership of George Michaelis, featured in John Train's book *The Money Masters*.[3] Michaelis became known for his method of valuing companies, called the Michaelis Ratio:[4]

$$\text{Michaelis total return} = \text{Yield} + \text{Growth}$$

where:
$$\text{Yield} = (\text{Return on equity} \times \text{Payout ratio}) \, / \, \text{Price to book value}$$
$$\text{Growth} = \text{Return on Equity} \times \text{Reinvestment rate}$$
$$\text{Payout ratio} = \text{Dividend per share} \, / \, \text{Earnings per share}$$
$$\text{Reinvestment rate} = 100\% - \text{Payout ratio}$$

In other words, there was a heavy emphasis on buying return on equity and steady growth, possibly at a discount to book value. This was an interesting compromise between Graham-Dodd–style investing and the growth investing with which Buffett and Munger often wrestled.

By 1975, the shares had doubled, and Buffett and Munger began to liquidate their position. They did this not because of any feelings about Michaelis (who ended up returning an average of 18 percent annually during his reign), but more as a result of the efforts to simplify their holdings. It was during this period that Buffett and Munger, to appease the SEC, began to merge their operations in Berkshire, Diversified Retailing, and Blue Chips Stamps into one unified public company under the umbrella of Berkshire Hathaway.

Another example of Buffett's investments in closed-end funds was the "Fund of Letters" in the late 1960s (see Exhibit 10.2). I say Buffett here, but it was really more Charlie Munger and one of Buffett and Munger's closest friends, Rick Guerin.

The Fund of Letters started in the late 1960s as a public venture capital fund. Because of the fees that brokers made during the public offering, the fund had started with $60 million in assets but immediately went to $54 million in assets when the brokers took their fees. This type of laissez-faire manage-

---

[3]John Train, *The Money Masters*, Harper Business, 1994.
[4]See www.psarasratio.com for more information.

EXHIBIT 10.2   Stock Certificate for 100 Shares of Fund of Letters, Inc. Issued in 1969

ment style caused shareholders to ultimately bail, with the fund ending up trading at a severe discount to NAV. At this point, Munger and Guerin bought up the shares and became activists, ultimately taking control of the fund.

They immediately changed the name of the fund to "The New America Fund" and changed the style to value investing. It is through this vehicle that they made purchases in Capital Cities and the Daily Journal, which is now the collection of legal newspapers in California that Munger still owns and runs. (It is public on the Nasdaq small-cap exchange under the symbol DJCO, as shown in Exhibit 10.3.)

Ultimately, New America Fund went from a low of $3.75 to a high of $100 per share by the time Munger and Guerin liquidated the fund in the late 1980s.

The story of New America Fund was repeated (but without the help of Buffett and Munger) during the dot-com boom as well, most notably with the closed-end fund MeVC, started by the venture capital (VC) fund Draper Fisher Jurvetson. Draper had had many successes in the late 1990s with early stage dot-com investments, most notably with free email provider hotmail.com, sold to Microsoft for $400 million shortly after the company started, when it had zero earnings.

EXHIBIT 10.3 Daily Journal, 1992–2004

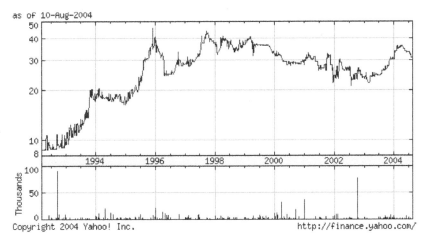

The fund went public with much fanfare in June 2000. The idea was that retail investors could now participate in all of the rich gains that their wealthier peers enjoyed during the late 1990s. At last, there was a high-tech, high-profile, VC firm available to the public! The stock opened above $19 and ultimately hit a low of $7.10 in August 2002, despite having an NAV at that time of approximately $12—a 40 percent discount to NAV!

Hedge fund Millenium Capital, run by Izzy Englander, began buying up shares of MeVC, ultimately ousting management and taking over the company. Shares have since rebounded to over $9 and now trade at a slight premium to NAV. Exhibits 10.4 and 10.5 demonstrate the premium/discount history of MeVC since its inception.

EXHIBIT 10.4 Premium/Discount History of MVC

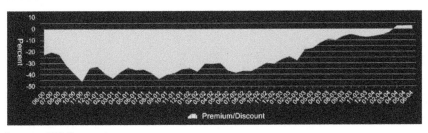

Source: ETF Connect.

EXHIBIT 10.5   Share Price/NAV History since Inception of MVC

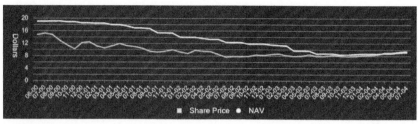

Source: ETF Connect.

If closed-end funds trade so often at a discount to their net asset value, then it stands to reason that there might be shorting opportunities with funds that trade at a premium. This is particularly the case at IPO time for a closed-end fund, since no fund will set its IPO at a discount to the net asset value.

A recent example is Apollo, the private equity firm run by Leon Black, who used to work for Michael Milken at Drexel Burnham. Apollo IPOed a business development corporation called Apollo Investment Corp on May 5, 2004, selling shares at $15. The stock immediately traded down and has been below NAV ever since (see Exhibit 10.6).

EXHIBIT 10.6   Apollo Investment Corp.

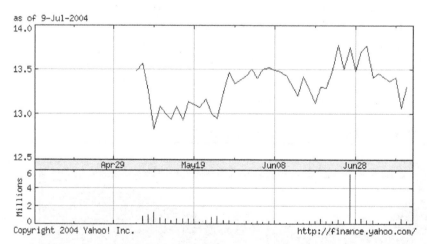

Source: Reproduced with permission of Yahoo! Inc. © 2004 by Yahoo! Inc. YAHOO! and the YAHOO! logo are trademarks of Yahoo! Inc.

EXHIBIT 10.7 Capital & Income Strategies Fund

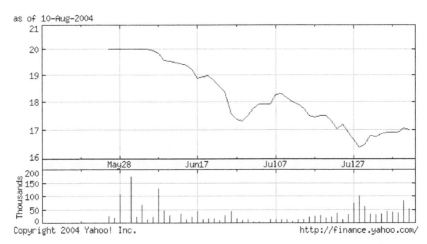

Source: Reproduced with permission of Yahoo! Inc. © 2004 by Yahoo! Inc. YAHOO! and the YAHOO! logo are trademarks of Yahoo! Inc.

Another interesting example is with closed-end bond funds such as Capital & Income Strategies Fund that usually IPO around $20 when their NAV is around $18. The stock usually hovers around $20 until finally breaking down.

The stock held steady at $20 until finally the bid was dropped and the stock immediately fell to its NAV and lower (see Exhibit 10.7).

Many critics of Berkshire Hathaway consider Berkshire a closed-end fund that should trade at a discount to its net asset value. Nothing could be further from the truth. Berkshire is an active business with over 50,000 employees spread out through its many subsidiaries and holdings.

CHAPTER 11

Interviews with Two Buffett-Style Hedge Fund Managers

INTERVIEW WITH ZEKE ASHTON

Zeke Ashton is a hedge fund manager at Centaur Capital, and a contributor to The Motley Fool investment Web site.

JA: Can you tell me a little about your background and how you got into the hedge fund business?

ZA: I started out in the risk-management business. I went to work after college for a little company called Wall Street Systems that specialized in basically treasury financial systems, mostly global financial risk management—things like foreign-exchange risk and interest-rate derivatives. We did various things like risk metrics, which was a big risk-control package that JP Morgan developed.

    I lived in Europe for about five years, most of it in Germany, and spent some time in Italy and Switzerland.

JA: What were you doing there?

ZA: Basically consulting work, building and installing these risk-management systems for the treasuries of large banks. In my case, my client was Siemens, which is kind of the General Electric of Germany.

    It has a tremendous amount of financial and various other risks to manage centrally there because it has plants in 80 countries and customers in 100 currencies, and it has to make sure that when it converts all that stuff back to its home currency, it doesn't lose a gazillion dollars in the process.

Interestingly enough, one of my coworkers gave me a Peter Lynch book back when I was an intern with the company, when I was still a student. I read that book in about four hours, and when I put it down, I thought to myself, "You know, in a perfect world, this is what I would love to do." That was just before the Internet became a popular phenomenon, and I didn't really know exactly how one got into that line of work.

I had this opportunity in front of me because I'd been overseas as a student and spoke some German, and this company needed somebody who was eager to learn and was willing to move to Germany and spoke a little bit of the language.

They hired me to do that out of school, sent me over to Europe and kind of threw me in there, and it was a great experience because I learned a tremendous amount about how the global financial markets—the foreign exchange market and the money market, interest rate derivatives market, the equities markets—are all sort of connected in a certain way. They're all assets that generate streams of cash flow.

That was helpful to me when I finally picked up some books to follow up on my interest in stock market investing back in '97 or '98. I picked up some books about Warren Buffett. I was a reader at the time of The Motley Fool, which was a very accessible source of investment information. So I got very serious about it as a hobbyist in early '98 and began to run my own portfolio, and I was so anal about it that I even wrote myself quarterly letters.

Buffettology was one of the first ones I read, and then *American Capitalist* by Roger Lowenstein, which is probably the best book on Warren Buffett.

You have one view of what Buffett is like, and then when you start to dig deeper, you realize that the way he runs money now and the way he sort of projects himself now as kind of this grandfatherly, "buy and hold 'til death do us part" sort of investor has really been taken to extreme lengths by the media.

And it's diametrically opposed to what he was doing earlier in his career, when he was really compounding money at the 20 percent to 25 percent range in sort of a bear-market environment from '56 to, you know, at least '73, '74, when the bear hit its kind of bottom.

He was out there buying net-net working capital stocks, as he'd been taught by Benjamin Graham, and when his problems went from too many ideas and not enough capital to too much capital and not enough ideas, he really was forced to make the transition into buying these much higher-quality businesses that he has the luxury of holding for a long period of time.

JA: Right.

ZA: I was very fascinated by having a case study of a man who, purely through rational capital allocation, was able to grow a very small amount of money and compound it at high rates of return over a 40- or 50-year period to become the world's second- or third-wealthiest man purely based on investing acumen, not based on building a company that turned into a global worldwide monopoly like Bill Gates. He didn't inherit a lot of money.

Something about that just really appealed to my nature, and I'm sort of a studious guy by design and love to get in there and figure out the system, find out what the probabilities are that this or that will work.

I came home from vacation when I was living in Switzerland and started a little limited partnership. I got a couple of coworkers who were in Europe with me—for whom it was very inconvenient to invest in mutual funds—to toss in $10,000 each or so, and I started managing the money.

Not long after that, I submitted an essay on investing to The Motley Fool. They liked it and published a couple of my things, and eventually they offered to hire me and move me to Alexandria, Virginia. I saw that as a huge opportunity to make the transition from the business that I was in, for which I was rapidly losing interest as well as losing its demand after the euro and the Y2K thing.

So I moved to The Motley Fool. I continued to run this little limited partnership on a pro bono basis in my spare time. I looked at 1,000 companies maybe in my two and a half years there and wrote a couple hundred articles. I tried to develop myself as an analyst and a money manager. Ultimately in August 2002, I did open up the fund to outside investors, changed the strategy a little bit to make it more of a hedge fund, and have been doing this for two years. Our track record has been very good.

Late last fall, Matthew Richey, who was a good friend of mine and helped to get me hired at The Motley Fool, came and joined me at

Centaur, and we're having a great time. We work very carefully and closely together and try to invest the capital that's been entrusted to us with a value sort of orientation, although we don't necessarily consider ourselves completely traditional.

We're willing to chase or go get value in whatever guise we think it happens to be in. We try to not to bind ourselves too rigidly by any one set of rules, but at the end of the day, it all comes down to how much cash you think an asset can produce over its life.

And so we try to reduce virtually everything that we can, in some way, shape, or form, to whether we think the price today is a good price and has a margin of safety that will give us a 15 percent annualized return, which is generally our equity hurdle rate.

JA: How do you quantify the margin of safety?

ZA: You know, it's hard. If we could put our strategy in certain buckets, we have one strategy where we look for smaller, high-quality companies that are trading at, say, single-digit price-to-free-cash-flow ratios and they have everything else right—strong balance sheets, good brands, some niches, [they are] managed correctly, this sort of thing.

If we had enough of those to go around all the time, we would do nothing but that. Some are growing at two percent a year and some are growing at eight percent a year. If you buy a group of those that are all high-quality, all managed by enlightened people who are shareholder-oriented, you pay an average of, say, seven times free cash flow for that group of fine companies, then you're going to do well over time.

JA: Let me just play devil's advocate. Wouldn't you say the market is pricing these companies in the single-digit cash flows because there's some anticipation that they're going to stop growing, or growth will be negative?

ZA: I don't think that's the case. Most are priced to low multiples because they're boring. I believe that in today's world, you can divide stocks into two groups: those with a buying constituency and those without a buying constituency.

For example, it's estimated that the U.S. mutual fund industry is about an $8 trillion industry. Somewhere around $2 trillion of that is either S&P 500 funds or S&P closet funds. So there's a $2 trillion constituency that has to buy only the companies in the S&P 500.

If you've ever been to a Berkshire Hathaway meeting, you sit there and think to yourself, "There are people lined up at six o'clock in the morning to listen to the CEO of this company answer questions for about five hours. The doors open and grown men and women run and knock each other over to try to get the best seats." I call it "the running of the bulls," and I think it's the funniest thing I've ever seen, that grown men and women are willing to do this.

They listen to this man whom they obviously worship—some in a more enlightened way than others—but you think to yourself, "How is it possible that Berkshire Hathaway can be undervalued when clearly there's this constituency of people who are going to buy the stock?"

The reason is that the constituency you see at the Berkshire Hathaway meeting is such a tiny, tiny drop of capital when you compare it to a constituency like all the S&P 500 index funds in the world.

As you know, Berkshire Hathaway is not in the S&P 500. And because it lacks that buying constituency, it's my theory that Berkshire Hathaway is occasionally very cheap relative to its intrinsic value, but even now, when it's trading at very high historical valuations relative to book value and whatever else you want to use, it's still trading at probably 80 cents on the dollar when you look at it from an intrinsic value standpoint.

You would think that there should be a premium to all of the relative metrics that we use as investors—simply because of the track record, the culture and the man who's running the money—but it doesn't have one.

Would you say it's because there's an expectation on the part of shareholders that Berkshire Hathaway's growth is going to stop? I would argue that it's not. It's just that Berkshire Hathaway does not have the huge buying constituency that, say, AIG might have.

JA: So with these companies—including Berkshire Hathaway—that don't have a constituency, it's not necessarily the case that there's going to be a future constituency. They might be forever valued cheap?

ZA: Yes.

JA: Until they have negative growth, and then they'll be valued less.

ZA: Yeah, the risk you're referring to is, of course, what we in value circles call the value trap.

I personally believe that if you have enlightened management that's shareholder-oriented, a value trap doesn't really exist. It can exist on a single-stock basis, perhaps. I'm willing to concede that. But on a portfolio of them? I don't believe that's possible because ultimately that enlightened management team will, if they're good capital allocators, make smart acquisitions. They will buy back stock at attractive prices. They will continue to pay out a higher and higher level of dividend until they bring in various people.

But you know what? As long as the stock continues to be relatively valued—i.e., if it never trades at more than eight times free cash flow on a per-share basis, but the company is reducing the outstanding shares by six percent a year and growing the business by three percent a year—you're going to still get a reasonable sort of equity return relative to the risk you're taking.

Again, a lot of these companies are excellent. Generally they're smaller, because they're neglected. Or they're small stocks or small companies. Some of them happen to compete in industries that don't get a lot of buzz. But ultimately, they get bought out by a bigger competitor, or something happens—the catalyst comes, as we say in value circles—and you end up making the money.

JA: Do you have an example?

ZA: The fall of 2002 was a very, very good time to be buying some of these stocks. It was kind of the nadir of the 2000–2002 bear market, which, depending on whom you talk to, may or may not be over yet.

In any case, Internet companies had fallen into such disrepute that nobody wanted to own an Internet stock anymore. There were jokes about them. It had almost become the new "swamp land in Florida" joke.

We noticed a little Internet advertising company called ValueClick and went out to visit the company. This was a true Ben Graham net-net working capital play. The company had $3 a share in cash and it was trading for $2.30. If you looked at the business from an operating standpoint, it was just barely breaking even, but it was profitable and cash-flow positive in general because its big cash balances were kicking off some interest income.

But the interesting thing it was doing was buying even smaller publicly traded Internet marketing companies at even bigger discounts to cash. The leader in the industry was DoubleClick, and even DoubleClick was pretty much hated and almost fell below cash at one point.

We looked at ValueClick's model and talked to its management team. The manager didn't strike us as a genius in capital allocation, but he was very, very good at the day-to-day operations of the business. He was not a big spender, and he knew how to keep costs in line with expenses.

The one thing we realized was that as soon as the advertising market turned around, a huge number of the advertising marketing players had been cleared off the table by consolidation, and many of them just went out of business. But those that were any good got taken over by Value Click, DoubleClick, and some of the other players.

Second, the business had a massive amount of scale to it, because it didn't cost them very much to run the advertisements out there once they had built their infrastructure.

The thing did turn around. About nine months later, the economy started to turn around a little bit and advertising went up. The scale of the business was becoming obvious. They had a couple of good quarters. The stock rocketed from $2.50 to $4.

We started selling because we thought the thing was only worth $4. I think we sold the last of our shares at $5, and the thing rocketed on to $12. It hovered there, but then the company announced earnings that weren't good enough and the stock's been knocked back since to the single digits again.

That's the way these things happen. The frustrating thing is that not only do they eventually get a catalyst and actually get catapulted in value, but generally once it gets going, it goes way beyond what you thought it could ever plausibly be worth.

My friend Whitney Tilson calls it the value investor's lament. You always sell too early, because you have to sell in order to keep the margin of safety. You always have to sell at fair value, or maybe the high end of fair value. But you never want to hold an overvalued stock because you could be holding ValueClick when it gets whacked back to the single digits. You don't want to do that to yourself after you've gotten the profit.

JA: Let's go back to, say, November 2003, and these Internet stocks have gone up 50 percent from their lows, and there aren't too many examples of companies trading below cash. How do you switch gears and find the margin of safety for your investors during a period like that?

ZA: The problem as an enlightened value investor is that you never want to deploy capital unless you really do see a) a reasonable discount to fair value, and b) a reasonable margin of safety in the stock price. So we, like a lot of value investors, inevitably started building up cash as we started selling the stocks that had kind of gone to fair value and above.

Fortunately, the market tends to be fairly merciful. I mean, there are 9,000 stocks that trade on the three major U.S. exchanges, and at some point or another, if you dig enough, there's always some trading at a significant discount to fair value. We have some statistical screens that we run through a computer software program that helps us identify the stocks that are obviously statistically cheap.

For example, we have one [based on] this net-net working capital strategy that Benjamin Graham popularized but that nobody really uses anymore. In the fall of 2002, we might have 40 names on that, and as we'd go through and look, for 30 to 35 of them there are legitimate reasons why the things are trading below net-net working capital. But for five, they were perfectly decent companies and not horrible assets, and they were clearly trading at below the value that they should have been trading.

Typically we prefer that most of that value is in cash, not in accounts receivable or inventories or that sort of thing. We also screen out those that have burnt a significant amount of cash.

When we ran that same screen at the end of 2003, there were only three names on it. And they were three names that we'd looked at previously and had decided there was something flawed enough about the business that even at that price there was no margin of safety. So these things do change.

You have to go where the ball is, and of course, if you're going to pay 10 times free cash flow, you have to get a higher-quality company with a little bit more growth or whatever it is that you're looking for.

JA: Can you give me an example from November or December '03?

ZA: We found a company—and the reason this one was available because it's just somewhat illiquid—called Atrion. The ticker symbol was ATRI, which is still in our portfolio today.

It's a little medical device company that grows the top line pretty significantly—or has over the last five or six years—but had actually bought back over a third of the shares in the last five years. And their capital allocation was phenomenal.

But nobody could own it because it was too small of a stock, and it actually dropped back a little bit on some top-line weakness. It was available in the $20 to $25 range, which made it at seven times free cash flow or something.

We continued to buy it—and we paid up to 11 times free cash flow for it—up into the mid-$30s because we thought it was a very high-quality company. We thought the management team was outstanding at both managing the business and allocating capital, which is a very, very tough combination to find.

The business was actually highly diverse and had a high margin for such a small company, and none of the big institutions could buy it because it just didn't have the liquidity. But for us, managing a smaller pool of capital, the liquidity wasn't an issue, and the company's located about 40 minutes north of us, so we were able to check around to make sure that their reputation matched our view of it. We're quite happy to get it, and we continue to hold it.

We bought a ton of Berkshire Hathaway in March 2000, which was probably the all-time best time to buy Berkshire Hathaway. The problem is that if you buy Berkshire Hathaway at a kind of once-in-a-lifetime opportunity—at least once-in-our-generation opportunity, when Warren Buffett's being raked over the coals for his refusal to buy technology stocks.

We bought these shares at perhaps $1,500 and now they're at $3,000, so four years later, you have a double, whereas if you buy a net-net working capital stock and something good happens, like it did to ValueClick, if we'd have sold at the right time, we could have had as much as a five-bagger. We ended up getting two bags in a nine-month period of time rather than a two-year period of time.

JA: What percentage of your fund do you typically put in the average position that you have?

ZA: We've gotten less concentrated than we used to be for a couple reasons. Number one, the bargains are probably less now than when we started doing it, but also just because we're not as comfortable holding, say, 10 percent positions as we used to be.

But if we have absolute confidence in, like, Berkshire Hathaway, it was upward of 10 percent of the fund, which was a very small fund at the time. So it probably doesn't even qualify as a fund. It was just a pool of friend-and-family capital when we did that.

But usually our maximum position, which we call the double, is 7.5 percent. Our standard position on what we think is a truly outstanding investment that will reach our 50 percent annualized hurdle rate and has a margin of safety is usually five percent.

On our net-net working capital strategy, you're buying a mediocre asset at best that's priced as if it's going out of business. So our position sizes there range between one and two percent, usually depending on the quality of the business.

JA: How many positions can you hold at any one time?

ZA: We'll hold between 25 and 30 long positions at any one period of time very easily.

JA: Here we are in August '04. How many positions do you have on right now?

ZA: We've got probably 27 longs and six shorts.

JA: How do you decide to short a stock?

ZA: We basically look for the mirror image of all the stuff we look for on the long side. We think of the market as this big bell curve. A bell curve is based upon value per dollar, per investing dollar that you get.

Most of the time, unlike a standard bell curve where the bulge is in the middle, in our markets, the bulge is usually on the right side, i.e., the overvalued side, because more stocks typically are overvalued or fairly valued than we would like for them to be.

We try to pick our long investments out of the far left end tail of that bell curve; that's just the cheapest stuff on the market and hopefully, in terms of value, to get the most value for the dollar.

When we're shorting, we try to pick out the five or the six stocks that we think are the most overvalued. We call it "the cream of the crap"—the most overvalued stocks with the worst business with the most hideous management that are doing everything that will basically guarantee their shareholders will never see a dime of their cash back.

We typically like it when they're a little bit bigger in size so there's enough float out there. A lot of scam companies will issue a press release or try to get their CEO on CNBC, and they're not above bringing on a boiler room shop to send out mass emails to people saying, "Hey, buy this stock at 80 cents. It's sure to go to $3 tomorrow." To protect ourselves from that, we try to get companies that have enough of a float that it would take a significant amount of buying power to push their stock up dramatically.

Typically we like to short them just after they've done one of these PIPEs or after they've done a secondary or something where they have brought in a significant amount of new investor base that's likely to not want to take any pain.

JA: What's an example of a short that you've done?

ZA: Commerce One Software was a $15 billion company back in 2000. This was the company that was going to be B2B. The share price reached over $1,500 per share, split adjusted. They'd done some reverse splits since.

We started shorting it at about $3 a share at a time when we basically knew this business was a cash incinerator. They were burning several hundred million dollars a quarter. They had taken out massive real estate liabilities at the top of the market to house their 1,000 employees, which are now down to 200. So the real estate was sitting empty, and they were paying the rents.

Their biggest customer was SAP, the big German software company with whom they'd done a partnership back in the heady days, and SAP had just terminated the partnership and was now their biggest competitor.

So they had about $300 million or $400 million left. They were burning it at somewhere close to $70 million a quarter. Their market was drying up. Nobody was paying for these things, and in fact, they ended up selling what was left of their original B2B software and are now trying to sell this new conductor software.

So we shorted it and let them burn cash for another seven or eight quarters. We covered at about 60 cents simply because it got so cheap that we were worried that SAP or somebody might decide to take it over.

We got a really good return on it. There was a tremendous amount of float out there, because this thing used to have a $15 billion market cap. There were still some institutional holders that were holding on, and we knew they had to sell at some point. It was burning so much cash. We knew there was no market for their software anymore. We could tell that all of their revenue, which used to be license revenue, which is what you get when you sell the software, was now maintenance revenue, which is just very low margin, and requires that you have a lot of highly skilled guys who will help support the software.

They were diluting the stock by about 20 percent a year. And they were in the capital-raising tailspin whereby they would have to do these kinds of toxic bonds or toxic equity offerings, where they would sell some stock at a buck a share, but then they would issue warrants for a similar number of shares if the stock went up above $1.30 or something.

One thing we've learned about shorting, though, is that the longer you short, the better the chance that something unexpectedly good can happen.

JA: What sort of screen do you use to find margin of safety in a short situation?

ZA: We have a screen that basically tells us which companies are running on fumes when it comes to cash flow. You've probably heard this analogy before, but cash flow is oxygen for the organisms we know as corporations. Businesses have to have positive cash flow to live, and anytime a company is burning a significant amount of cash, particularly if they don't have very much left in the bank, then they're going to eventually die of cash asphyxiation.

Only two things can happen with a company that's burning cash and [whose] business is not working. They're either going to be able to raise more capital, which usually means the shareholders are going to be massively diluted, which is good for the shorts, or they're not going to be able to raise additional capital, which means it's going to be good for the shorts, because the company then goes to zero.

I've been amazed at how many ways there are in the modern capital markets for these companies to try and get more capital and stay alive another quarter. So that's why we never try to hold them to zero anymore.

You know? As soon as they—we look at shorting as an IRR game. We try to maximize our annualized return. So basically if we're short a stock and the thing takes a 30 percent dive, you know, in six weeks or eight weeks, we typically are gone.

We never invest based on ideas that are kicked out by a mechanical screen. There's always a very, very intense qualitative review that goes along with it. The screens are just designed to kick out candidates, nothing more.

INTERVIEW WITH MOHNISH PABRAI

This section is an interview with a hedge fund manager who focuses on Buffett-style investments. Mohnish Pabrai is manager of Pabrai Investments and also a frequent contributor to RealMoney.com and TheStreet.com.

JA: Give me a little background on yourself and how you went from the IT services business to Buffett-style investing and the hedge fund business.

MP: You know, first of all, I cringe whenever anyone says hedge fund, but—

JA: Why is that?

MP: Well, I think the connotation is that [the fund is] in some way hedging, leveraging, shorting, or delving into derivatives. The fund does none of those things, so basically a better description of it is a private mutual fund or a private investment partnership. That's just semantics, but people just short-form all private investment partnerships as hedge funds.

JA: Did Warren Buffett consider his partnership a hedge fund?

MP: I was surprised when he talked about it recently. He basically said, "Well, you know, Charlie Munger and I ran a hedge fund of sorts." I think he used that as a sort of short-form. But I think if you go back to the Buffett partnership letters, there's no such term; it's very clearly a private investment partnership. Again, the style of that fund included either special situations or just great businesses at a discount. But all the action and all the money are in the workouts in special situations.

JA: You mentioned in one of your letters that Laser Mortgage takes up intellectual energy. You know, it allows him to keep his hands dirty so he doesn't have to mess around with Berkshire's $50 billion in these situations.

MP: That's right, and I think Munger's exact quote was, "One hundred and seventy thousand employees and $150 billion of capital are inadequate to utilize that motor." So we need all these other special situations to keep Warren amused. A few years back, there was a charity event where they auctioned off his wallet, and he put a stock tip in the wallet, and the stock tip was First Industrial Realty, a REIT.

JA: All right, so tell me how you got into all this.

MP: I had an IT services company that I sold in '98 and then got more into investing and the fund business. My entry to investment funds was very accidental. I think when you learn about Buffett, it's like peeling an onion. There are many layers that you have to go through before you get to the essence, and I think I'm still not at the essence because all these nuances about management and so on are more difficult to grasp onto.

The first layer for Buffett is that he just buys these great businesses at a discount to what they're worth and holds them forever. I was very intrigued by that in the mid-'90s, and I thought, "OK, this thing is pretty simple." I love figuring businesses out.

I was still running my IT services company at the time, and I had a million dollars of cash with me in '95. So I said, "I'm going to start investing this million in public markets, and I think it will do better than market indexes." I wanted to find out how much better I could do. If you compound money at a healthy rate—let's say 20 percent or 30 percent a year—it grows pretty spectacularly. So I thought it'll be just interesting to see where this million ends up, and if I were to compound it [at] 26 percent and I ignored taxes, it would double every three years.

So I said, "Let's play a 30-year game." I was 30 years old at the time, and I said, "Let's see at 60 how close I can get to a billion." My thinking was that even if I missed it by 80 percent or 90 percent, that'd still be fine.

JA: That's not bad, right.

MP: So I started to spend about 15 or 20 hours a week doing investment research and starting a concentrated portfolio—a few big bets, and that did very well. I think from '95 to 2000, I averaged 60 percent a year. I would tell a bunch of friends, "Hey, I found this great business; you should buy the stock." And these guys also made a lot of money making some of these investments.

In early '99, a group of them approached me and said, "Look, you tell us stuff, and we sometimes act on it, sometimes don't." They wanted to set up a fund for the friends, and they wanted me to manage it. So they said, "We'll give you $100,000 each, pull together a million bucks, and you can manage that money. That way, we're not dealing with stock tips and whatnot." And I thought for me to manage another pool of capital would be basically no work, because I was already doing the research for my own assets anyway.

I said I would do it if they let me set it up in a format exactly like the Buffett partnership. I like those partnership rules—no fee until six percent and then one-fourth profit above that comes to me, three-fourths to partners, no disclosure of holdings, and I like that format of writing a letter to partners and so on. They didn't really care, so that's how the fund got started. I was still running my business at the time, and it was really a part-time endeavor with a million dollars. In 2000, the business got sold, and in the fall of 2000, I went full-time into running the funds.

I have a rule that if on Monday morning, I'm not fired up to go to work, then I do two things. One is I don't go to work, and the second is I hit the reset button on my life. So in early '99, I was getting so much more ingrained into Buffett and whatnot, and with declining interest in IT services, that I didn't feel like going to work. So I started a search to bring in a CEO [for the IT firm], and I actually then applied for a job with Buffett to learn from him. I got turned down.

JA: Did you go out to meet Buffett?

MP: No, no, I just sent him a letter with a résumé, and he sent me a response in a week saying, "Look, I work alone, and the kind of position you seek doesn't exist at Berkshire." So he says, "Good luck reorganizing your life; I'm not the answer."

I was very disappointed when I got the letter, but after I got it, a friend said, "Look, why don't you set up your own fund and get the CEO search going?" I never thought of the fund as being a full-time vocation; I thought it'll be something on the side. By November '99, the CEO I brought in had started at the company, and then I think in early 2000, he said that he got a phone call from someone who wanted to buy the business. So now the buyer was looking at this new CEO as continued new management—not me, which was awesome. So then we did a transaction, this person stayed on, and they didn't even talk to me about any sort of employment contract. In hindsight, just dumb luck worked very well.

In the fall of 2000, the fund had about two and a half or three million [dollars] in assets, and I really wanted to spend full-time on just the investment funds. At that time, I thought, "You know, let's run this for at least 13 years and see how close we can get to the Buffett partnership."

There were two or three nuances. One is that he went from $100,000 to $100 million in 13 years without spending much time raising money, and he had a 29-percent-a-year return. Both of them were spectacular, so I said, "I just want to see how close I can get to both benchmarks." The fund rules won't allow you to advertise or solicit or anything, so I was just curious to find out if you just sort of put your head down and run the fund, will your partners actually send you money and will they refer you to others? On both counts, it's worked out far better than I thought.

The way I look at it, I'm about three years ahead of schedule. I have a spreadsheet that shows me the Buffett partnership's increase in assets over time, and then I did a CPI index delta for inflation from then until now, and I think I'm about three years ahead in terms of assets versus where he was. Amazingly, the returns so far have been ahead, though I think if I end up anywhere close to him, that'd be just awesome.

That's some of the history, but when the fund started, the focus—
and, in fact, even my understanding of the Buffett workouts in special
situations—wasn't that great. I think I'd read about it, but I never really
grasped onto the power of the model. I think in the fall of 2000, I visited
one of the authors, Timothy Rick. I had read his book and noticed he
was in Munster, Indiana, which is pretty close, and I just emailed him
and said, "If you'd like to get together for lunch someday. . ."

I met with him and then subsequently he was the one who really
highlighted for me how the special situations route was the way to go.
If you look at investing in terms of probabilistic terms, those are the
ones that do have the highest probabilities, absolute no-brainers,
et cetera. So in absolute returns, a buy-and-hold-forever strategy—
even if you buy a company at a discount—would, in general, be somewhat inferior to the special situations, especially if you held it forever.

The concept is really simple. Let's say you take a business like
Coca-Cola, and say you buy it at half of what it's worth and you held
it forever. What would happen is that your eventual return would
approximate the return in equity the company was generating. It
wouldn't matter what discount you bought it at, because over time it
would get to full price. The gains in stock price you would see would
be approximately mid-range gains and return on equity.

JA: Have people done research on this and proved that to be true for companies over time?

MP: It's intuitively obvious. Let's say you buy an apartment building for a
million dollars, and let's say it's generating $100,000 a year in cash
flow for you. Let's say that cash flow goes up at 10 percent a year; the
value of the building will track with that cash flow. It will go to $1.1
million or $1.2 million, and I'm assuming discount rates are the same,
interest rates are the same, and all of that. But if you take all those
variables out, returns on investment will track return of equity.

That's one edict, and the second edict is that there's no business
on the planet that can generate returns in equity in excess of, let's say,
30 percent a year and be able to forever redeploy the capital that it's
generating. Take a business like Microsoft. Historically, Microsoft's
return on equity used to be well over 30 percent, but the problem is
that when they generate all the cash, they're not able to redeploy it
back. That's why they've got such a big cash hoard.

So if they're not able to redeploy the cash back, now that cash is
earning one percent. So your return on equity does not compound at

30 percent a year at Microsoft. It can only compound at 30 percent or 35 percent a year for the amount of actual capital deployed in the business, and the actual capital deployed in the business is not able to absorb all the capital that the business is generating.

There is no business that I'm aware of—in the country or in the world—that can endlessly generate return on equity over 20 percent and redeploy all the cash to generate. From that, you will infer that the upper-limit returns that you can generate, if you made no mistakes whatsoever, would be 20 percent a year. There's an upper-limit bound on buy-and-hold-forever, and the upper-limit bound is about 20 percent.

In reality, it's actually less, because when you get to a portfolio and you get to mistakes and you get to management redeploying capital with some mistakes themselves—when you get to all those real-world situations, the real number is much below 20 percent. So let's look at Sequoia Fund, probably the best research shop on the planet that I know of and probably the best buy-and-hold investors that I know of. Sequoia Fund generated 16 percent or 17 percent a year for the last 32 years.

If you take Berkshire out of the portfolio, the returns on their investment excluding Berkshire Hathaway are about 13 percent a year. So the best buy-and-hold investors, with the best research team, just kick ass in what they do. Look at the portfolio of businesses— they buy amazing businesses—it's banging out 14 percent or 13 percent a year.

And now the flip side. You go to special situations and you just flip the map, or you just say, "OK, I'm going to buy a dollar for 50 cents, and when it gets appraised at a dollar or 90 cents, I'm going to get rid of it." Now your returns are simply a function of how long it takes to get to convergence. If you bought a dollar for 50 cents and sold it for a dollar, and convergence took one year, you would generate a hundred percent return. If convergence took two years, you would generate a 37 percent or something return. If convergence took three years, you would generate 26 percent, and if convergence took four years, you would generate 18 percent. So up to four years of convergence beats buy-and-hold. This very simple math became obvious, and the fact is that buying great businesses is all good because you have a few more tax efficiencies and all of that. But really, the pop in terms of getting better returns on assets is first of all to sell fully priced—or near fully priced—assets, whether they're special situations or not, and then go back and buy at 50 cents on the dollar.

JA: What do you think of Buffett's saying, "My favorite holding period is forever"?

MP: I think Berkshire has the model. The problem with special situations is you have to continuously be able to find these opportunities to take advantage of the market—what I would call market anomalies. If you have a huge pool of capital, it becomes a problem because you can put a lot of capital to work in a company like Coca-Cola, American Express, or Gillette, but the Finovas, the MCIs, or the First Industrials of the world—those sorts of investments are very random. They're not very good to look at in a portfolio that is a hundred and fifty billion.

Generally speaking, you'll have a very hard time trying to put that amount of capital to work in these sorts of situations. Typically, a lot of the special situations are going to get just thinner and thinner as the market caps go higher. I think Munger said that the first few hundred million at Berkshire Hathaway came from running a Geiger counter over everything. You know, you're at the beach trying to find metal under the sand, and you're running over everything and find something. But he says that subsequent billions have come from making a few select investments. I think if you have unlimited capital, then the special situations isn't going to work so well because you will not be able to deploy capital.

Buffett made a statement two years back. He said, "If you gave me a million dollars of capital to manage, I would pretty much almost guarantee that I will make 50 percent a year." For a guy who's very humble, that's a pretty cocky statement. But I think the reason he makes that statement is he would just make 100 percent doing special situations.

JA: How do you go about, right now, finding special situations?

MP: You don't. You let the game come to you. So basically, you do nothing, just read and think, and occasionally, you read the paper and you'll see something. For example, I think I made an investment in a company called Front Line. Front Line was a case where the value of the company was, I think, $14 or $15 a share. It was losing money in the near-term market, and the price went from $15 to $3, and so there was mispricing.

Basically, you're looking for market anomalies. Whenever there's extreme fear in some sector, or whenever there's some big clouds over some companies, you're likely to get mispricing. The question is, "Am I able to see through the clouds, and do I know the business well enough to be able to see beyond the temporary negativity of an industry or a company and see what the value of the business is versus the price at which it's being offered, and if it is enough of a delta, step in?"

If you look at broad-based special situations, like a Front Line, or I bought a funeral services company three or four years back called Stewart Enterprises for less than two times cash flow—there were clouds over those businesses when they were bought, and they're OK businesses. I mean, Front Line is not such a great business because it's eventually a commodity. Stewart has some mood around its business, but in both cases, the primary driver for buying the business was an ultra-cheap price and a huge discount to what it was worth.

JA: What were the valuation parameters? How did you analyze it?

MP: Well, let's go through Stewart for example.

This is going further back. The thing with Stewart is that there was a big rollup in the '80s and '90s of these funeral services operators, and the three big ones were Service Corp., Stewart Enterprises, and Carriage Services, and in the glory days, they took on a lot of debt, issued a lot of stock, and bought a zillion companies—small mom-and-pop funeral homes. Stewart ended up with like a thousand funeral homes, about a billion [dollars] in revenue, and about a billion in debt.

The debt load was such that they had—in the year 2000, I believe—a $500 million note coming due in 2002, about 22 or 23 months away. The company was generating about a hundred million a year in cash after all interest payments and everything. So in two years, they were generating $200 million, but they were still $300 million short, and there was no clear answer as to exactly how that note would get settled. The existing lenders in that space had taken so many losses in that area that they were not willing to make any additional loans or roll over existing debt. So Stewart would have to refinance, pay the debt off or find another lender.

The Street had just witnessed one bankruptcy out of these three big players, and so they painted them all with the same brush, and all the funeral-services stocks collapsed. In fact, Stewart went from, I think, $28 to $2 a share in about an 18-month period. I looked at it at $1.91 a share. This was a company that was generating a hundred million in cash flow, after all, and it had a market cap of a $190 million. So you could buy a business for less than two times cash flow, which is unheard of, right?

This is a very predictable business because you know exactly how many people are going to die each year. Maybe they'll charge 300 basis points more or whatever else, but someone will be willing to make this loan because the economics of the business are so solid. So I said, "First of all, I don't believe that this debt is not yet settled." Second, I said, "Even if there's no lender on the planet willing to lend to them, it's not a single street plant. It's 1,000 different funeral homes, each of which has the same brand it had when it was born."

So what I decided is I need $300 million. I can go to the first: I just put 200 funeral homes on sale, go back to the people I bought them from, and say, "I'll sell it back to you at half the price I paid you." I think that easily two or three hundred of these guys would take that business back in a heartbeat. So my sense was that they could sell these funeral homes pretty much back to the people they bought them from, get the cash, pay the debt, and move on, and still retain a lot of value in the business and still be underpriced.

So we put assets into Stewart, and literally less than two months after I made the investment, the company announced that it was going to sell all its international funeral homes. They had about 300 funeral homes overseas, and they said that those funeral homes, because they were in so many different countries, were not generating any cash flow to the business. So the hundred million a year they were generating would be unaffected by that sale, and they estimated that that sale would bring in three or four hundred million at least. The stock went from $2 to $3 on that news.

Another few weeks later, they said there were three definitive buyers fighting over who would be able to buy the 300 homes, and the bidding had gotten the price up to five, six hundred million. The stock went to like $3.50 or something, and then when they closed the transaction, it went to about $4.50 a share. Stewart subsequently went to between $6 and $8 a share after that. So that was a classic no-brainer, no-downside, significant upside investment.

JA: Let's say you're the average retail investor right now. Other than reading the newspaper, are there any other techniques that you can use to try to find these opportunities?

MP: I do look at the New York Stock Exchange every day, and I look for names that are familiar. Then if something piques my interest, I'll do a drill-down. In general, you want to look at stuff that's hated and unloved, like I had bought Level 3 bonds. That's another classic—

well, actually amazing—special situation because that one is going to give you like a 45 percent return a year for seven years, which is just unheard of.

JA: Did you buy prior to Buffett getting in?

MP: Yes, about a year before. There was a rumor circulating at that time that he might have invested, but it was confirmed a year later when he did the convertible issue with Longleaf and Bill Miller. I felt good about being ahead of the Messiah.

[Laughter]

JA: On a slightly different topic, basically these are mostly Graham-Dodd-style plays as opposed to the '70s or '80s Buffett-style plays, when he did Coca-Cola, for instance. How do you reconcile the fact that most of Graham's money he made actually on Geico, which was more or less a buy-and-hold-forever play for him completely outside the boundaries of how he normally can add value?

MP: Most of the money on Geico was made because it was a great business. But if you look at, again, if you look at Buffett's purchase of Geico, a huge portion was bought when Geico was under severe distress. He was buying at like about a buck a share. Geico's very unusual, and to find those sorts of investments is very rare. This was a company that was available undervalued, and some would argue even today that it has a sliver of the market share that it eventually will. It's got an ability to grow its business pretty dramatically over a very long period of time.

From my point of view, there are a couple of things that come in. One is, can you actually see it? Coke is a good example. If I look at that business independently, I just won't be able to see a long, huge runway and all that growth ahead of it without hitting blips and other major issues along the way and even changes in consumer behavior.

All these issues would cloud my judgment about something like that. So I think that if you can identify a Geico—but I'm thinking if you look at Graham, how many did he find?

JA: One.

MP: Exactly. And when the investment in Geico was made, it was at a time when Geico was undervalued.

I think that sometimes it's dumb luck. From my perspective, I think sitting around trying to find a Geico and just waiting until you make that investment is somewhat foolish because it's very, very hard to find. You are going to learn more about the business after it becomes part of your portfolio. And I think Geico is that type of company.

In fact, the very best investments are great businesses that are bought at times when they are under severe distress. So Buffett did that with American Express, right? He put 40 percent of his partnership assets into American Express in the '60s, right? But again, he sold it out. He never kept the stock through all that run.

My sense is that any special situation is fine as long as your math is giving you two-to-one returns in two or three years or less. In some sliver of them, you actually buy great businesses—and I look for that. The ideal situations are the ones that actually have an underlying great business, because then there's a decent chance that you'll have increases in intrinsic value while you're holding the business, which means that you never get to the point where it gets all valued. Ideally, the thing is going along at a slight discount to what the market price is. And that works out great.

But most of them are what the market's going to do. If you look at Front Line, for example, it went from $15 to $3 a share. When it got close to $12 or $13, I was selling. It's close to 40 bucks a share today.

JA: Wow.

MP: So if you had a Geico in your portfolio and it was worth $15 and went to $3 and you sold at $15, that would look like a reasonable decision. And then subsequently the Street takes it to two times intrinsic value. What do you do then, right? From my point of view, it's better to sell it rather than trying to play mental games.

JA: You brought up an interesting point about American Express: how Buffett put 40 percent of his assets in that situation, something which Graham almost certainly would never do in terms of that size of his portfolio. What are your feelings on diversification?

MP: I am not confident enough to put 40 percent into a single asset—mainly because I think I'm not Mr. Buffett. I feel that I want 10 bets, ideally uncorrelated, in 10 different industries, and I'm very happy to leave it at that. I know if I take 10 down to eight, my returns will go up. I just feel that there are macro factors and even macro events that cannot be analyzed. I'm just not willing to go above 10 percent.

CHAPTER 12

P/E Ratios, Market Timing, and the Fed Model

While Warren Buffett is usually considered the "world's greatest value investor," he has repeatedly stated that simple indicators—such as P/E ratios, P/Book ratios, and so on—are completely useless.

Despite this, fund managers, investors, and the media, have repeatedly hopped on the price/earnings (P/E) bandwagon when making macro predictions about the direction of the markets. For instance, a recent book about investing has asserted that the U.S. markets are "in a bubble" because the trailing 12-month ratio of the S&P 500 is 25. Analysts and pundits have also pointed to the 1974 and 1982 bear market bottoms when the market P/E ratio was less than 10.

Assume that the 50-year average P/E ratio is 15 and that the market tends to mean-revert, as asserted by all the people who claim P/E ratios are too high at any given point. I did the following experiment in order to test if Buffett's claim that P/E ratios are meaningless is true.

Since 1900, this simulation uses the S&P 500 total return index (the index plus dividends) and uses P/E data compiled by global financial data to buy the S&P 500 whenever the P/E ratio is lower than 10 and to sell when it is higher than 20. See Exhibit 12.1. P/E ratios are in the top pane and the S&P 500 total return index is in the bottom pane.

EXHIBIT 12.1

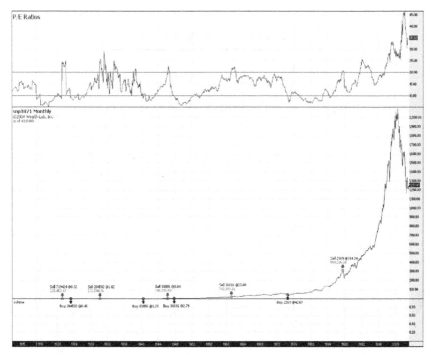

Source: Fidelity Investments. Charts created by using Wealth-Lab Developer software.

The five trades that occurred were all successful, as shown in Exhibit 12.2.

And it is interesting to note that the "system" caught most of the bull move of the 1920s, the 1950s, and bought at the bottom in the 1970s. However, this method underperformed the method of simply buying on January 1, 1900, and holding until now by a factor of 6,000.

EXHIBIT 12.2

Entry Date	Entry Price	Exit Date	Exit Price	% Change
12/1/1907	0.15	3/1/1921	0.32	116.81
3/1/1923	0.48	3/1/1930	1.82	275.19
7/1/1940	1.25	3/1/1946	3.04	143.46
10/1/1947	2.79	4/1/1961	23	724.92
7/1/1974	42.67	7/1/1987	314.34	636.6

Changing the parameters didn't result in anything better. I tried making the higher parameter 25, 30, and 35. I changed the lower parameter to 15. At the risk of curve-fitting, I tried stepping through the parameters in an attempt to "optimize" the result. Nothing beat the buy-and-hold method. Nor did shorting help. In the above example, if you had shorted rather than sold the market every time P/E ratios hit higher than 20, the result would have been five unsuccessful short trades.

Does this mean buy-and-hold is the best strategy? Absolutely not. For one thing, there were several periods of longer than 10 years (the most recent being from 1964 to 1981) where the market was completely flat and almost any other investment would have been better. But it does mean that P/E is mostly useless when not taking into account any other aspect of the market.

Buffett has said that he is not a market timer. For instance, in his 1992 letter to shareholders, he wrote:

We've long felt that the only value of stock forecasters is to make fortune tellers look good. Even now, Charlie and I continue to believe that short-term market forecasts are poison and should be kept locked up in a safe place, away from children and also from grown-ups who behave in the market like children.

And yet, as excellent Buffettesque investor Whitney Tilson[1] has pointed out, Buffett has made market calls no less than six times.

MARKET CALL #1

In 1969, Buffett "retired" from the hedge fund business, and returned his investors' money with the statement:

I just don't see anything available that gives any reasonable hope of delivering such a good year and I have no desire to grope around, hoping to "get lucky" with other people's money. I am not attuned to this

---

[1]"Buffett's Prescient Market Calls," Whitney Tilson, 1999, Motley Fool Web site (www.fool.com).

market environment, and I don't want to spoil a decent record by try-
ing to play a game I don't understand just so I can go out a hero.

Over the next six years the market returned –11.8 percent, topping off
a huge bull market run that essentially ended in the late 1960s.

Although his market call was dead on and he left the hedge fund business at this time, I do think his bearishness was more excuse than reason
for his decision. He was already the controlling shareholder of Berkshire
Hathaway and he had already decided that the economics of insurance
were much better than the economics of running a hedge fund.

In a hedge fund you only get 20 percent of the profits. In insurance,
assuming the cost of float is kept to a minimum (and to his great credit,
Buffett over the past 40 years has been particularly good at this), the owners of an insurance company get to keep 100 percent of the investing profits. By 1970, rather than having to split the profits with the limited partners
in his hedge fund, Buffett was now the majority shareholder. Only one percent of the profits of Berkshire Hathaway in 1970 came from textiles, the
rest was from insurance, banking, and investments.

MARKET CALL #2

In 1974, Buffett made his famous quote to *Forbes*, "I feel like an oversexed
man in a harem," when referring to all of the buying opportunities out there.
1975 was one of the biggest bull market moves ever, with the S&P going up
over 70 percent over the next two years.

MARKET CALL #3

Tilson reminds us of Buffett's quote in the August 6, 1979, issue of *Forbes*
where he states:

Stocks now sell at levels that should produce long-term returns far
superior to bonds. Yet pension managers, usually encouraged by cor-

porate sponsors they must necessarily please, are pouring funds in record proportions into bonds. Meanwhile, orders for stocks are being placed with an eyedropper.

Can better results be obtained over, say, 20 years from a group of 9½ percent bonds of leading American companies maturing in 1999 than from a group of Dow-type equities purchased, in aggregate, at around book value and likely to earn, in aggregate, around 13 percent on that book value?... How can bonds at only 9½ percent be a better buy?

In typical self-deprecating fashion, Buffett referred to this market call in a July 2001 speech when he said,

Now, if you had read that article in 1979, you would have suffered—oh, how you would have suffered!—for about three years. I was no good then at forecasting the near-term movements of stock prices, and I'm no good now. I never have the faintest idea what the stock market is going to do in the next six months, or the next year, or the next two.

MARKET CALL #4

Tilson quotes Buffett from the 1986 annual meeting:

I still can't find any bargains in today's market. We don't currently own any equities to speak of [except for the core holdings of GEICO, the Washington Post Co., and Capital Cities/ABC].

Although he more or less cruised past the crash of 1987 because of this prescience, it was during this period that he figured he could weather a more than 10 percent correction by making "pseudo" equity investments in the form of convertible preferreds. He did this with Salomon, Gillette, and Champion, where in each case he was able to get a preferred stake in each company paying between 9- and 10-percent yields and convertible into equity should the stocks rise. Happily, they all did, at different points over the next decade. (See more on this in Chapter 7.)

MARKET CALL #5

Tilson reports that in the 1992 annual report Buffett writes:

> *Charlie Munger, Berkshire's vice chairman and my partner, and I are virtually certain that the return over the next decade from an investment in the S&P index will be far less than that of the past decade...Making [this] prediction goes somewhat against our grain: We've long felt that the only value of stock forecasters is to make fortune tellers look good. Even now, Charlie and I continue to believe that short-term market forecasts are poison and should be kept locked up in a safe place, away from children and also from grown-ups who behave in the market like children. However, it is clear that stocks cannot forever overperform their underlying businesses, as they have so dramatically done for some time, and that fact makes us quite confident of our forecast that the rewards from investing in stocks over the next decade will be significantly smaller than they were in the last.*

Tilson prophetically concludes this market call with the statement: "The next three years will have to be pretty grim to validate Buffett's prediction." His article was written in 1999 and up to that point, the decade following Buffett's 1992 call was outperforming the prior ten years.

However, the next three years did turn out to be pretty grim, and with this prediction Buffett was also correct. From December 1992 to December 2002 the S&P 500 was up a sliver below 100 percent. From December 1982 to December 1992 the S&P 500 was up 210 percent.

MARKET CALL #6

In the November 22, 1999, issue of *Fortune,* Buffett predicted that the stocks were about to "fall dramatically." When he wrote that the Dow was at 11,194 and two years later it was at 9,900.

MARKET CALL #7

Buffett wasn't through yet and the December 2001 issue of *Fortune* reprinted a speech he had given at the July 2001 Allen & Co. Sun Valley Conference. In it he stated his reasons for being somewhat bearish on the market for the next 17 years and reaffirmed his belief that over the next decade we can expect to see seven percent annual returns.

So you can't really have it both ways. Buffett might not make specific investing decisions based on market timing (for instance, there is no evidence he uses puts or any hedging techniques to hedge his portfolio when he thinks the market is going down). However, he does make macro-level portfolio decisions or even huge personal life decisions (his decision in 1969 to close his fund) based on his feelings about the market. One can argue that this is not the case: When the market is frothy it is evident in his portfolio from a bottoms-up approach—that is, his investing for those years is scarce simply because there are fewer opportunities. However, diving into his July 2001 speech, as reprinted by *Fortune*, it is evident that Buffett does at least develop macro-level explanations for why there might be a dearth of investment prospects.

Specifically, he notes first that the stock market is not necessarily related to growth in the economy. For example, from 1964 to 1981, when the market gained "one-tenth of one percent" over a 17-year period, he noted that the gain in gross national product (GNP) during that time was 373 percent as opposed to only 177 percent from 1981 to 1998 when the market went up over 9,000 percent. To quote Buffett:

> *So what was the explanation? I concluded that the market's contrasting moves were caused by extraordinary changes in two critical economic variables—and by a related psychological force that eventually came into play. Here I need to remind you about the definition of "investing," which, though simple, is often forgotten. Investing is laying out money today to receive more money tomorrow. That gets to the first of the economic variables that affected stock prices in the two periods—interest rates. In economics, interest rates act as gravity behaves in the physical world. At all times, in all markets, in all parts*

of the world, the tiniest change in rates changes the value of every financial asset.

He notes further that from 1964 to 1981, interest rates on long-term government bonds went from 4.2 to 13.65 percent and from 1981 they went from 13.65 to 5.09 percent.

Putting this further to the test, let's look at long-term government bonds and P/Es dating back to 1900 and buy the market whenever 1/(P/E) (the earnings yield) is greater than bonds. In other words, an investment in the average company yields a greater dollar amount than a similar passive investment in a bond. There are modifications we will make to this initial assumption, but first let's test out the basic so-called Fed Model.

Before examining the numbers in detail lets take a closer look at the Fed Model in Exhibit 12.3.

In Exhibit 12.3, the S&P 500 monthly chart from 1900 to 2004 is represented in the bottom pane. The top pane is the earnings yield of the S&P 500 represented by the thick black line; the thin gray line is the yield of the 10-year government bond. The horizontal axis is the timeline from 1900 to 2004. The question an investor has at any given point is, *Will investing in companies yield me more money than I can safely get in government bonds?* If a government bond is yielding 10 percent, for example, and that's money I can put in my pocket safely, and the average company is only earning me five percent on my money, then there's no need to invest in stocks. This is an extreme example, but it expresses the point.

As we can see in the graphic, the question did not really come into play for the first seven decades of the twentieth century. There was a slight flirtation with it in the late 1920s, however, which erupted into the Great Depression. And then earnings yields were higher by a fairly wide margin until the late 1960s.

And why were these yields higher by such a wide margin? People assumed that since bonds were so safe and a company's earnings were so volatile and unpredictable, the only way to get the prescribed margin of safety would be if earnings were significantly higher than what could be achieved by the appropriate risk-free bond. However, Buffett's point, repeating a point made in the 1920s by Keynes when analyzing Edgar Lawrence Smith's book *Common Stocks as Long-Term Investments*, is that

EXHIBIT 12.3 Fed Model

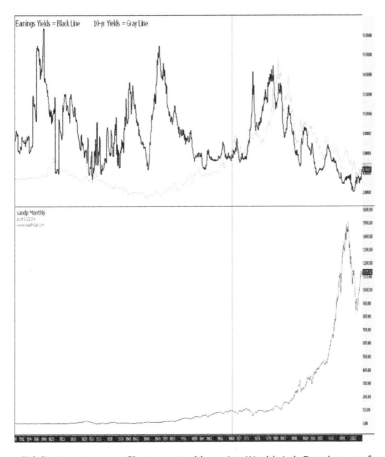

Source: Fidelity Investments. Charts created by using Wealth-Lab Developer software.

companies retain their earnings. Then they reinvest the capital so they could then return even more. In other words, their earnings compound, as opposed to a government bond, which only returns a fixed coupon. It is this point that makes stocks a more attractive investment than bonds, even when the earnings yield is lower than the government bond yield.

However, when the earnings yield first breached the 10-year yield in 1969 (the vertical line in the graph), this flashed a warning sign to Buffett, who promptly shut down his hedge fund and decided to watch the action.

When the earnings yield was significantly higher than the 10-year yield (the second vertical line in Exhibit 12.4), Buffett got his "buy signal" and made his "oversexed in a harem" comment.

After another brief dip and subsequent lift in the earnings yield representing the 1980–82 bear market, the earnings yield went more or less permanently under the 10-year yield. At any point, a traditional value investor using the Fed Model could have argued that the market was overvalued, and many investors did, in fact, argue that. But other than brief pauses, the market was basically a skyrocket until early 2000. It is this "regime shift"

EXHIBIT 12.4

Source: Fidelity Investments. Charts created by using Wealth-Lab Developer software.

that occurred around 1982 that makes the traditional Fed Model difficult to use as a forecasting method for stock prices.

However, just because there is a regime shift does not necessarily mean there is no longer any relationship between bonds and earnings. From 1982 on, it is more important to look at the relative relationship between the two. In other words, if bond yields move quickly relative to earnings or vice versa, then the market is most likely being either irrationally pessimistic with regard to the earnings potential of stocks, or irrationally optimistic.

To prove my theory, I plotted the earnings yield (trailing 12-month core earnings) of the S&P 500 back to 1982, and did the same for the 10-year note. Then I divided the bond yield by the earnings yield and bought the stock market whenever the ratio hit 1.5 standard deviations below its 10-day moving average. Given that the yields are correlated, I'm simply buying the market when bond yields tank faster than earnings yields (or when earnings yields go up faster than bond yields), regardless of whether one is above the other. I'm then selling the market when the ratio gets back to its 10-day moving average.

To summarize the results shown in Exhibit 12.5, 14 trades were made, 10 of which were profitable (giving the system a 71 percent success rate). The average gain per trade was 11 percent.

EXHIBIT 12.5

Trades Executed 1983–2002 (based on extreme shifts in Fed Model)				
Entry Date	**Price**	**Exit Date**	**Exit Price**	**% Change**
2/1/1984	163.41	6/1/1984	150.55	−7.87
7/2/1984	153.16	3/1/1985	181.18	18.29
3/3/1986	226.92	6/2/1986	246.04	8.43
8/1/1986	236.12	10/1/1986	231.32	−2.03
12/1/1987	230.32	3/1/1989	288.86	25.42
7/3/1989	317.98	9/1/1989	351.45	10.53
10/1/1990	306.1	3/1/1991	367.07	19.92
9/1/1992	414.03	3/1/1994	467.19	12.84
12/1/1994	453.55	2/1/1996	636.02	40.23
11/1/1996	705.27	1/2/1997	740.74	5.03
9/1/1998	957.28	1/4/1999	1,229.23	28.41
3/1/2000	1,366.42	5/1/2000	1,452.43	6.29
8/1/2000	1,430.83	6/1/2001	1,255.82	−12.23

The overall point, it seems, is that relative difference is of more interest than static difference between the yields, contrary to what the Fed Model suggests.

Basically, it is clear that purely looking at P/Es or purely looking at the Fed Model, which dates back to 1900, doesn't do us any good. But it is also clear that through the years Warren Buffett has made some very prescient calls timing the market, and his justification for these calls was some derivative of the Fed Model. The public's expectation of earnings growth and the compounded value of that earnings growth might change over time, as well as the market's feelings about earnings versus bond yields. However, any sudden movement (and by "sudden," I mean over the course of months or even years) could result in one of Buffett's famous signals. The key is not simply waiting for a P/E of five or interest rates less than two percent, but to aggressively act when the spread, in whatever direction, becomes irrational.

CHAPTER 13

Buffett and
Disasters

A t the time of this writing halfway into 2004, the Nasdaq and Dow are down on the year and the S&P is slightly positive. Volume is increasingly petering out and the daily ranges are hitting new record lows. One of the reasons given for this lack of exuberance is the threat of terrorism. If terrorists strike again on American soil, nobody wants to be left holding the bag. Although the United States has been spared a second major attack until now, with so much bloodshed having gone on in places such as Spain and Russia, the idea that Al Qaeda might still be able to launch a major attack is seen as an overhang on global markets.

After September 11, 2001, when the markets shut down for almost a week, nobody had any idea what would happen to the U.S. markets when they opened. Many wondered if they would even be able to open? To Dick Grasso's credit, he was able to organize the reopening of the New York Stock Exchange and instill confidence back into the U.S. markets that business would continue as usual. However, even with the reopening of the markets, to say people were nervous about the future prices of their stock portfolios would be a severe understatement.

It was into this void of confidence that Warren Buffett went on television and said "If you were a holder of stocks and a believer in the long-term growth of the U.S. economy on September 10, then you should be a believer on September 12." The idea is this: We have seen this before. The United States had not experienced the specific psychological and financial damage caused by September 11, but the nation has nevertheless undergone shocks to the system that we have survived, and will continue to survive, thanks to gradual increases in the overall stability of the system.

With the help of my colleague Omid Malekan, I took a look at ten potentially systemic shocks that have occurred over the past 70 years. In each case, we looked at where the S&P 500 was the day before the shock, the day after, the panic low during the ensuing week, and then where the market was one week later, one month later, and six months later. A summary table of the results appears in Exhibit 13.11 at the end of this chapter.

THE INVASION OF POLAND (SEPTEMBER 1, 1939)

The market barely blinked at the invasion, reaching its panic low a few days after the event and then not looking back for almost the next year (see Exhibit 13.1). Several possible explanations for this are:

- Some sort of crisis event with Germany was certainly expected and built into the market.
- Perhaps the United States felt that the situation with Germany would be somewhat contained with the countries immediately surrounding it.
- After a 10-year depression, there might have been an expectation that war in Europe (for which we would be supplying the arsenal) would be a boost to the economy.

THE BOMBING OF PEARL HARBOR (DECEMBER 7, 1941)

Perhaps the worst event in the United States' history up until the 9/11 attacks, the bombing of Pearl Harbor brought the threat of an attack on American soil

EXHIBIT 13.1 Effects of the Invasion of Poland

Source: Fidelity Investments. Charts created by using Wealth-Lab Developer software.

to life. The market took several years to recover, although again a "buy during the dip" strategy would have worked well (see Exhibit 13.2).

THE NORTH KOREAN INVASION OF SOUTH KOREA (JUNE 25, 1950)

This was the first real clash with the post-WWII Soviet Empire that spread into the global Cold War. The market fell from $19.14 to $18.11 the day after,

EXHIBIT 13.2　　Effects of the Bombing of Pearl Harbor

Source: Fidelity Investments. Charts created by using Wealth-Lab Developer software.

reaching a low of $17.27 a month later until rallying up to $21.03 six months later (see Exhibit 13.3).

KENNEDY'S ANNOUNCEMENT OF NUCLEAR MISSILES IN CUBA (OCTOBER 22, 1962)

The idea that nuclear weapons were being aimed at the American shores from just 90 miles away was enough to send the market down several per-

EXHIBIT 13.3   Effects of North Korea Invading South Korea

Source: Fidelity Investments. Charts created by using Wealth-Lab Developer software.

centage points (see Exhibit 13.4). What is most interesting is the ferocity with which the market rallied in only a few months. The Cuban Missile Crisis did not begin and end the threat in one week. The threat, emboldened by a policy of MAD (mutual assured destruction), continued for the next 30 years and is still not an issue that the world can ignore. And yet, the market more or less determined that if a nuclear war resulted, there would be bigger problems than the stock market, so the party started in 1962 and continued for the next seven years, resulting in the biggest bull market in history, until the 1990s came along.

EXHIBIT 13.4   Effects of Kennedy Announcing Nuclear Missiles in Cuba

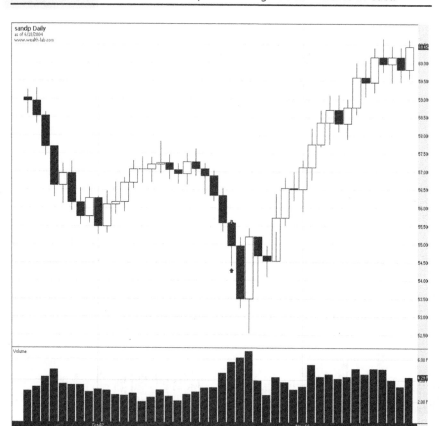

Source: Fidelity Investments. Charts created by using Wealth-Lab Developer software.

THE KENNEDY ASSASSINATION (NOVEMBER 22, 1963)

Everybody who was alive then has an "I remember that moment" story about when Kennedy was assassinated. The impact struck the United States to the core: Our young, youthful president who had stood up to the Soviets and made them back off, was dead. It was inconceivable, and the market reacted appropriately that day, closing almost three percent down from its prior day close. But the bull market that had begun under Kennedy's reign had another six years to go, and a week later the market was higher than it had been on

EXHIBIT 13.5 Effects of the Kennedy Assassination

Source: Fidelity Investments. Charts created by using Wealth-Lab Developer software.

November 21. Six months later it had gone from a low of $69.48 on the day of the assassination to $80.73 (see Exhibit 13.5).

OIL EMBARGO (OCTOBER 17, 1973)

While a host of events served as a prelude to October 19, 1973, the actual announcement by OPEC that it was raising oil prices almost 70 percent sent the market into a swoon unrivaled until 1987 (see Exhibit 13.6). The market quickly fell to its panic low three percent lower, and then 17 percent lower six months later. However, it is interesting that one week after the embargo, the S&P 500 was actually two percent higher than it had been the day before

EXHIBIT 13.6   Effects of the Oil Embargo

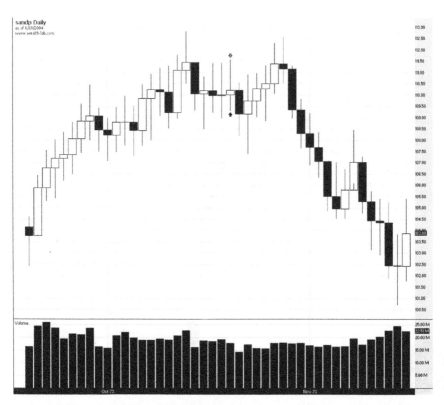

Source: Fidelity Investments. Charts created by using Wealth-Lab Developer software.

the embargo. One shock was not enough to bury the market. However, at the time there was a series of negative events, including:

- The Arab-Israeli war, which began on October 6, 1973.
- A recession caused, in part, by the 8.5 percent inflation in consumer prices.
- The ongoing investigation into the Watergate scandal.

HOSTAGE CRISIS IN IRAN (NOVEMBER 4, 1979)

The idea that somebody could, without fear of massive punishment, take American citizens hostage, was enough to send the market down several

EXHIBIT 13.7 Effects of Hostages Taken in Iran

Source: Fidelity Investments. Charts created by using Wealth-Lab Developer software.

percent during the days immediately after (see Exhibit 13.7). However, despite the fact that we were still in a languishing economy and a series of bear markets, the market was able to rebound one week later, and was still several percent higher one month and six months later.

IRAQ'S INVASION OF KUWAIT (AUGUST 2, 1990)

Perhaps fearful of the slide that occurred in the 1970s when the oil embargo started, the market immediately slid off when Iraq invaded Kuwait, going from $355.52 on the day before the invasion to a low of $294.51 on October 11, 1990 (see Exhibit 13.8). After the war began and once initial fears proved

EXHIBIT 13.8   Effects of Iraq Invading Kuwait

Source: Fidelity Investments. Charts created by using Wealth-Lab Developer software.

unjustified about both the potential length of the war and the effect on oil prices, the market rebounded sharply, going to $409.52 six months to the day after the invasion, and setting the stage for the bull market of the 1990s.

THE FIRST BOMBING OF THE WORLD TRADE CENTER (FEBRUARY 26, 1993)

This is the best example of a crisis that instilled panic but was largely forgotten (to everyone's regret) almost immediately. The market began a sharp dip immediately following the bombing, going from a close of $442.34 the day before to a low of $440.98 right after the bombing, three percent

EXHIBIT 13.9   Effects of the First Bombing of the World Trade Center

Source: Fidelity Investments. Charts created by using Wealth-Lab Developer software.

lower, to actually closing higher on the day at $443.98 by the end of the day. Worries that there would be a repeat incident were largely unfelt as the market moved upwards the rest of the year, closing at $461.04 six months later (see Exhibit 13.9).

THE TERRORIST ATTACKS OF SEPTEMBER 11, 2001

This event really was the worst of every situation. We were already in a recession and severe bear market. The attack on American soil was the

worst ever, and it was an attack against the heart of the financial capital of
the country. Additionally, oil prices spiked immediately afterward and the
market closed for the longest period since the beginning of World War I.
The panic was severe, resulting in a low of $944.75 compared with the
market close of $1092.54 on September 10, 2001 (see Exhibit 13.10). In
addition, the next six months saw the bankruptcy of Enron and the splin-
tering apart of stock market favorites Tyco, WorldCom, and dozens of
other companies. And yet, the market closed at 1165.55 six months later on
March 18, 2002. Exhibit 13.11 shows a summary of the figures for each of
the preceding events.

EXHIBIT 13.10   Effects of 9/11

Source: Fidelity Investments. Charts created by using Wealth-Lab Developer software.

EXHIBIT 13.11 Summary of Effects of Catastrophic Events on the Stock Market

Event	Date	S&P at Prior Close	Closing Price Next Day	Panic Low	1 week later	1 month later	6 months later
Invasion of Poland	9/1/1939	11.18	11.29	None	12.69	12.88	12.06
Bombing of Pearl Harbor	12/7/1941	9.35	8.97	8.4	8.74	8.88	8.47
North Korea invades South Korea	6/25/1950	19.14	18.11	17.44	17.64	17.27	21.03
Kennedy Announces Nukes in Cuba	10/22/1962	55.59	53.49	52.55	55.72	60.81	70.14
Kennedy Assassination	11/22/1963	71.62	69.61	69.48	73.23	73.81	80.73
Oil Embargo	10/19/1973	110.01	109.16	107.4	111.38	100.73	93.75
Hostages Taken In Iran	11/4/1979	102.51	101.82	99.49	103.51	106.79	106.38
Iraq invades Kuwait	8/2/1990	355.52	344.86	332.22	339.94	323.09	409.53
First WTC Attack	2/26/1993	442.34	443.38	440.98	446.11	447.78	461.04
9/11/2001	9/11/2001	1092.54	1038.77	944.75	1003.45	1077.09	1165.55

DON'T FIGHT THE MARKET

In its history, the United States has been attacked several times and threatened with nuclear weapons. Its leaders have been assassinated and financial shocks have been inflicted on its markets. The world has been in peril on many occasions over the past century as well. Each time, however, the market has absorbed the shock and moved past the event. Perhaps the purveyors of doom and gloom can claim that next time, things will be different. But I doubt they will be.

In the book *Trade Like a Hedge Fund*,[1] I analyzed the results of simply buying every dip that occurred, both on stocks and on the markets as a whole. Although Buffett never uses mean reversion as the sole basis of a trade, it is helpful to know that simply using the mean reversion in a decision to buy has a high probability of success, regardless of the other factors that Buffett uses to decide on a trade. The mean reversion nature of stocks adds to the margin of safety when making a trade or an investment based on fundamental factors, such as liquidation value or P/E.

THE 10 PERCENT PULLBACK

This system involves the following two steps:

1. Buy a stock that is 10 percent lower than the prior day close.
2. Sell at the end of the day.

The data includes all S&P Mid-cap 400 stocks over the past five years. I chose mid-cap to avoid any "size effect," but the same test can obviously be performed on any subset of stocks. Five years is not long enough if you are developing a thorough trading system. That said, a five-year period does take us through some rises and falls in the bull market of the 1990s as well the nonstop bear market of the 2000s.

---

[1]*Trade Like a Hedge Fund*, James Altucher, John Wiley & Sons, Inc., 2004.

As for our position size, let's assume we start off with $1 million and use $50,000 per trade (five percent of portfolio per trade). The results are shown in Exhibits 13.12 and 13.13.

Since January 1, 1997, the 10 percent pullback system did about 8,200 trades, 60 percent of which were profitable, with an average profit per trade of 1.4 percent. The maximum drawdown of the system was –3.5 percent as opposed to –40 percent for a buy-and-hold strategy (as evidenced by the thick blue line in the equity curve in Exhibit 13.13).

EXHIBIT 13.12 10% Pullback System

	All Trades	Buy & Hold
Starting Capital	$1,000,000.00	$1,000,000.00
Ending Capital	$6,744,820.50	$1,998,198.00
Net Profit	$5,744,820.50	$998,198.00
Net Profit %	574.48%	99.82%
Exposure %	7.50%	100%
Risk Adjusted Return	7,663.94%	99.82%
All Trades	8,197	397
Average Profit/Loss	$700.84	$2,514.35
Average Profit/Loss %	1.42%	99.85%
Average Bars Held	1.00	1,499.00
Winning Trades	4968 (60.61%)	282 (71.03%)
Gross Profit	$12,969,821.00	$1,101,028.75
Average Profit	$2,610.67	$3,904.36
Average Profit %	5.30%	155.07%
Average Bars Held	1.00	1,499.00
Max Consecutive	41	14
Losing Trades	3229 (39.39%)	115 (28.97%)
Gross Loss	$–7,224,984.00	$–102,831.17
Average Loss	$–2,237.53	$–894.18
Average Loss %	–4.54%	–35.56%
Average Bars Held	1.00	1,499.00
Max Consecutive	25	5
Max DrawDown	–3.54%	–40.43%
Max DrawDown $	$–142,059.75	$–1,107,053.25
Max DrawDown Date	4/14/2000	10/9/2002
Standard Error	$335,618.53	$258,692.67
Risk Reward Ratio	3.35	0.91
Sharpe Ratio of Trades	3.24	0.16

Source: *Trade Like a Hedge Fund*, James Altucher. Copyright © 2004 John Wiley & Sons, Inc.

EXHIBIT 13.13   Equity Curve for the 10% Pullback System

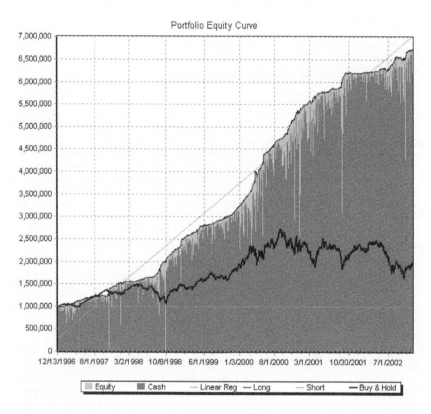

Source: *Trade Like a Hedge Fund*, James Altucher. Copyright © 2004 John Wiley & Sons, Inc.

AN ALTERNATIVE PULLBACK METHOD

Use the same procedure as above, except instead of holding for one day, hold for one month. The data set includes 11 Nasdaq 100 stocks over the past eight years. The simulation starts with $1,000,000, using $2,000 (0.2 percent of equity) per trade.

The results are shown in Exhibits 13.14 and 13.15.

EXHIBIT 13.14 Chart of Annual Returns of 10% Pullback Method #2

Period Starting	$ Return	% Return	% Max DD	Exposure	Entries	Exits
1/24/1995	99,167.25	9.92	−1.48	5.76	351	301
1/2/1996	108,217.50	9.85	−2.86	8.24	569	598
1/2/1997	70,164.13	5.81	−2.12	8.25	637	605
1/2/1998	358,756.75	28.08	−5.51	12.44	989	986
1/4/1999	247,274.00	15.11	−2.01	8.91	921	919
1/3/2000	168,689.00	8.96	−14.45	23.24	3,112	2,799
1/2/2001	565,377.88	27.55	−16.89	18.73	2,475	2,770
1/2/2002	153,366.75	5.86	−7.50	12.49	1,867	1,764

Average annual return	13.89%
Standard Deviation of returns	9.07
Sharpe Ratio	1.53
Average return per trade	8.16%
Average return per winning trade	28.82%
Average return per losing trade	−18.67%

Source: *Trade Like a Hedge Fund*, James Altucher. Copyright © 2004 John Wiley & Sons, Inc.

EXHIBIT 13.15 Equity Curve for the 10% Pullback Method #2

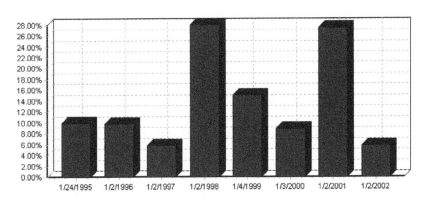

Source: *Trade Like a Hedge Fund*, James Altucher. Copyright © 2004 John Wiley & Sons, Inc.

EXTREME ADVANCES/DECLINES

The system involves:

1. Buy the Mid-cap ($MDY) index at the close of the market if the number of advancing stocks minus the number of declining stocks is lower than −300.
2. Sell in two months.

Since 1996, the system makes the trades shown in Exhibit 13.16.

Not a lot of trades are generated—only nine, six of which are profitable. However it is interesting to see that those days of extreme market reactions to the downside, where everyone was selling everything, called significant market bottoms over the past six years.

Even in the midst of disaster, it is important to take a step back from the panic and remember that we've most likely seen similar levels of panic in the past. It is times like these, whether it was during the oil crisis of the mid-1970s, or even the aftermath of 9/11, that investors like Warren Buffett often make their best purchases.

EXHIBIT 13.16   Extreme Advances/Declines System

Entry Date	Entry Price	Exit Date	Exit Price	% Change	Bars Held
10/27/1997	308.70	12/24/1997	319.28	3.41	41
8/27/1998	305.25	10/26/1998	322.30	5.56	41
4/14/2000	431.37	6/14/2000	489.55	13.47	41
3/12/2001	478.61	5/9/2001	510.71	6.69	41
6/14/2001	509.98	8/13/2001	501.93	−1.60	41
9/17/2001	445.19	11/13/2001	479.45	7.67	41
6/3/2002	515.82	7/31/2002	441.27	−14.47	41
8/2/2002	419.70	10/3/2002	399.18	−4.91	41
10/4/2002	389.47	Open	Open	15.18	40

Source: *Trade Like a Hedge Fund,* James Altucher. Copyright © 2004 John Wiley & Sons, Inc.

CHAPTER 14

Life and
Death

T he idea of paying someone for his or her life insurance policy, in the hopes that the individual dies fast enough to generate financial gain for the purchaser, seems oddly unsettling. And yet, the secondary market for life insurance policies has blossomed, going from $50 million ten years ago in acquired policies to over $1.8 billion by 2002. This is precisely when Warren Buffett, through a division of Berkshire Hathaway called Gen Re Securities, entered the game. In February 2002 the division announced that it would provide financing of up to $400 million to a Minnesota firm, Living Benefits Financial Services. This company would in turn use the money to buy life insurance policies of senior citizens.

The "life-settlement" business is an extension of the earlier viatical business. A viatical was the purchase of the life insurance policy of a terminally ill patient, typically an AIDS patient. Investors would put up money and viatical firms would aggregate many of these policies almost in the same manner that firms specializing in mortgage-backed securities aggregate many mortgages into one security. The early problem with viaticals was that improvements in AIDS medicines elongated the life of AIDS patients, forcing the viatical firms to continue making payments longer than their investors were willing to fund those payments. This drastically reduced the returns of those companies and forced many of them into insolvency.

After that, the industry switched focus to life-settlement—buying the life insurance policies of seniors over 65 who had experienced a sudden decline in health. As morbid as this may appear, the addition of a secondary market in life insurance policies greatly increased the economic value of life insurance policies to seniors who preferred having the money. Prior to the creation of a secondary market, the life insurance market was similar to what the housing market would be if you could only sell your house back to the person who sold the house to you. In other words, it was non-completive and often reduced the benefits to the policyholder, particularly if the policyholder needed to access the economic value of the policy before his or her death.

How do you determine the value of a policy? The same way Warren Buffett calculates the investment value and margin of safety of every other transaction: by using a combination of interest rates and probabilities. If the risk-free rate is eight percent and a policy is worth $10 million, then the value of that policy is $10 million discounted using the risk-free rate over the expected lifespan of the policyholder. And companies like Gen Re have spent countless hours in building models of life expectancies for every type of demographic and medical condition. In a secondary market, you get an increased margin of safety if you have a better model than your investors for determining life expectancy. Also, the ability to aggregate policies and diversify across various demographics and medical conditions also increases the probability that, in aggregate, your models will pay off as expected.

Although this is a small part of Buffett's overall investment portfolio, it does exemplify his ability to seek out and find uses of capital that are uncorrelated to the traditional modes of investing. At the same time, he still has his sought-after margin of safety. To get involved in this secondary market, visit the Viatical and Life-Settlement Association of America at www.viatical.org for a list of brokers and firms that participate in this marketplace.

CHAPTER 15

Fixed-Income Arbitrage

D espite Buffett's aversion to both derivatives and leverage, he has on occasion made the decision to dip into these areas by allocating to fixed-income arbitrage strategies. In 1998, Buffett made an investment of several hundred million dollars in the hedge fund run by Mark Byrne, son of former GEICO CEO Jack Byrne. West End Capital Management, Mark Byrne's fund, focuses on several fixed-income strategies. Nor was this Buffett's only foray into fixed-income arbitrage.

During the Long Term Capital Management (LTCM) disaster, of which the largest losses were in the fixed-income arbitrage portions of the portfolio, Buffett made an offer to buy the assets of the firm. The offer was rejected, but this shows that Buffett saw that there was some value there; he was willing to accept the risk of a highly leveraged fixed-income portfolio. Even before the LTCM doings, Buffett had been involved in fixed-income arbitrage when he became chairman of Salomon Brothers. This was shortly after the scandal that had erupted on their fixed-income desk involving a trader working for John Meriwether, who later started LTCM.

Fixed-income arbitrage is not one strategy, but a family of strategies involving the buying and selling of fixed-income instruments in order to capture a very small gain, usually a difference in yield between the two investments.

As a very simple example, if a corporate bond is yielding six percent and a U.S. Treasury note that expires the same time as the corporate bond is yielding five percent, then it is possible to go long the corporate bond and short the Treasury note, capturing the one percent difference. Why do this and not just go long the corporate bond? Leaving aside the issue of default risk for a second, both notes are at risk if interest rates change. If you were to go long the corporate bond and interest rates rose, the face value of that corporate bond would fall. However, assuming the hedging is done correctly (and this is no simple matter), hedging the interest rate risk inherent in owning a corporate bond by shorting the Treasury note would allow you to capture the one percent in a relatively risk-free manner (assuming there is no default risk on the corporate note).

There are several types of fixed-income strategies:

- Government versus corporate spread trades, as described above.
- Yield curve bets, where the investor goes long one part of the yield curve and short another part, making a directional bet on where he or she thinks the yield curve is heading.
- Municipal versus treasury spread trades.
- Cash versus futures trades. For whatever reason, there are moments when demand for bond futures as opposed to demand for the actual bonds creates an inefficiency that can be exploited.
- Various spread trades between asset-backed securities and other types of fixed-income instruments. An example of an asset-backed security is a mortgage-backed security.

Risks that need to be hedged in a fixed-income arbitrage strategy include:

- *Credit risk:* the risk that one of the counterparties can default.
- *Interest rate risk:* the risk that interest rates can rise.
- *Foreign exchange risk:* If you are short a bond in one currency and long a bond in another currency, then changes in the relative values of those currencies can affect the return on the strategy.
- *Prepayment risk:* If you are short a Treasury bond and long an asset-backed bond and the seller of the asset-backed bond pays early, then an investor in the spread trade can be stuck making the payments on

the Treasury bond without the corresponding payment on the asset-backed bond.

As can be seen in the previous example, the possible returns (here, one percent annually) can be quite small, and so heavy amounts of leverage are often used (10 to 25 times or more). For instance, when trading the spread that sometimes occurs between a bond and its corresponding bond futures contract, the spread might be just a few basis points (each basis point is $\frac{1}{100}$ of one percent). In LTCM's case, it was using up to 100:1 leverage. Myron Scholes—Nobel Prize winner, developer of the Black-Scholes model for modeling options, and one of the founders of LTCM—described it as "as if it were vacuuming nickels that others couldn't see." The issue is this: Is the fixed-income arbitrageur picking up those nickels in the face of an upcoming steamroller? Exhibit 15.1 shows the returns for the CSFB/Tremont Hedge Fund Index for Fixed-Income Arbitrage.

EXHIBIT 15.1 CSFB/Tremont Hedge Fund Index for Fixed Income Arbitrage

Monthly Performance

	Jan	Feb	Mar	Apr	May	Jun	Jul	Aug	Sep	Oct	Nov	Dec	Annl	S&P 500 Total Return	MSCI World $
2004	1.23%	0.87%	-0.49%	1.34%	0.63%	0.71%	0.70%	N/A	N/A	N/A	N/A	N/A	5.09%	0.02%	0.43%
2003	1.26%	0.99%	0.42%	1.25%	1.28%	0.34%	-0.98%	0.21%	1.16%	0.46%	0.52%	0.80%	7.97%	28.68%	33.76%
2002	1.03%	0.87%	0.63%	1.35%	1.44%	0.65%	1.08%	1.23%	-1.14%	-2.27%	-0.53%	1.32%	5.75%	-22.10%	-19.54%
2001	1.42%	0.53%	0.24%	1.32%	0.52%	0.50%	0.91%	0.64%	0.18%	1.55%	-0.27%	0.23%	8.04%	-11.89%	-16.52%
2000	0.54%	0.57%	-0.15%	0.93%	0.02%	0.93%	0.55%	0.67%	0.75%	0.29%	0.70%	0.32%	6.29%	-9.10%	-12.92%
1999	1.90%	1.52%	1.34%	1.63%	0.88%	0.75%	0.49%	-0.41%	0.74%	0.91%	0.78%	0.97%	12.11%	21.04%	25.34%
1998	-0.84%	0.81%	1.61%	-0.01%	-0.21%	-1.08%	0.48%	-1.46%	-3.74%	-6.96%	1.55%	1.73%	-8.16%	28.58%	24.80%
1997	1.48%	1.10%	0.72%	1.24%	1.01%	0.87%	1.09%	0.82%	1.15%	-1.58%	0.40%	0.71%	9.34%	33.36%	16.23%
1996	1.43%	1.06%	0.77%	1.35%	1.09%	1.25%	1.34%	1.04%	1.47%	1.16%	1.17%	1.75%	15.93%	22.96%	14.00%
1995	0.27%	0.65%	-0.44%	2.02%	2.01%	0.52%	1.12%	0.77%	1.04%	1.14%	1.68%	1.07%	12.50%	37.58%	21.32%
1994	1.30%	-2.00%	-1.68%	-0.20%	0.79%	-0.40%	-0.18%	-0.09%	0.70%	0.89%	0.69%	0.57%	0.31%	1.32%	5.58%

Index data begins January 1994. Sharpe ratio calculated using a rolling 90-Day T-bill rate.

Net Performance	HEDG Fixed Income Arb	S&P 500 Total Return	MSCI World $
1 Month	0.70%	-3.31%	-3.24%
3 Months	2.06%	-0.08%	-0.24%
6 Months	3.82%	-1.78%	-1.18%
1 Year	8.45%	13.17%	18.11%
2 Years	11.86%	25.22%	29.13%
3 Years	22.81%	-4.37%	1.99%
3 yr Avg	**7.09%**	**-1.48%**	**0.66%**
5 years	41.97%	-10.72%	-9.13%
5 yr Avg	**7.26%**	**-2.24%**	**-1.90%**
Since Inception	102.98%	185.68%	108.57%
Incep Avg Annl	**6.92%**	**10.43%**	**7.19%**

Statistics	HEDG Fixed Income Arb	S&P 500 Total Return	MSCI World $
Avg Month	0.57%	0.93%	0.67%
Best Month	2.02%	9.78%	9.06%
Worst Month	-6.96%	-14.46%	-13.32%
Mth Std Dev	1.12%	4.47%	4.16%
Mth Std Dev, Ann'd	**3.87%**	**15.50%**	**14.42%**
Beta(vs S&P 500)	**0.01**	**0.97**	**0.86**
Sharpe	**0.77**	**0.42**	**0.22**

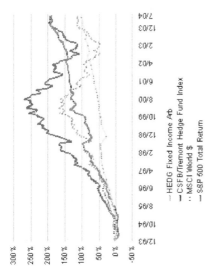

— HEDG Fixed Income Arb
— CSFB/Tremont Hedge Fund Index
·· MSCI World $
— S&P 500 Total Return

— HEDG Fixed Income Arb
— CSFB/Tremont Hedge Fund Index
— MSCI World $
— S&P 500 Total Return

EXHIBIT 15.1 *(continued)*

Correlations	HEDG Fixed Income Arb	S&P 500 Total Return	MSCI World $
Dow	0.05	0.93	0.89
MSCI World $	0.03	0.94	1.00
MSCI EAFE $	0.03	0.77	0.94
S&P 500 Total Return	0.03	1.00	0.94
NASDAQ	0.05	0.80	0.78

CHAPTER 16

Trade Like Bill Gates

M
ost people think of Bill Gates as the guy who built up a small fortune writing word processing programs and operating systems. But the big question on Gates' mind when he goes to work every day is not figuring out the many ways he can outperform Real Networks (RNWK), but *How can I diversify my $50,000,000,000.00?*

Fortunately, his first major investment worked out fine, as shown in Exhibit 16.1, which charts Microsoft (MSFT) stock from IPO to the present.

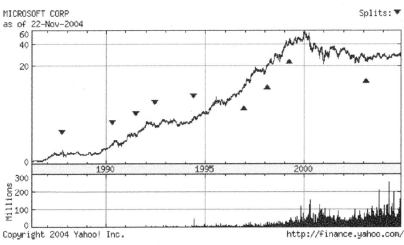

Source: Reproduced with permission of Yahoo! Inc. © 2004 by Yahoo! Inc. YAHOO! and the YAHOO! logo are trademarks of Yahoo! Inc.

But how has Gates attempted to achieve diversification as well as capital appreciation over the past few years? First, as we will see, he has been greatly influenced by his friend and bridge partner, Warren Buffett—and the approach to investing that Buffett takes.

There are three primary ways to look at Gates' investing prowess:

1. **The investments that Microsoft makes.** Microsoft is sitting on a hoard of more than $20 billion in cash and often makes investments in other companies in the technology sector. From Microsoft's viewpoint on the industry, these investments can be very telling and are probably worthwhile to analyze. However, it is also hard to tell if these investments are made for the capital appreciation potential or, in some cases, for the strategic potential to Microsoft. An individual investor almost never makes a strategic investment. For example, McDonald's is not going to give you a deal on their Happy Meals just because you are a shareholder.

2. **The investments of Gates' charitable foundation.** The Gates Foundation is among the largest family foundations in the world with an estimated endowment worth more than $10 billion. Appraising the foundation's worth, however, might not be the best way to study Gates' investment style; the foundation is extremely conservative with its funds, putting almost 85 percent in short-term government bonds and treasuries with the occasional AAA corporate bond.

3. **Cascade Investments represents Gates' personal money outside of Microsoft and the Foundation.** Run by money manager Michael Larson, it is this portfolio that seems the most "Buffett-like" in its approach, and we will study these investments.

The one qualifier, as usual, is that we don't really know for sure what Cascade has invested in for the simple reason that in most cases, the company is not obligated to tell us. In cases where it accumulates over five percent of a public company, it must do an SEC filing saying so. More recently Cascade has been filing "Schedule 13-H" forms, detailing all of the investments that represent more than five percent ownership in a firm. That said, we are not privy to the company's smaller investments.

EXHIBIT 16.2 Cascade's Holdings

Company	Value	No. of Shares
Alaska Air Group	$17 million	792,400
Avista Corp	$42 million	2,982,200
Boca Resorts	$26 million	2,047,704
Canadian National Railway	$506 million	10,485,000
Cox Communications	$780 million	24,463,986
Extended Stay America	$76 million	5,692,000
Fisher Communications	$22 million	455,700
Four Seasons Hotel	$19 million	441,500
ICOS Corp	$201 million	5,359,501
Nextel Partners	$93 million	12,766,106
Otter Tail	$40 million	1,503,200
Pain Therapeutics	$11 million	1,851,700
Pan American Silver	$36 million	5,105,000
PNM Resources	$98 million	3,694,100
Republic Services	$409 million	18,078,000
Schnitzer Steel	$21 million	495,200
Seattle Genetics	$17 million	3,521,088
Six Flags	$69 million	10,210,600

Exhibit 16.2 shows the positions listed in Cascade's more recent 13-HR forms (filed November 14, 2003): airlines, energy companies, hotels and resorts, biotech, steel, and the occasional technology stock. A couple of very Buffett-like things to note are:

1. **He is diversified, but not overly diversified.** With more than $5 billion to put to work, one can clearly own hundreds of stocks. However, Cascade has significant positions in only 18 companies, which is much less than is needed to really achieve full diversification.

2. **The companies, on the whole, represent very "boring" sectors of industry.** Republic Services is a garbage collection company. Canadian National Railway operates about 18,000 miles worth of railroad. This is a sector that has not been popular since the 1850s and yet Gates' Cascade has made a significant bet here. One great thing about the company is its relatively low correlation to the overall market, as demonstrated by the five-year chart in Exhibit 16.3—not a bad steady return, even with a few blips.

EXHIBIT 16.3   Canadian National Railway

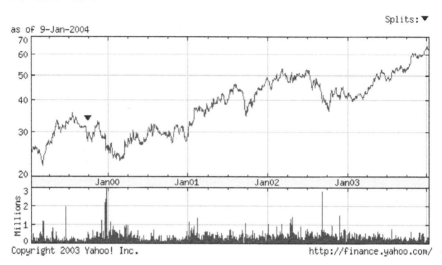

Source: Reproduced with permission of Yahoo! Inc. © 2004 by Yahoo! Inc. YAHOO! and the YAHOO! logo are trademarks of Yahoo! Inc.

Gates' investment in Pan American Silver came shortly after Buffett's investment in silver. The key difference here is that he bought a mine instead of the commodity itself. Since Buffett dabbled in Kaiser Aluminum in the early 1980s, he has stayed away from the commodity companies, and prefers to buy and store the commodity itself. Gates and Michael Larson, the manager of Cascade, probably figured that their time would be better spent focusing elsewhere rather than worrying about the logistics of storing all that silver.

3. Energy companies make up a significant portion of the portfolio. While Buffett has gone in more for the pipeline companies, Gates has become a pretty big player in the utility sector, owning greater than five percent stakes in Otter Tail (a utility in the Dakotas), PNM (a utility in New Mexico), and Avista (a utility in Washington).

4. There is also a shared activism. In Buffett's early days, if he didn't like what was going on in a company he would go in, buy up enough shares to have a say, and take charge before beginning his usual liquidations. Berkshire Hathaway is a good example of this, as is Dempster Mining.

With Schnitzer Steel, Gates has been fighting the Schnitzer family since 2002 to nominate more independent directors. A 2002 proposal Cascade made was defeated by stockholders (largely members of the Schnitzer family), even though 80 percent of common shareholders approved the proposal. In that proposal Cascade states:

> *In fiscal 2001, Schnitzer Steel paid at least $15.39 million to companies owned and controlled by members of the Schnitzer family. These payments range from leasing major facilities and headquarters office space to management and administrative services to shipping costs. For example, the proxy statement acknowledges that Schnitzer Steel paid $13.5 million for vessel charter expenses to two companies controlled by members of the Schnitzer family.*
>
> *Investors need to have confidence that the Schnitzer Steel board has the independence necessary to examine closely these conflict-of-interest and self-dealing transactions. Is the board asking the hard questions about the payments? Are there competitive alternatives? Should there be competitive bidding for those contracts? Is the status quo being maintained to protect those contracts?*

Perhaps as a direct result of this activism the stock has gone up fairly steadily, allowing Gates to reduce his holdings from 12 percent to 6 percent of the company. Exhibit 16.4 shows the two-year chart on Schnitzer.

EXHIBIT 16.4   Schnitzer Steel Industries

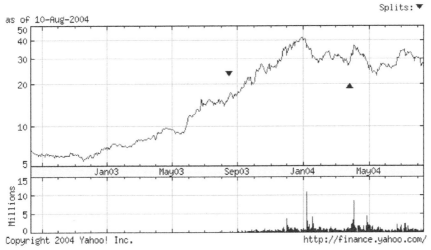

Of course, the average retail investor is not likely to engage in activist behavior, but by checking *Barron's* each week one can see which stocks are being "plagued" by activist shareholders who are submitting hostile proposals to the board.

To be fair, Michael Larson, not Gates, has made most of these stock picks. Larson has been managing Gates' portfolio since 1994. Gates has said that Larson has total discretion over the funds and most of the stock picks are his. That said, the two men meet at least once every six weeks and discuss every investment so it is likely that Gates is at least sympathetic to Larson's choices.

However, the one area where Gates makes the picks is biotechnology. SGEN, PTIE, and ICOS are all Gates' picks. At the time of this writing, none of these companies has developed significant revenues. PTIE, a developer of painkillers, has zero revenues and is burning cash fast. In the biotech arena, Gates seems to be making a basket or VC-style approach as opposed to Buffett-style. If one of these companies achieves a significant medical breakthrough, then the results will be well worth it—its stock will appreciate significantly, even if the other companies fail completely.

It is also worth noting that like Berkshire Hathaway, Gates and Cascade allocate some of their investing to others including Blue Ridge Capital, a New York hedge fund run by ex-Tiger employee John Griffin and VC firm Integral Capital Partners.

It is difficult to know exactly what positions Gates is in. And while his portfolio has suffered some changes over the past few years, it is interesting to note that most of his picks are largely uncorrelated to the market. They have not done as poorly as MSFT has during the recent 2000–2002 bust in tech stocks as well as the overall market. So, for a diversification play (and we should all be so lucky to have to diversify in this manner), the Cascade portfolio has withstood the test of time.

CHAPTER 17

Jealousy

L et's face it: Many people are jealous of Warren Buffett. Although Freud insists that all emotional problems stem from feelings about sexuality, the reality is that money is either a close second or, more likely, a winner by a long shot. And when a guy from the middle of Nebraska accumulates the sum of $42,000,000,000.00, well, that stimulates a lot of jealousy.

We have all heard that money cannot buy happiness. But, in fact, this is not really true. As my father-in-law tells me, "Money doesn't solve all of your problems, but it does solve your money problems." And money problems are not trivial. Money buys the two basic needs, food and shelter. And $42 billion buys *a lot* of food and shelter.

The most common statement said about Warren Buffett is that he was lucky. The other day, a friend of mine who is a stockbroker at Morgan Stanley said this to me. He also said, "Anybody who put their money in the market 47 years ago made a ton of money." This is certainly correct, although there are a lot of things wrong with this statement, which we will see shortly. However, I partly agree with my friend's statement. Warren Buffett certainly is lucky. Among top-ranked chess players there is a saying, "Only the good players are lucky." People tend to find their luck and Buffett has certainly spent a lot of time looking for the pot of gold at the end of the rainbow. That time spent searching has paid off.

For instance, in 1963, Buffett placed a very large bet (40 percent of his partnership) on American Express in the middle of the Salad Oil Scandal. There was a potential for American Express to go bankrupt, or at least to have major financial problems for years to come. If American Express had gone bankrupt, I most likely would not be writing this book about Warren Buffett right now, nor would you have any interest in reading a book about him. And yet the company did not go bankrupt; within two years he had made about 100 percent on his investment. Since nobody knows the future, it is quite possible to say Buffett was "lucky" when he bought the stock that American Express did not go bankrupt later. However, there are two important reasons why I don't think this is the case:

1. He saw the strength of the brand when he sat behind the cashier at Ross's Steakhouse in Omaha and saw that people were still using their American Express card despite the scandal in the news.

2. He analyzed the value of the float generated by the American Express traveler's checks. People pay for the traveler's checks and then it might be months or even years before they cash those checks and spend that money. In the meantime, American Express is like a hedge fund that gets to keep 100 percent of the profits on the money they make from investing that float. Nor is Buffett lucky that he stumbled into a company with such great economics as American Express had with their float. Buffett has staked his 50-year career on investing in companies with similar float characteristics. This pattern started in 1951 when he visited GEICO to understand more about the interest that his mentor Ben Graham had in such companies.

But now let's look at the statement "Warren Buffett is lucky" from both a quantitative and qualitative view. Exhibit 17.1 shows his returns from his partnership days.

Buffett returns, after partnership fees, an average of 25.3 percent per year; the Dow Jones Industrial Average returned an average of 10 percent. Buffett beat the Dow every year but one. Assume that the average stock is able to return more or less what the Dow does each year. Randomly throwing a dart at the stock charts in the *New York Times* will give an investor a 50-50 shot at beating the Dow. Buffett did it for ten years in a row during the

EXHIBIT 17.1 Returns of Buffett Partnership

Year	Buffett Partners	Dow	Value Added
1957	9.3%	(8.4%)	17.7
1958	32.2	38.5	(6.3)
1959	20.9	20.0	.9
1960	18.6	(6.2)	24.8
1961	35.9	22.4	13.5
1962	11.9	(7.6)	19.5
1963	30.5	20.6	9.9
1964	22.3	18.7	3.6
1965	36.9	14.2	22.7
1966	16.8	(15.6)	32.4
1967	28.4	19.0	9.4
1968	45.6	7.7	37.9
Total Return	1403.5	185.7	1217.8
Average Annual	25.3	9.1	16.2

Source: *Warren Buffett Wealth*, Robert Miles, © 2004 by Robert P. Miles. Reprinted with permission of John Wiley & Sons, Inc.

last ten years of his partnership. The odds of that happening are 1 in 1,024. This does not take into account the fact that he beat the Dow, on average, by 15 percentage points a year. Nor does it take into account the fact that he continued to beat the Dow for the next 30 years. The odds head into the one-in-billions range very quickly.

Let's give the skeptics the benefit of the doubt. Let's say that the odds against Buffett's success are one in a billion and that of the six billion people on the planet, one billion of them like to play in the sandbox and invest. So the odds are that someone with Buffett's track record would exist eventually, and lo and behold, here he is in the middle of Nebraska. Who'd have thought?

On a qualitative level, it is definitely true that we create our own luck. Having a methodology, sticking to it with discipline, and working day and night towards identifying stocks and opportunities that fit specific criteria are all part of creating that luck.

I'm not jealous of Buffett because of the money. In fact, I would probably jump off the carousel well before I had earned $42 billion. However, I am jealous of the fact that he clearly has fun day in and day out. As he has stated, "I tap dance to work every day."

Warren Buffett has built up friendships over the last fifty years. In a cut-throat environment like the business world this seems like a difficult thing to do. You could argue that he is everybody's friend because he helped so many people make money. But I have found that even helping people make money doesn't necessarily make them your friend. In many cases, it makes them the exact opposite.

Also, we can see from his many admirers (some of whom are interviewed in this book) that they, too, have succeeded by following Buffett's various methods. It is this community of mentor and students that is very inspirational as well.

I must admit that I started this book as a skeptic. The primary thing I was skeptical of was that Buffett's homespun "Buffett-isms" seemed perhaps for show. For instance, he does not buy and hold forever. There are many, many examples where he actively trades, and only a few exceptions. But so what? His point remains the same. Not everyone is going to go out and do risk arbitrage or find the latest liquidations or have the opportunity to play the PIPEs that he plays. If you can find 20 stocks that are like Coca-Cola, then all the better. Also, he plainly admits that his biggest mistakes were mistakes of omission. Why didn't he chase Wal-Mart up a few points? Or hold onto his Disney stock in the 1960s? Or keep McDonald's? Maybe he would have $90 billion if he had done that instead of $42 billion. And I'm not being facetious.

I was a bit upset at him when, shortly after the terrorist attacks of September 11, 2001, he stated that there was an almost near certainty of a nuclear attack on American soil within the next 50 years. From a man who seldom likes to predict the future, this is a bold statement—particularly considering that there are no relevant statistics or historical events on which to base this claim. It is just a guess. Meanwhile, we all had a horrible experience on 9/11. I lived a few blocks away from the World Trade Center and was right outside the North Tower when I watched the first plane crash into it. I was unhappy with Buffett's claim that something similar would happen again.

But, again, this is my problem. From Buffett's perspective, he had to protect the fact that he has billions of dollars on the line insuring against the mega-catastrophe of a nuclear attack on American soil. And his point was purely mathematical. Even if there were a 1 in 10,000 chance for there to be a nuclear attack in any given year, the odds do quickly add up to near certainty by the time fifty years elapse. So why not charge for that statistic?

Another big criticism of Buffett is that he doesn't invest in new technology. Why not invest in the growth engine of the United States? Why not invest in the vehicle that has driven this economy for 200 years, whether it is the cotton gin, railroads, computers, the Internet, or biotech? However, history is our guide. The Dow Jones Railroad Index was flat from 1846 to 1910. The computer craze that swept the market in the 1960s saw computer companies like Xerox lose 80 percent of their market value when the Nifty 50 turned into the "Iffy" 50 in the early 1970s. And the results of the Internet boom do not have to be repeated here. The reality is that most technologies that spur the economy do not necessarily result in investment success. Hundreds of automobile companies that went public in the early 1920s ended up in bankruptcy. Only the big three remained. If you had the skill set (and the luck) to pick General Motors, you would have done quite well. But most other companies that were around then are gone today. An excellent book that covers this topic is *Tomorrow's Gold* by Marc Faber. He writes that the U.S. market during technology booms behaves very similarly to Third World markets that enjoy their boom and bust periods—they go up multiples of 100 percent and then have a tendency to go straight to zero.

This doesn't mean that it is bad to invest in technology. But the luck factor plays a larger role. Who could have known that Yahoo! would be the successful company and that Excite (which was older than Yahoo!) would file for bankruptcy? The same can be said for my favorite search engine in 1993—the World Wide Web Worm.

In *Technical Analysis of Stocks & Commodities*, a monthly magazine about trading, there was a recent article about a man in the late 1990s who turned $10,000 into $40 million in just a few years. In the resulting bear market he gave a lot of it back, but he still has a fair amount of money. He proved his results by showing audited returns to the magazine. His approach for years had been to buy breakouts with leverage and options, and perhaps add to his positions as they went up. Ninety-five percent of the time this approach failed, but he was able to capitalize on the dot-com boom of the late 1990s and really multiply his money.

Is he a better investor or trader than Warren Buffett? Maybe. Certainly during the years he went from $10,000 to $40 million he was, and I don't think Buffett would disagree. But there are a lot of reasons why one would prefer the Buffett approach to investing and trading. And I don't mean the advice of buying great companies and holding them forever, but rather the idea of looking for a margin of safety in many different types of investments, then trading around that idea. Why would one prefer this to going from $10,000 to $40 million in a few years? Who knows? But maybe making $40 million in a few years requires a little too much luck.

Index